WHERE
THE STRESS
FALLS

Susan Sontag

WHERE
THE STRESS
FALLS

e s s a y s

FARRAR, STRAUS AND GIROUX

NEW YORK

Farrar, Straus and Giroux
19 Union Square West, New York 10003

Copyright © 2001 by Susan Sontag
Distributed in Canada by Douglas & McIntyre Ltd.
Printed in the United States of America
First edition, 2001

Library of Congress Cataloging-in-Publication Data

Sontag, Susan, 1933–
    Where the stress falls : essays / Susan Sontag.— 1st ed.
    p.   cm.
    ISBN 0-374-28917-4 (hardcover : alk. paper)
    I. Title.

PS3569.O6547 W48 2001
814'.54—dc21

                                           2001033704

Designed by Cassandra J. Pappas

for Elizabeth Hardwick

Continent, city, country, society:
the choice is never wide and never free.
And here, or there . . . No. Should we have stayed at home,
wherever that may be?

—ELIZABETH BISHOP
"Questions of Travel"

CONTENTS

Contents

READING

A Poet's Prose

"**I** WHO WOULD BE nothing without the Russian nineteenth century . . . ," Camus declared, in 1958, in a letter of homage to Pasternak—one of the constellation of magnificent writers whose work, along with the annals of their tragic destinies, preserved, recovered, discovered in translation over the past twenty-five years, has made the Russian twentieth century an event that is (or will prove to be) equally formative and, it being our century as well, far more importunate, impinging.

The Russian nineteenth century that changed our souls was an achievement of prose writers. Its twentieth century has been, mostly, an achievement of poets—but not only an achievement *in* poetry. About their prose the poets espoused the most passionate opinions: any ideal of seriousness inevitably seethes with dispraise. Pasternak in the last decades of his life dismissed as horribly modernist and self-conscious the splendid, subtle memoiristic prose of his youth (like *Safe Conduct*), while proclaiming the novel he was then working on, *Doctor Zhivago,* to be the most authentic and complete of all his writings, beside which his poetry was nothing in comparison. More typically, the poets were committed to a definition of poetry as an enterprise of such inherent superiority (the highest aim of literature, the highest condition of language) that any work in prose became an inferior venture—as if prose were always a communication, a service activity. "Instruction is the nerve of prose," Mandelstam wrote in an early essay, so that "what may be meaningful to the prose writer or essayist, the poet finds absolutely meaningless." While prose writers are obliged to address themselves to the concrete audience of their contemporaries, poetry as a whole has a more or less distant, unknown addressee, says Mandelstam: "Exchanging signals with the planet Mars . . . is a task worthy of a lyric poet."

Tsvetaeva shares this sense of poetry as the apex of literary endeavor—which means identifying all great writing, even if prose, as poetry. "Pushkin was a poet," she concludes her essay "Pushkin and Pugachev" (1937), and "nowhere was he the poet with such force as in the 'classical' prose of *The Captain's Daughter*."

The same would-be paradox with which Tsvetaeva sums up her love for Pushkin's novella is elaborated by Joseph Brodsky in his essay prefacing the collected edition (in Russian) of Tsvetaeva's prose: being great prose, it must be described as "the continuation of poetry with other means." Like earlier great Russian poets, Brodsky requires for his definition of poetry a caricatural Other: the slack mental condition he equates with prose. Assuming a privative standard of prose, and of the poet's motives for turning to prose ("something usually dictated by economic considerations, 'dry spells,' or more rarely by polemical necessity"), in contrast to the most exalted, prescriptive standard of poetry (whose "true subject" is "absolute objects and absolute feelings"), it is inevitable that the poet be regarded as the aristocrat of letters, the prose writer the bourgeois or plebeian; that—another of Brodsky's images—poetry be aviation, prose the infantry.

Such a definition of poetry is actually a tautology—as if prose were identical with the "prosaic." And "prosaic" as a term of denigration, meaning dull, commonplace, ordinary, tame, is precisely a Romantic idea. (The *OED* gives 1813 as its earliest use in this figurative sense.) In the "defense of poetry" that is one of the signature themes of the Romantic literatures of Western Europe, poetry is a form of both language and being: an ideal of intensity, absolute candor, nobility, heroism.

The republic of letters is, in reality, an aristocracy. And "poet" has always been a *titre de noblesse*. But in the Romantic era, the poet's nobility ceased to be synonymous with superiority as such and acquired an adversary role: the poet as the avatar of freedom. The Romantics invented the writer as hero, a figure central to Russian literature (which does not get under way until the early nineteenth century); and, as it happened, history made of rhetoric a reality. The great Russian writers *are* heroes—they have no choice if they are to be great writers—and Russian literature has continued to breed Romantic notions of the poet. To the modern Russian poets, poetry defends nonconformity, freedom, individuality against the social, the wretched vulgar present, the communal drone. (It is as if prose in its true state were, finally, the State.) No wonder they go on insisting on the absoluteness of poetry and its radical difference from prose.

PROSE IS TO POETRY, said Valéry, as walking is to dancing—Romantic assumptions about poetry's inherent superiority hardly being confined to the great Russian poets. For the poet to turn to prose, says Brodsky, is always a falling off, "like the shift from full gallop to a trot." The contrast is not just one of velocity, of course, but one of mass: lyric poetry's compactness versus the sheer extendedness of prose. (That virtuoso of extended prose, of the art of anti-laconicism, Gertrude Stein, said that poetry is nouns, prose is verbs. In other words, the distinctive genius of poetry is naming, that of prose, to show movement, process, time—past, present, and future.) The collected prose of any major poet who has written major prose—Valéry, Rilke, Brecht, Mandelstam, Tsvetaeva—is far bulkier than his or her collected poems. There is something equivalent in literature to the prestige the Romantics conferred on thinness.

That poets regularly produce prose, while prose writers rarely write poetry, is not, as Brodsky argues, evidence of poetry's superiority. According to Brodsky, "The poet, in principle, is 'higher' than the prose writer . . . because a hard-up poet can sit down and compose an article, whereas in similar straits a prose writer would hardly give thought to a poem." But the point surely is not that writing poetry is less well paid than writing prose but that it is special—the marginalizing of poetry and its audience; that what was once considered a normal skill, like playing a musical instrument, now seems the province of the difficult and the intimidating. Not only prose writers but cultivated people generally no longer write poetry. (As poetry is no longer, as a matter of course, something to memorize.) Modern performance in literature is partly shaped by the widespread discrediting of the idea of literary virtuosity; by a very real loss of virtuosity. It now seems utterly extraordinary that anyone can write brilliant prose in more than one language; we marvel at a Nabokov, a Beckett, a Cabrera Infante—but until two centuries ago such virtuosity would have been taken for granted. So, until recently, was the ability to write poetry as well as prose.

In the twentieth century, writing poems tends to be a dalliance of a prose writer's youth (Joyce, Beckett, Nabokov . . .) or an activity practiced with the left hand (Borges, Updike . . .). Being a poet is assumed to be more than writing poetry, even great poetry: Lawrence and Brecht, who wrote great poems, are not generally considered great poets. Being a poet is to define oneself as, to persist (against odds) in being, only a poet. Thus, the one generally acknowledged instance in twentieth-century literature of a great prose writer who was also a great poet, Thomas Hardy, is someone who renounced writing novels in order to write poetry. (Hardy ceased to be a prose writer. He became a poet.) In that sense the Romantic notion of the poet, as someone who has a maximal relation to poetry, has prevailed; and not only among the modern Russian writers.

An exception is made for criticism, however. The poet who is also a master practitioner of the critical essay loses no status as a poet; from Blok to Brodsky, most of the major Russian poets have written splendid critical prose. Indeed, since the Romantic era, most of the truly influential critics have been poets: Coleridge, Baudelaire, Valéry, Eliot. That other forms of prose are more rarely attempted marks a great difference from the Romantic era. A Goethe or Pushkin or Leopardi, who wrote both great poetry and great (non-critical) prose, did not seem odd or presumptuous. But the bifurcation of standards for prose in succeeding literary generations—the emergence of a minority tradition of "art" prose, the ascendancy of illiterate and para-literate prose—has made that kind of accomplishment far more anomalous.

Actually, the frontier between prose and poetry has become more and more permeable—unified by the ethos of maximalism characteristic of the modern artist: to create work that goes as far as it can go. The standard that seems eminently appropriate to lyric poetry, according to which poems may be regarded as linguistic artifacts to which nothing further can be done, now influences much of what is distinctively modern in prose. Precisely as prose, since Flaubert, has aspired to some of the intensity, velocity, and lexical inevitability of poetry, there seems a greater need to shore up the two-party system in literature, to distinguish prose from poetry, and to oppose them.

Why it is prose, not poetry, that is always on the defensive is that the party of prose seems at best an ad hoc coalition. How can one not be suspicious of a label that now encompasses the essay, the memoir, the novel or short story, the play? Prose is not just a ghostly category, a state of language defined negatively, by its opposite: poetry. (*"Tout ce qui n'est point prose est vers, et tout ce qui n'est point vers est prose,"* as the philosophy teacher in Molière's *Le Bourgeois Gentilhomme* proclaims, so that the bourgeois can discover that all his life he has been—surprise!—speaking prose.) Now it is a catchall for a panoply of literary forms that, in their modern evolution and high-speed dissolution, one no longer knows how to name. As a term used to describe what Tsvetaeva wrote that couldn't be called poetry, "prose" is a relatively recent notion. When essays no longer seem like what used to be called essays, and long and short fictions no longer like what used to be called novels and stories, we call them prose.

ONE OF THE GREAT EVENTS of twentieth-century literature has been the evolution of a particular kind of prose: impatient, ardent, elliptical, usually in the first person, often using discontinuous or broken forms, that is mainly written by poets (or if not, by writers with the standard of poetry in mind). For some poets, to write prose is to practice a genuinely different activity, to have a different (more persuasive, more reasonable) voice. The criticism and cultural journalism of Eliot and Auden and Paz, excellent as they are, are not written in poet's prose. The criticism and occasional pieces of Mandelstam and Tsvetaeva are. In contrast to Mandelstam—who wrote criticism, journalism, a poetics ("Conversation about Dante"), a novella (*The Egyptian*

Stamp), a memoir (*The Noise of Time*)—Tsvetaeva in her prose offers a narrower range of genres, a purer example of poet's prose.

Poet's prose not only has a particular fervor, density, velocity, fiber. It has a distinctive subject: the growth of the poet's vocation.

Typically, it takes the form of two kinds of narrative. One is directly autobiographical. The other, also in the shape of a memoir, is the portrait of another person, either a fellow writer (often of the older generation, and a mentor) or a beloved relative (usually a parent or grandparent). Homage to others is the complement to accounts of oneself: the poet is saved from vulgar egoism by the strength and purity of his or her admirations. In paying homage to the important models and evoking the decisive encounters, both in real life and in literature, the writer is enunciating the standards by which the self is to be judged.

Poet's prose is mostly about being a poet. And to write such autobiography, as to be a poet, requires a mythology of the self. The self described is the poet self, to which the daily self (and others) is often ruthlessly sacrificed. The poet self is the real self, the other one is the carrier; and when the poet self dies, the person dies. (To have two selves is the definition of a pathetic fate.) Much of the prose of poets—particularly in the memoiristic form—is devoted to chronicling the triumphant emergence of the poet self. (In the journal or diary, the other major genre of poet's prose, the focus is on the gap between the poet and the daily self, and the often untriumphant transactions between the two. The diaries—for example, Baudelaire's or Blok's—abound with rules for protecting the poet self; desperate maxims of encouragement; accounts of dangers, discouragements, and defeats.)

Many of Tsvetaeva's writings in prose are portraits of the self as poet. In the memoir of Max Voloshin, "A Living Word about a Living Man" (1933), Tsvetaeva evokes the bespectacled, defiant schoolgirl with a shaved head who has just published her first book of poems; Voloshin, an established poet and critic, having praised her book, arrived unannounced to call on her. (The year is 1910 and Tsvetaeva is eighteen. Like most poets, unlike most prose writers, she was in precocious command of her gifts.) The fond evocation of what she calls Voloshin's "insatiability for the genuine" is, of course, Tsvetaeva's avowal about herself. The more directly memoiristic texts are also accounts of the growth of the poet's vocation. "Mother and Music" (1935) describes the birth of the poet's lyricism through the household's immersion in music; Tsvetaeva's mother was a pianist. "My Pushkin" (1937) recounts the birth of the poet's capacity for passion (and its peculiar bent—"all the passion in me for unhappy non-reciprocal love") by recalling the relation Tsvetaeva had, in the very earliest years of her childhood, with the image and legend of Pushkin.

The prose of poets is typically elegiac, retrospective. It is as if the subject evoked belongs, by definition, to the vanished past. The occasion may be a literal death—the memoirs of both Voloshin and Bely. But it is not the tragedy of the exile, not even the atrocious privation and suffering endured by Tsvetaeva in exile and up to the time she returned to the Soviet Union in 1939 (where, now an internal exile, she committed suicide in August 1941), that accounts for this elegiac register. In prose the poet is always mourning a lost Eden; asking memory to speak, or sob.

A poet's prose is the autobiography of ardor. All of Tsvetaeva's work is an argument for rapture; and for genius, that is, for hierarchy: a poetics of the Promethean. "Our whole relation to art is an exception in favor of genius," as Tsvetaeva wrote in her stupendous essay "Art in the Light of Conscience." To be a poet is a state of being, elevated being: Tsvetaeva speaks of her love for "what is highest." There is the same quality of emotional soaring in her prose as in her poetry: no modern writer takes one as close to an experience of sublimity. As Tsvetaeva points out, "No one has ever stepped twice into the same river. But did anyone ever step twice into the same book?"

[1983]

Where the Stress Falls

for P.D.

IT **BEGINS**, this great American novel (let's not call it "this great American short novel"), with the voice of recollection; that is, the voice of uncertainty:

The Cullens were Irish; but it was in France that I met them and was able to form an impression of their love and their trouble. They were on their way to a property they had rented in Hungary; and one afternoon they came to Chancellet to see my great friend Alexandra Henry. That was in May of 1928 or 1929, before we all returned to America, and she met my brother and married him.

Needless to say, the twenties were very different from the thirties, and now the forties have begun. In the twenties it was not unusual to meet foreigners in some country as foreign to them as to you, your peregrination just crossing theirs; and you did your best to know them in an afternoon or so; and perhaps you called that little lightning knowledge, friendship. There was a kind of idealistic or optimistic curiosity in the air. And vagaries of character, and the various war and peace that goes on in the psyche, seemed of the greatest interest and even importance.

To cite the decade—the novel was published in 1940, so the forties had barely begun—puts an additional glaze on the story, investing it with the allure of the untimely; supervening World Events, it's suggested, have wilted the importance of the "war and peace that goes on in the psyche." This is to be merely some stuff about private lives, digested in record time: "an afternoon or so" is exactly the duration of the story, for the Cullens arrive after lunch, around two-thirty, and bolt just as an elaborate dinner is about to be served. In these few hours—a good deal less than the entire day and evening of *Mrs. Dalloway*—a storm of feelings will batter the constraints of gentility, and the ferocious indissoluble union of the Cullens, "their love and their trouble," will have been subjected to a cunningly thorough examination. "Lightning knowledge"—what kind of knowledge is that?

The novel, still neglected, ever astonishing, is *The Pilgrim Hawk* by Glenway Wescott. It belongs, in my view, among the treasures of twentieth-century American literature, however untypical are its sleek, subtle vocabulary, the density of its attention to character, its fastidious pessimism, and the clipped worldliness of its point of view. What's thought to be typically American is brash, broad, and a little simple, even simpleminded, particularly about such venerable subjects of European discernment as marriage, and *The Pilgrim Hawk* is anything but simple about marriage.

Of course, American literature has always provided complex performances of the moral imagination, some of which are dramas of intricate psychic violence as observed and mulled over by a witnessing consciousness. The job of the "I" who narrates *The Pilgrim Hawk* is to watch, to reflect, to understand (which also means to be puzzled by) what is going on. Who are this bluff, fleshy, self-conscious man and this exquisitely dressed woman with a full-grown hooded falcon, or pilgrim hawk, clinging to the rough gauntlet on her wrist? The narrator finds their presence, their derangements, stimulating. He is quick with eloquent summary assessments of their character. These evolve as their turmoil unfolds.

The opening of the novel suggests the uncanny speed at which an omnivorous observer might form "an impression" of two hitherto-unknown people: "you did your best to know them." It also proposes a masterly vagueness about when this impression was formed: "That was in May of 1928 or 1929, before we all returned to America . . ." Why would Wescott choose to make the narrator unsure of the year? It could be to mute the import of 1929, the year of the Crash, for such as his two idle-rich American expats—not Zelda and Scott Fitzgerald rich but seriously rich, as in a Henry James novel about Americans "doing" Europe. Or maybe this vagueness is simply the good manners of someone assigned the all too Jamesian name of Alwyn Tower. And good manners may dictate the narrator's fits of doubt about his own acuity: an Alwyn Tower would not wish to appear to be merely trying to be clever.

Name follows function. Detached, more than that, disabused, and virtually pastless (we don't learn what has exiled him from loving and being loved; we don't even learn his last name until nearly halfway through the book, and to divine his first name we have to know that Alwyn Tower is the central figure in Wescott's early autobiographical novel, *The Grandmothers*), the narrator is nevertheless not as mysterious as he might seem. In fact, *The Pilgrim Hawk*'s "I" is a familiar personage, the shadowy bachelor friend of one or more of the principal characters who, in kindred versions, narrates Hawthorne's *The Blithedale Romance*, James's *The Sacred Fount*, and Fitzgerald's *The Great Gatsby*. All these recessive narrators are abashed to some degree by the more reckless or vital or self-destructive people they observe.

The narrator as spectator is, necessarily, something of a voyeur. Gazing can become snooping, or at least seeing more than one is supposed to see. Coverdale, the creepy narrator of *The Blithedale Romance*, observes his friends from a treetop mirador and also from his post at a hotel room window where he can see into the windows of a house opposite. *The Sacred Fount* is the consummate narrator-at-the-peephole novel. The key revelation in *The Pilgrim Hawk*, Cullen's hatred of his wife's creature, comes when Tower happens to look out a window and sees Cullen, stealthily approaching the falcon, who has been removed to the garden after a bloody meal, pulling out a knife, unhooding her, and then slicing through her leash to set her free.

Marriage is the normative tie in this world of couples that includes not only the Cullens and a stormily mated pair of servants but the pseudo-couple formed by Alex Henry and her opaquely sexed, ruminative friend and houseguest. Maybe Tower's unease with the working of his own understanding proceeds from his awareness of being outside the deep experiences of coupledom, and alone. "Life is almost all perch. There is no nest; and no one is with you, on exactly the same rock or out on the same limb. The circumstances of passion are all too petty to be companionable." His is the arid wisdom of a profoundly unmarried consciousness. "Whether or not I finally arrive at a proper understanding of people, I often begin in the way of a vexed, intense superficiality."

Tower is describing the vagaries of novel writing as much as the pitfalls of understanding. All these valetudinarian narrators are also writers' self-portraits and exercises in writers' self-mortification. Coverdale, Hawthorne's "frosty bachelor," is a poet. Wescott's bachelor narrator is still embittered by his failure to become a "literary artist" ("no one warned me that I really did not have talent enough"), which does not stop him from thinking like a novelist, observing like a novelist, flaunting a novelist's volatility of judgment. "Sometimes I am as sensitive as a woman to others' temper or temperament; and it is a kind of sensitivity which may turn, almost by chance, for them or against them."

There is no smugness in Tower's acknowledgment of a novelist's ambivalence toward his subject, in contrast to Coverdale's chilling reflection:

> The thought impressed itself upon me, that I had left duties unperformed. With the power, perhaps, to act in the place of destiny, and avert misfortune from my friends, I had resigned them to their fate. That cold tendency, between instinct and intellect, which made me pry with a speculative interest into people's passions and impulses, appeared to have gone far towards unhumanizing my heart.
>
> But a man cannot always decide for himself whether his own heart

is cold or warm. It now impresses me that, if I erred at all in regard to Hollingsworth, Zenobia, and Priscilla, it was through too much sympathy, rather than too little.

Tower is able to make his mixed feelings about the couple he is observing more explicit. He feels repelled. He sympathizes, sometimes with the wife, sometimes with the husband—she so driven and sexually vibrant, he so desperate and dejected. The Cullens themselves seem to dissolve and re-form several times as the balance of power between them alters. (The neurasthenic, fragile wife even appears to change body type, becoming robust, coarse, indomitable.) Sometimes Tower seems in arrears of their ever more interesting natures, sometimes he seems to be imposing more complexity on their story than is plausible, and the narration risks becoming a story about him, his tortuous and self-torturing way of seeing—in the manner of late Henry James. But Wescott does not go that far. He is content to stay with the benefits, for the advancement of the story, of so self-conscious a narrator. A novelist with a painful story to tell will want to furnish it with complex characters who reveal themselves only gradually. What more ingenious, economical method than to make the complexity of a character the result of the instability of a first-person narrator's perceptions? For this purpose Tower could hardly be better suited. His appetite for discovering and repudiating significances is insatiable.

There is only one way for such a narrator to conclude: with yet another recoil from his own knowingness. After the drunken confidences and weeping and shouting and dangerous flirting, after a large revolver has been brandished (and flung into a pond), after nervous farewells have papered over the abyss and the Cullens and the hawk have spun off into the night in the long dark Daimler, after Tower and Alex have wandered into the garden to muse on all this unruly behavior, Tower recalls to himself the visions of rapacity and inhumanity he has mustered throughout the Cullens' visit—recalls, that is, the book we have been reading:

> . . . and I blushed. Half the time, I am afraid, my opinion of people is just guessing; cartooning. Again and again I give way to a kind of inex-

act and vengeful lyricism; I cannot tell what right I have to be avenged, and I am ashamed of it. Sometimes I entirely doubt my judgment in moral matters; and so long as I propose to be a story-teller, that is the whisper of the devil for me.

Is this frenetic reflectiveness distinctively American? I think so, without being able to prove it. The only English novel I know with something of these tones—the tormented diffidence and the muffled anguish—is one that plainly served Wescott as a partial inspiration for *The Pilgrim Hawk*: Ford Madox Ford's *The Good Soldier* (1915). Ford's novel is also both a story of marital agony breaking through the routines of idleness and a project of recollection undertaken by an American expatriate whiling away his life on the Continent. At the center of the drama is an English couple abroad, friends of a rich American couple. It is the American husband, now a widower—his wife has died since the time of the "sad affair" he is recalling—who tells the story.

Both in fiction and in autobiography, first-person narrating generally needs a pretext—also known as a justification—to begin. To talk about oneself used to be considered unseemly: the classic autobiographies and the classic novels that pretend to be somebody's memoir all begin by offering extenuating reasons for doing something so egotistical. Even now, when self-centeredness hardly requires an apology, a book of self-examination, a novel cast as a personal recollection, continues to invite a self-justifying explanation. It's useful to others. It's all I know how to do. It's all that's left for me to do. There is something I don't understand, and I want to understand. I'm not really talking about myself but about them.

The Good Soldier starts with its deracinated narrator explaining that he sits down "today" in order "to puzzle out" what he lamentably did not understand when it was happening. "My wife and I knew Captain and Mrs. Ashburnham as well as it was possible to know anybody, and yet, in another sense, we knew nothing at all about them." Not to know then—by the rules of fiction, where (unlike life) something *has* to happen—is to know now. The narrator may restate his bewilderment, fret from time to time over his inability to describe properly, worry that he has not got some fact quite right. There is no way for readers to take these avowals of deficient understanding other than as evidence that he sees—or, rather, allows us to see—the doomed Captain Ashburnham all too well.

MARRIAGES ARE CENTRAL MATERIAL in most great novels and are likely to activate the generalizing impulse. In novels recounted in the third person, a good place to sound the trumpet call of a generalization is right at the beginning.

"It is a truth universally acknowledged, that a single man in possession of a good fortune must be in want of a wife." Who is saying this? The author, sarcastically. And the denizens of the small world in which Austen sets her story actually think it—which makes this maxim something less than "a truth universally acknowledged."

And who is saying "All happy families are alike; each unhappy family is unhappy in its own way"? Again, the author. Or, if you will, the book. There's only a touch of irony in the opening line of Tolstoy's synoptic marriage novel. But does anyone, inside or outside the novel, actually think this? No.

The authority of the renowned first sentences of *Pride and Prejudice* and *Anna Karenina* depends on their floating free from any particular speaker, as if it were the nature of wisdom to be impersonal, oracular, anonymous, overbearing. Neither assertion is actually true. Both seem unchallengeably mature and pertinent as impatient observations about the cruelties of the marriage market and the despair of a naïve wife upon discovering her husband's infidelity. This is a strong hand with which to open a novel, some axiom about human behavior offered preemptively or ironically as an eternal verity. ("It *is* a truth . . ." "All happy families *are* . . .") Knowingness about human nature, old-style, is always in the present tense.

Wisdom in the contemporary novel is more likely to be retrospective, intimate-sounding. The vulnerable, self-doubting voice is more appealing and seems to be more trustworthy. Readers crave the display—the intrusion—of personality; that is, of weakness. Objectivity is suspect; it's thought to be bogus or cold. Generalizations can be proposed, but wryly. (Pathos and self-doubt are always welcome flavors.) Certitude seems like arrogance. "This is the saddest story I have ever heard" is the famous opening sentence of *The Good Soldier*. Sad stories exude signs, like sweat, which a squeamish narrator voice will undertake, with many hesitations and doubts, to decipher.

While a narration conducted in the third person can create the illusion of a story happening now, freshly told, a first-person narrator's story is inevitably one from the past. Telling is retelling. And where there is self-conscious retelling, witnessing, there is always the possibility—no, the likelihood—of error. A first-person novel with anything to mourn on its mind will be a feast of reflection on what makes that backward look so error-prone: the fallibility of memory, the impenetrability of the human heart, the obscuring distance between past and present.

Evoking that distance at the start of a novel narrated in the first person is a strong new opening move. Thus *The Pilgrim Hawk* gives us a blur of a year, "May of 1928 or 1929," since which so much has changed, and follows that with a bit of decade-mongering: the twenties, which were, "needless to say," very different from the thirties and the "now" of the forties. Elizabeth Hardwick's novel *Sleepless Nights* (1979) opens with another tease of a time-marker:

> It is June. This is what I have decided to do with my life just now. I will do this work of transformed and even distorted memory and lead this life, the one I am leading today. Every morning the blue clock and the crocheted bedspread with its pink and blue and gray squares and diamonds. How nice it is—this production of a broken old woman in a squalid nursing home. The niceness and the squalor and sorrow in an apathetic battle—that is what I see. More beautiful is the table with the telephone, the books and magazines, the *Times* at the door, the birdsong of rough, grinding trucks in the street.
>
> If only one knew what to remember or pretend to remember. Make a decision and what you want from the lost things will present itself. You can take it down like a can from a shelf. Perhaps. One can would be marked Rand Avenue in Kentucky . . .

The weird specificity of a month, June, minus the year; the statement of the project ("transformed and even distorted memory"); the inventory of homely comforting objects (clock and bedspread) followed by the plunge into the world of the disfavored (the broken old woman in the nursing home), a foretaste of much of the book's raw feeling and unease; the brave assumption of possibly erroneous subjectivity ("that is what I see"); the return to the comforts enjoyed by the narrator with a more sophisticated inventory (books, magazines, the *Times* at the door); the worry about knowing what to attempt to retrieve, in memory, from the past; and, finally, the wistful stipulativeness of the venture ("this is what I have decided to do with my life just now")—such incomparably rapid modulations of tone and tale are a signature aspect of Hardwick's method as a writer.

Like *The Pilgrim Hawk*, *Sleepless Nights* is a book of judgments about human relations, with special attention to marriage, and, like Wescott's novel, is told by a somewhat veiled first-person narrator who is (what else?) a writer. Hardwick's feat is to make that narrator—a version of herself—both the protagonist of the book and the voice of detached, brilliant spectatorship. In *Sleepless Nights* there is not one narrative but many, and the "I" is not at the center but to the side of most of the stories she chooses to retell—conjuring up, talking to, reproving, grieving over ghosts.

"Back to the 'long ago.'" Trawling through the past, memory makes a narrow, arbitrary-seeming selection of what to relate ("You can take it down like a can from a shelf"), then, guided by the steady streaming and fitful damming up of associations, makes a montage of that. There is remembering for remembering's sake. You can even remember for others. ("Dear old Alex: I will remember this for you.") To remember is to voice—to cast memories into language—and is, always, a form of address. There is more invocation of others than self-description, and none of the usual appetite in autobiographical fiction for the describing of injury to the self. The injuries described—and there are many—are those borne by others.

Many of the memories are discomfiting; some reek of spent painfulness. In contrast to what understanding accomplishes in *The Pilgrim Hawk*, the awareness garnered in *Sleepless Nights* is cathartic. It is felt and it is composed, written down, wrung out, speeded up. In *The Pilgrim Hawk*, the narrator has only himself to talk to, a self—one has the impression—he doesn't really like (or at any rate upon whom he is reluctant to seem to be bestowing any kind of approval). In *Sleepless Nights*, the narrator has the gallery of all the people who are remembered, fondly or ruefully, to talk to, and the wry magnanimity she extends to most of those she describes she extends to herself as well. Some memories are brought to life and quickly dismissed, while others are allowed to dilate and fill many pages. Everything is there to be questioned; everything, in retrospect, is drenched with poignancy. Not a breath of complaint (and there is much to complain of): whatever it was, it's gone now, part of the past, the nothing-to-be-done, the was-it-really-like-that, all retold in a voice that is both absorbed by and indifferent to self. ("Can it be that I am the subject?") The doubts and the pungent astuteness complement each other.

When the commenting, summing-up observer is impervious to doubts, the register inevitably shifts to the comic. Take that most assured of fictional people-watchers, the "I" voice of Randall Jarrell's awesomely witty *Pictures from an Institution* (1954). It starts by being unidentified, although, as cultural conventions would have it, a voice that is so attractively superior—reflective, learned, cheeky—would be assumed to be that of a man. All we do come to know is that he (and it is a he) is on the faculty of Benton College, a "progressive" college for women not far from New York City, where the famous novelist Gertrude Johnson has arrived to teach for a semester, and that he is married.

It's even a while before we realize there is a first-person narrator, someone with a small role in the story. Recounting matters that only an omniscient narrator could know, the novel's first seven pages point irrefutably in the other direction. Then, speeding through a hilarious riff on the vanity and presumption of his writer-monster, Jarrell delivers a little surprise:

> Gertrude thought Europe overrated, too; she voyaged there, voyaged back, and told her friends; they listened, awed, uneasy somehow. She had a wonderful theory that Europeans are mere children to us Americans, who are the oldest of men—why I once knew: because our polit-

ical institutions are older, or because Europeans skipped some stage of
their development, or because Gertrude was an American—I forget.

Who is this "I" who once knew, who forgets? Not someone worried
about his memory lapses. Though the first-person voice of *Pictures
from an Institution* pipes up belatedly, it is in canonical fashion, with an
avowal of incertitude. But this is a mock avowal, surely, by a nimble
and self-possessed mind. We wouldn't expect the narrator to recall
every one of Gertrude's glib pronouncements; to have forgotten some
is rather to his credit. In the world of Jarrell's novel, genuinely doubt-
ridden narrators need not apply.

Only the tragic—or the bleak—can accommodate, even promote,
incertitude. Comedy depends on certitude, the certitude about what is
foolish and what is not, and on characters who are "characters," that
is, types. In *Pictures from an Institution* they come in pairs (for this,
too, is a marriage novel): Gertrude and her husband; the composer, the
sociologist, the college's professionally boyish president, and their
amusingly discontented or complacent spouses—all in residence at this
school of fools and apt targets, all, for the narrator's genial, inspired
mockery. To poke fun at *everyone* might have made Jarrell seem churl-
ish. He obviously preferred to risk being sentimental, and added to the
mix a paragon of sincerity and niceness by the name of Constance. No
bashfulness about showing himself to be feverishly erudite, proteanly
intelligent, terminally droll, and a wizard phrase-maker. On the contrary (*autre temps, autres mœurs*), these were clearly glorious assets. But
perhaps there was a shade of anxiety about being, or being thought to
be, too mordant. An adorable, tenderhearted young woman who is first
glimpsed working in the office of the president, Constance sees gener-
ously what the narrator sees fiercely. Her indulgence allows him to go
on.

The true plot of Jarrell's novel, such as it is, consists of the flow of
coruscating descriptions of characters—above all, the inexhaustibly
fascinating, appalling Gertrude. Characters need to be described over
and over, not because they ever act "out of character" and so surprise
us, or because the narrator, like Tower in *The Pilgrim Hawk*, changes
his mind about them. (The characters in Wescott's novel can't be types:

it's precisely the function of the narrator's attention to them to make them ever more complicated.) In *Pictures from an Institution*, the "I" keeps on describing his characters because he continues to devise new, ingenious, giddy, ever more hyperbolic phrases to sum them up. They keep on being foolish, and he—the narrative voice—keeps on being inventive. His restlessness is lexical, or rhetorical, not psychological or ethical. Is there yet one more way to pin these follies down verbally? Forward!

HOW TO CIRCUMSCRIBE and refine a story and how to open up a story are two sides of the same task.

To explain, to inform, to amplify, to connect, to color in—think of the essayistic digressions in *Lost Illusions* and *A Harlot High and Low*, *Moby-Dick*, *Middlemarch*, *The Egoist*, *War and Peace*, *In Search of Lost Time*, *The Magic Mountain*. Such pursuit of completeness plumps out a novel. Is there a verb "to encyclopedize"? There has to be.

To condense, to pare away, to speed up, pile up, to be ready to renounce, to distill, to leap ahead, to conclude (even if one intends to conclude again and again)—think of the aphoristic glitter of *The Pilgrim Hawk*, *Pictures from an Institution*, *Sleepless Nights*. Such pursuit of celerity brings a novel's weight and length down drastically. Novels driven by the need to summarize, to intensify inexorably, tend to be single-voiced, short, and often not novels at all in the conventional sense. Occasionally, they will go after the deadpan, mock smoothness of an allegory or fable, as does Donald Barthelme's *The Dead Father*. Is there a verb "to angularize"? Or "to ellipsify"? There ought to be.

Compressed first-person narrations don't tell any kind of story; they tend to project a few distinctive moods. A surfeit of experiences that bring worldly wisdom (and, usually, disenchantment) is often intimated. It's hard to imagine a naïve narrator with a penchant for trenchant summary. Such moods color the whole span of the narration, which can darken but does not, strictly speaking, develop. In fictions narrated by a resident observer the end lies much closer to the beginning than in fictions enhanced by digressions. Not just because the novel is shorter but because the look is retrospective and the tale one whose end is known from the beginning. However straightforward the narration tries to be, it can't help registering a few tremors of anticipated pathos: the pathos of the already known, and the not prevented. The beginning will be an early variant on the end, the end a late, somewhat deflating variant on the beginning.

Stories kept lean by ellipsis and refined judgments rather than fattened by essayistic expansiveness may look like a quicker read. They're not. Even with sentences that are fired like bullets, attention can wander. Every exquisite linguistic moment (or incisive insight) is a moment of stasis, a potential ending. Aphoristic finalities sap forward momentum, which thrives on more loosely woven sentences. *Sleepless Nights* —a novel of mental weather—enchants by the scrupulousness and zip of the narrative voice, its lithe, semi-staccato descriptions and epigrammatic dash. It has no shape in the usual novelistic sense. It has no shape as the weather has no shape. Like the weather, it arrives and departs, rather than, in the usual structured way, begins and ends.

A first-person voice devoted to looking and reflecting is likely to be drawn to reporting its displacements, as if that were mainly what a solitary consciousness does with its time. These fictions with melancholy or frankly superior narrators are often travelers' tales, stories of a wandering of some sort, or a halt in that wandering. *The Pilgrim Hawk* takes place among the peripatetic rich. The staid academic village depicted in *Pictures from an Institution* is full of successful professionals coming from or on their way to somewhere else. Such well-oiled travels are about as dramatic as the story gets. Perhaps the fictions that condense have to be relatively plotless, large brawling events being better accommodated in fat books.

Many displacements are recorded in *Sleepless Nights*, none unconnected with a lifetime of incessant reading, fat books and thin:

> From Kentucky to New York, to Boston to Maine, to Europe, carried along on a river of paragraphs and chapters, of blank verse, of little books translated from the Polish, large books from the Russian—all consumed in a sedentary sleeplessness. Is that sufficient—never mind that it is the truth.

The voyaging of the bookish, undoubtedly a source of many keen pleasures, is nevertheless an occasion for irony, as if one's life had failed to meet an agreed standard of interest. A career of mental traveling, illustrated by a fair bit of real traveling in safety and relative comfort, doesn't make for a very exciting plot. "It certainly hasn't the drama of: I saw the old, white-bearded frigate master on the dock and signed up for the journey. But after all"—best to name the formidable constraint unknown to other representatively brilliant first-person narrators—" 'I' am a woman."

COMPARED WITH BEGINNINGS, endings of novels are less likely to resound, to have an aphoristic snap. What they convey is the permission for tensions to subside. They are more like an effect than a statement.

The Pilgrim Hawk starts with the Cullens' arrival and must go on until they leave and stop very soon after they do. *Pictures from an Institution* also draws to a close with a departure, actually two departures. To the joy of all, Gertrude and her husband are on the train back to New York City the moment the spring term ends. Then we learn that the narrator himself, having accepted the offer of a better job at another college, will be leaving Benton soon, with some regret and more than a little relief.

The Pilgrim Hawk signs off with an ambiguous reflection about marriage. Tower claims to be worrying about the effect on Alex of the spectacle of the Cullens' torment:

> "You'll never marry, dear," I said, to tease Alex . . . "You'll be afraid to, after this fantastic bad luck."
>
> "What bad luck, if you please?" she inquired, smiling to show that my mockery was welcome.
>
> "Fantastic bad object lessons."
>
> "You're no novelist," she said, to tease me. "I envy the Cullens, didn't you know?" And I concluded from the look on her face that she herself did not quite know whether she meant it.

For last lines, Wescott's novel confects a flurry of doubts about what is meant and what is felt, an exchange of teasing untruths: "You'll never marry." "You're no novelist." To readers who have retained a piece of information dropped into the very first paragraph (Alex will soon meet and marry the narrator's brother) and to those still gripped by the histrionic misery of the Cullens as parsed by the joyless narrator, the ending may seem light; perhaps too light. Or too neatly *da capo*.

Pictures from an Institution finishes as do the great comedies, with a celebration of marriage. It's the no-name narrator, until now the most revved up of observers, who has the becalmed last scene of the novel all to himself. Summer vacation has started; the campus is deserted; he has been in his office going through books and papers ("I worked hard for the rest of the afternoon: I threw away and threw away and threw away . . ."). Then he leaves:

> When at last I went downstairs everything was hollow and silent; my steps echoed along the corridor, as I walked down it looking at the sunlight in the trees outside. There was nobody in the building—nobody, I felt, in all the buildings of Benton. I stood in the telephone-booth on the first floor, dialed the number of my house, and my wife's *hello* was small and far-off in the silence; I said, "Can you come get me now, darling?" She answered, "*Of course* I can. I'll be right over."

For all that we know virtually nothing of the narrator, still less about his entirely notional wife, it seems appropriate that this novel about comic and pathetic (but never tragic) marriages ends as it does, with that italicized *Of course*, which evokes, with exquisite economy, the shelter and rightness of a true marriage.

And here are the last lines of *Sleepless Nights*, which, having no single story to tell, has no obvious place to end. *The Pilgrim Hawk* and *Pictures from an Institution* move forward in an announced, framed length of time: an afternoon and early evening; a spring semester. *Sleepless Nights* stretches over decades, darting backward and forward in time, its gallantly de-married narrator accumulating solitudes. Best to affirm solitude—writing, the work of memory—while also acknowledging the longing to reach out, to write letters, to telephone.

Sometimes I resent the glossary, the concordance of truth, many have about my real life, have like an extra pair of spectacles. I mean that such fact is to me a hindrance to memory.

Otherwise I love to be known by those I care for. *Public assistance*, beautiful phrase. Thus, I am always on the phone, always writing letters, always waking up to address myself to B. and D. and C.—those whom I dare not ring up until morning and yet must talk to throughout the night.

So *Sleepless Nights* ends with a departure, too. It ends by leaving—that is, delicately excluding—the reader ("I love to be known by those I care for"), who is presumed to read intrusively, looking for the concordance of truth about a "real life."

AN AUTOBIOGRAPHICAL FICTION in the guise of a journal (Rilke's *Notebooks of Malte Laurids Brigge*), a memoir in poet's prose (Pasternak's *Safe Conduct*), and a volume of stories (Isherwood's *Berlin Stories*) have all been mentioned by Hardwick as books she found emboldening when she came to write the genre-buster that is *Sleepless Nights*.

To be sure, fiction of all kinds has always fed on writers' lives. Every detail in a work of fiction was once an observation or a memory or a wish, or is a sincere homage to a reality independent of the self. That both the pretentious novelist and the pretentious women's college in *Pictures from an Institution* have well-known models illustrates familiar practices of fiction. (In a satire this is the norm: it would be surprising if Jarrell did not have a real novelist, a real college, in mind.) And authors of first-person narratives will often be discovered to have lent to that voice a few stray bio-facts. For instance, it helps explain the end of *The Pilgrim Hawk* to recall having been told that Alex Henry will marry. But that she will marry the narrator's brother, of whom nothing is ever said in the novel, seems like noodling. It's not. The great friend who inspired the character Alex, a rich 1920s-era American expatriate with a house near Paris in fashionable Rambouillet (the village renamed Chancellet), did, after returning home, marry Wescott's brother.

Many first-person narrators are endowed with enough traits to make a pleasantly self-regarding resemblance to their authors. Others are there-but-for-the-grace-of-God creations, what the author believes (or hopes) he or she has escaped being. Wescott, though not—like Tower—a failed writer, often reproached himself for being a lazy one, and it is odd that someone capable of a book as marvelous as *The Pilgrim Hawk* would only once in a long life write at the top of his form. Hawthorne was always wrestling with the Coverdale in himself. Writing to Sophia Peabody in 1841 from Brook Farm, the model for the cooperative community depicted in *The Blithedale Romance*, Hawthorne blesses his future wife for imparting a sense of life's "reality" and keeping "a feeling of coldness and strangeness" from creeping into his heart; in other words, for rescuing him from being someone like Coverdale.

But what about when the "I" and the author bear the same name or have identical life circumstances, as in *Sleepless Nights,* or in V. S. Naipaul's *The Enigma of Arrival* and W. G. Sebald's *Vertigo*? How much fact from the author's life can be sponged up without our becoming reluctant to call the book a novel? Sebald is the writer who plays most daringly with this project now. His narratives of mental haunting, which he wants to be regarded as fiction, are related by an emotionally distressed alter ego who presses the claim of solemn factuality to the point of including photographs of himself among the many photographs that annotate his books. Of course, almost everything that would normally be disclosed in an autobiographical work is absent from Sebald's books.

Actually, secretiveness—which might be called reticence, or discretion, or withholding—is essential to keeping these anomalous works of fiction from tipping over into autobiography or memoir. You can use your life, but only a little, and at an oblique angle. We know the narrator of *Sleepless Nights* draws on a real life. Kentucky is the birthplace of the writer named Elizabeth Hardwick, who did meet Billie Holiday soon after coming to live in Manhattan in the 1940s, did spend a year in Holland in the early 1950s, did have a great friend named M—, did live in Boston, has had a house in Maine, has lived for many years on the

West Side of Manhattan, and so on. All this figures in her novel, as glimpses—the telling designed as much to conceal, to put readers off the track, as to reveal.

To edit your life is to save it, for fiction, for yourself. Being identified with your life as others see it may mean that you come eventually to see it that way, too. This can only be a hindrance to memory (and, presumably, to invention).

There is more freedom to be elliptical and to abridge when the memories are not set down in chronological order. The memories— fragments of memories, transformed—emerge as chains of luxuriant notations that wind around, and conceal, the kernel of story. And Hardwick's art of acute compression and decentering is simply too fast-paced to tell only a single story at a time; too fast, sometimes, to relate any story at all, especially where one is expected. For instance, there is much about marriage, notably a long-running soap opera starring the philandering husband in a Dutch couple, friends of the narrator and her then husband when they lived in Holland. Her own marriage is announced thus on the fifth page: "I was then a 'we' . . . Husband-wife: not a new move to be discovered in that strong classical tradition." The ensuing silence about the "we"—a declaration of independence that has to be intrinsic to the fashioning of the authoritative, questing "I" capable of writing *Sleepless Nights*—lasts until a sentence some fifty pages later: "I am alone here in New York, no longer a *we*. Years, decades even, have passed." Maybe books devoted to exalted standards of prose will always be reproached for not telling readers *enough*.

But it's not an autobiography, not even of this "Elizabeth," who is made out of materials harvested from, but not identical with, Elizabeth Hardwick. It's about what "Elizabeth" saw, what she thought about others. Its power is linked with its refusals, and its distinctive palette of sympathies. Her assessments of long-term sufferers in lousy marriages are pitiless, but she is kind to Main Street, touched by inept wrongdoers and class traitors and self-important failures. Memory conjures up a procession of injured souls: foolish, deceiving, needy men, some briefly lovers, who have been much indulged (by themselves and by women) and come to no good end, and humble, courteous, simple women in archaic roles who have known only hard times and been indulged by nobody. There are desperately loving evocations of the narrator's mother, and several meanderingly sustained, *Melanctha*-like portraits of women who are invoked like muses:

> When I think of cleaning women with unfair diseases I think of you, Josette. When I must iron or use a heavy pot for cooking, I think of you, Ida. When I think of deafness, heart disease and languages I cannot speak, I think of you, Angela. Great washtubs full of sheets remind me of more than one.

The work of memory, this memory, is choosing, most emphatically, to think about women, especially women serving out lives of hard labor, those whom exquisitely written books customarily ignore. Justice requires that they be remembered. Pictured. Summoned to the feast of the imagination and of language.

Of course, you summon ghosts at your peril. The sufferings of others can bleed into your soul. You try to protect yourself. Memory is inventive. Memory is a performance. Memory invites itself, and is hard to turn away. Hence the ravishing insight that gives the book its title: that remembering is intimately connected with insomnia. Memories are what make it hard for you to sleep. Memories procreate. And the uninvited memories always seem to the point. (As in fiction: whatever is included is connected.) The boldness and virtuosity of Hardwick's associativeness intoxicate.

On the last page, in the peroration with which *Sleepless Nights* concludes, the narrator observes, in a final summative delirium:

> Mother, the reading glasses and the assignation near the clammy faces, so gray, of the intense church ladies. And then a lifetime with its mound of men climbing on and off.
>
> The torment of personal relations. Nothing new there except in the disguise, and in the escape on the wings of adjectives. Sweet to be pierced by daggers at the end of paragraphs.

Nothing new except language, the ever found. Cauterizing the torment of personal relations with hot lexical choices, jumpy punctuation, mercurial sentence rhythms. Devising more subtle, more engorged ways of knowing, of sympathizing, of keeping at bay. It's a matter of adjectives. It's where the stress falls.

[2001]

Afterlives:
The Case of Machado de Assis

IMAGINE A WRITER WHO, in the course of a moderately long life in which he never traveled farther than seventy-five miles from the capital city where he was born, created a huge body of work . . . a nineteenth-century writer, you will interrupt; and you will be right: author of a profusion of novels, novellas, stories, plays, essays, poems, reviews, political chronicles, as well as reporter, magazine editor, government bureaucrat, candidate for public office, founding president of his country's Academy of Letters; a prodigy of accomplishment, of the transcending of social and physical infirmity (he was a mulatto and the son of a slave in a country where slavery was not abolished until he was almost fifty; he was epileptic); who, during this vividly prolific, exuberantly national career, managed to write a sizable number of novels and stories deserving of a permanent place in world literature, and whose masterpieces, outside his native country, which honors him as its greatest writer, are little known, rarely mentioned.

Imagine such a writer, who existed, and his most original books, which continue to be discovered more than eighty years after his death. Normally, the filter of time is just, discarding the merely celebrated or successful, rescuing the forgotten, promoting the underestimated. In the afterlife of a great writer—this is when the mysterious questions of value and permanence are resolved. Perhaps it is fitting that this writer, whose afterlife has not brought his work the recognition it merits, should have had himself so acute, so ironic, so endearing a sense of the posthumous.

WHAT IS TRUE of a reputation is true—should be true—of a life. Since it is only a completed life that reveals its shape and whatever meaning a life can have, a biography that means to be definitive must wait until after the death of its subject. Unfortunately, autobiographies can't be composed under these ideal circumstances. And virtually all the notable fictional autobiographies have respected the limitation of real ones, while conjuring up a next-best equivalent of the illuminations of death. Fictional autobiographies, even more often than real ones, tend to be autumnal undertakings: an elderly (or, at least, loss-seasoned) narrator, having retired from life, now writes. But, close as old age may bring the fictive autobiographer to the ideal vantage point, he or she is still writing on the wrong side of the frontier beyond which a life, a life story, finally makes sense.

I know only one example of that enthralling genre, the imaginary autobiography, which grants the project of autobiography its ideal—as it turns out, comical—fulfillment, and that is the masterpiece called *Memórias póstumas de Brás Cubas* (1880), introduced into English under the pointless, interfering title *Epitaph of a Small Winner*. In the first paragraph of Chapter 1, "The Death of the Author," Brás Cubas announces gaily: "I am a deceased writer not in the sense of one who has written and is now deceased, but in the sense of one who has died and is now writing." Here is the novel's first, framing joke, and it is about the writer's freedom. The reader is invited to play the game of considering that the book in hand is an unprecedented literary feat. Posthumous reminiscences written in the first person.

Of course, not even a single day, much less a life, can ever be recounted in its entirety. A life is not a plot. And quite different ideas of decorum apply to a narrative constructed in the first person and to one in the third person. To slow down, to race ahead, to skip whole stretches; to comment at length, to withhold comment—these done as an "I" have

another weight, another feel, than when said about or on behalf of someone else. Much of what is affecting or pardonable or insufferable in the
first person would seem the opposite if uttered in the third person, and
vice versa: an observation easily confirmed by reading aloud any page
from Machado de Assis's book first as it is, a second time with "he" for
"I." (To sample the fierce difference *within* the codes governing the third
person, then try substituting "she" for "he.") There are registers of feeling, such as anxiety, that only a first-person voice can accommodate. And
aspects of narrative performance as well: digressiveness, for instance,
seems natural in a text written in the first person, but amateurish in an
impersonal, third-person voice. Thus, any piece of writing that features
an awareness of its own means and methods should be understood as in
the first person, whether or not the main pronoun is "I."

To write about oneself—the true, that is, the private story—used to
be felt to be presumptuous, and to need justifying. Montaigne's *Essays*,
Rousseau's *Confessions*, Thoreau's *Walden*, and most of the other spiri-
tually ambitious classics of autobiography have a prologue in which the
author directly addresses the reader, acknowledging the temerity of the
enterprise, evoking scruples or inhibitions (modesty, anxiety) that had
to be overcome, laying claim to an exemplary artlessness or candor, al-
leging the usefulness of all this self-absorption to others. And, like real
autobiographies, most fictional autobiographies of any stylishness or
depth also start with an explanation, defensive or defiant, of the decision to write the book the reader has just begun—or, at least, a flourish
of self-deprecation, suggesting an attractive sensitivity to the charge of
egotism. This is no mere throat-clearing, some polite sentences to give
the reader time to be seated. It is the opening shot in a campaign of seduction in which the autobiographer tacitly agrees that there is something unseemly, brazen, in volunteering to write at length about oneself
—exposing oneself to unknown others without any evident interest (a
great career, a great crime) or without some documentary ruse, such as
pretending that the book merely transcribes existing private papers,
like a journal or letters, indiscretions originally destined for the smallest, friendliest readership. With a life story offered straight-out, in the
first person, to as many readers as possible (a "public"), it seems only
minimal prudence as well as courtesy for the autobiographer to seek

permission to begin. The splendid conceit of the novel, that these are memoirs written by someone who is dead, just puts an additional spin on this regulatory caring about what the reader thinks. The autobiographer can also profess not to care.

Still, writing from beyond the grave has not relieved this narrator from showing an ostentatious amount of concern about the reception of his work. His mock anxiety is embodied in the very form, the distinctive velocity of the book. It is in the way the narrative is cut and mounted, its stop-and-start rhythms: 160 chapters, several as brief as two sentences, few longer than two pages. It is in the playful directions, usually at the beginning or end of chapters, for the best use of the text. ("This chapter is to be inserted between the first two sentences of chapter 129." "Please note that this chapter is not intended to be profound." "But let us not become involved in psychology," et cetera.) It is in the pulse of ironic attention to the book's means and methods, the repeated disavowal of large claims on the reader's emotions ("I like jolly chapters"). Asking the reader to indulge the narrator's penchant for frivolity is as much a seducer's ploy as promising the reader strong emotions and new knowledge. The autobiographer's suave fussing over the accuracy of his narrative procedures parodies the intensity of his self-absorption.

Digression is the main technique for controlling the emotional flow of the book. The narrator, whose head is full of literature, shows himself adept at expert descriptions—of the kind flattered with the name of realism—of how poignant feelings persist, change, evolve, devolve. He also shows himself understandably beyond all that by the dimensions of the telling: the cutting into short episodes, the ironic, didactic overviews. This oddly fierce, avowedly disenchanted voice (but then what else should we expect a narrator who is dead to be?) never relates an event without drawing some lesson from it. Chapter 133 opens: "The episode serves to illustrate and perhaps amend Helvetius' theory that . . ." Begging the reader's indulgence, worrying about the reader's attentiveness (does the reader get it? is the reader amused? is the reader becoming bored?), the autobiographer continually breaks out of his story to invoke a theory it illustrates, to formulate an opinion about it—as if such moves were needed to make the story more interesting. Brás Cubas's socially privileged, self-important existence is, as such lives often are, starkly uneventful; the main events are those which did not happen or were judged disappointing. The rich production of witty opinions exposes the emotional poverty of the life, by having the narrator seem to sidestep the conclusions he ought to be drawing. The digressive method also generates much of the book's humor, starting with the very disparity between the life (modest in events, subtly articulated) and the theories (portentous, blunt) he invokes.

The Life and Opinions of Tristram Shandy is of course the principal model for these savory procedures of reader awareness. The method of the tiny chapters and some of the typographical stunts, as in Chapter 55 ("The Venerable Dialogue of Adam and Eve") and Chapter 139 ("How I Did Not Become a Minister of State"), recall the whimsical narrative rhythms and pictographic witticisms of *Tristram Shandy*. That Brás Cubas begins his story after his death, as Tristram Shandy famously begins the story of his consciousness before he is born (at the moment of his conception)—that, too, seems an homage to Sterne by Machado de Assis. The authority of *Tristram Shandy*, published in installments between 1759 and 1767, on a writer born in Brazil in the nineteenth century should not surprise us. While Sterne's books, so celebrated in his lifetime and shortly afterward, were being reassessed in England as too peculiar, occasionally indecent, and finally boring, they continued to be enormously admired on the Continent. In the English-speaking world, where in this century he has again been thought very highly of, Sterne still figures as an ultra-eccentric, marginal genius (like Blake) who is most notable for being uncannily, and prematurely, "modern." When looked at from the perspective of world literature, however, he may be the English-language writer who, after Shakespeare and Dickens, has had the greatest influence; for Nietzsche to have said that his favorite novel was *Tristram Shandy* is not quite as original a judgment as it may seem. Sterne has been an especially potent presence in the literatures of the Slavic languages, as is reflected in the centrality of the example of *Tristram Shandy* in the theories of Viktor Shklovsky and other Russian formalists from the 1920s forward. Perhaps the reason so much commanding prose literature has been issuing for decades from Central and Eastern Europe as well as from

Latin America is not that writers there have been suffering under monstrous tyrannies and therefore have had importance, seriousness, subjects, relevant irony bestowed on them (as many writers in Western Europe and the United States have half enviously concluded) but that these are the parts of the world where for over a century the author of *Tristram Shandy* has been the most admired.

Machado de Assis's novel belongs in that tradition of narrative buffoonery—the talkative first-person voice attempting to ingratiate itself with readers—which runs from Sterne through, in our own century, Natsume Sōseki's *I Am a Cat*, the short fiction of Robert Walser, Svevo's *Confessions of Zeno* and *As a Man Grows Older*, Hrabal's *Too Loud a Solitude*, much of Beckett. Again and again we meet in different guises the chatty, meandering, compulsively speculative, eccentric narrator: reclusive (by choice or by vocation); prone to futile obsessions and fanciful theories and comically designed efforts of the will; often an autodidact; not quite a crank; though sometimes driven by lust, and at least one time by love, unable to mate; usually elderly; invariably male. (No woman is likely to get even the conditional sympathy these ragingly self-absorbed narrators claim from us, because of expectations that women be more sympathetic, and sympathizing, than men; a woman with the same degree of mental acuity and emotional separateness would be regarded as simply a monster.) Machado de Assis's valetudinarian Brás Cubas is considerably less exuberant than Sterne's madcap, effusively garrulous Tristram Shandy. It is only a few steps from the incisiveness of Machado's narrator, with his rueful superiority to the story of his own life, to the plot malaise that characterizes most recent fiction in the form of autobiography. But storylessness may be intrinsic to the genre—the novel as autobiographical monologue—as is the isolation of the narrating voice. In this respect the post-Sternean anti-hero like Brás Cubas parodies the protagonists of the great spiritual autobiographies, who are always profoundly, not just by circumstances, unmarried. It is almost a measure of an autobiographical narrative's ambition: the narrator must be, or be recast as, alone, certainly without a spouse, even when there is one; the life must be unpeopled at the center. (Thus, such recent achievements of spiritual autobiography in the guise of a novel as Elizabeth Hardwick's *Sleepless*

Nights and V. S. Naipaul's *The Enigma of Arrival* leave out the spouses who were actually there.) Just as Brás Cubas's solitariness is a parody of a chosen or an emblematic solitude, his release through self-understanding is, for all its self-confidence and wit, a parody of that sort of triumph.

The seductions of such a narrative are complex. The narrator professes to be worrying about the reader—whether the reader gets it. Meanwhile, the reader can be wondering about the narrator—whether the narrator understands all the implications of what is being told. A display of mental agility and inventiveness which is designed to amuse the reader and purportedly reflects the liveliness of the narrator's mind mostly measures how emotionally isolated and forlorn the narrator is. Ostensibly, this is the book of a life. Yet, despite the narrator's gift for social and psychological portraiture, it remains a tour of the inside of someone's head. Another of Machado's models was a marvelous book by Xavier de Maistre, a French expatriate aristocrat (he lived most of his long life in Russia) who invented the literary micro-journey with his *Journey around My Room*, written in 1794, when he was in prison for dueling, and which recounts his diagonal and zigzag visits to such diverting sites as the armchair, the desk, and the bed. A confinement, mental or physical, that is not acknowledged as such can make a very funny story as well as one charged with pathos.

At the beginning, in a flourish of authorial self-knowingness that graciously includes the reader, Machado de Assis has the autobiographer name the eighteenth-century literary models of his narrative with the following somber warning:

> It is, in truth, a diffuse work, in which I, Brás Cubas, if indeed I have adopted the free form of a Sterne or of a Xavier de Maistre, have possibly added a certain peevish pessimism of my own. Quite possibly. The work of a man already dead. I wrote it with the pen of Mirth and the ink of Melancholy, and one can readily foresee what may come of such a union.

However modulated by whimsy, a vein of true misanthropy runs through the book. If Brás Cubas is not just another of those repressed, desiccated, pointlessly self-aware bachelor narrators who exist only to be seen through by the full-blooded reader, it is because of his anger—which is by the end of the book full-out, painful, bitter, upsetting.

The Sternean playfulness is lighthearted. It is a comic, albeit extremely nervous, form of friendliness with the reader. In the nineteenth century this digressiveness, this chattiness, this love of the little theory, this pirouetting from one narrative mode to another, takes on darker hues. It becomes identified with hypochondria, with erotic disillusionment, with the discontents of the self (Dostoyevsky's pathologically voluble Underground Man), with acute mental distress (the hysterical narrator, deranged by injustice, of Multatuli's *Max Havelaar*). To natter on obsessively, repetitively, used to be invariably a resource of comedy. (Think of Shakespeare's plebeian grumblers, like the porter in *Macbeth*; think of Mr. Pickwick, among other inventions of Dickens.) That comic use of garrulousness does not disappear. Joyce used garrulousness in a Rabelaisian spirit, as a vehicle of comic hyperbole, and Gertrude Stein, champion of verbose writing, turned the tics of egotism and sententiousness into a good-natured comic voice of great originality. But most of the verbose first-person narrators in the ambitious literature of this century have been radically misanthropic. Garrulousness is identified with the baleful, aggrieved repetitiveness of senility (Beckett's prose monologues that call themselves novels) and with paranoia and unslakable rage (the novels and plays of Thomas Bernhard). Who does not sense the despair behind the loquacious, sprightly musings of Robert Walser and the quirkily erudite, bantering voices in the stories of Donald Barthelme?

Beckett's narrators are usually trying, not altogether successfully, to imagine themselves as dead. Brás Cubas has no such problem. But then Machado de Assis was trying to be, and is, funny. There is nothing morbid about the consciousness of his posthumous narrator; on the contrary, the perspective of maximum consciousness—which is what, wittily, a posthumous narrator can claim—is in itself a comic perspective. Where Brás Cubas is writing from is not a true afterlife (it has no geography), only another go at the idea of authorial detachment. The neo-Sternean narrative hijinks of these memoirs of a disappointed man do not issue from Sternean exuberance or even Sternean nervousness.

They are a kind of antidote, a counterforce to the narrator's despondency: a way of mastering dejection considerably more specialized than the "great cure, an anti-melancholy plaster, designed to relieve the despondency of mankind" that the narrator fantasizes about inventing. Life administers its hard lessons. But one can write as one pleases—a form of liberty.

Joaquim Maria Machado de Assis was only forty-one when he published these reminiscences of a man who has died—we learn at the opening of the book—at sixty-four. (Machado was born in 1839; he makes his creation Brás Cubas, the posthumous autobiographer, more than a generation older, born in 1805.) The novel as an exercise in the anticipating of old age is a venture to which writers of a melancholy temperament continue to be drawn. I was in my late twenties when I wrote my first novel, which purports to be the reminiscences of a man then in his early sixties, a *rentier*, dilettante, and fantasist, who announces at the beginning of the book that he has reached a harbor of serenity where, all experience finished, he can look back on his life. The few conscious literary references in my head were mostly French—above all *Candide* and Descartes's *Meditations*; I thought I was writing a satire on optimism and on certain cherished (by me) ideas of the inner life and of a religiously nourished inwardness. (What was going on unconsciously, as I think about it now, is another story.) When I had the good fortune to have *The Benefactor* accepted by the first publisher to whom I submitted it, Farrar Straus, I had the further good luck of having assigned to me as my editor Cecil Hemley, who in 1952, in his previous incarnation as the head of Noonday Press (recently acquired by my new publisher), had brought out the translation of Machado's novel that really launched the book's career in English. (Under that title!) At our first meeting Hemley said to me: "I can see you have been influenced by *Epitaph of a Small Winner*." Epitaph of a what? "By, you know, Machado de Assis." Who? He lent me a copy and several days later I declared myself retroactively influenced.

Although I have since read a good deal of Machado in translation, *Memórias póstumas de Brás Cubas*—the first of five late novels (he lived twenty-eight years after writing it) generally thought the summit of his genius—remains my favorite. I am told it is the one that non-Brazilians often prefer, although critics usually pick *Dom Casmurro* (1899). I am astonished that a writer of such greatness does not yet occupy the place he deserves. Up to a point, the relative neglect of Machado outside Brazil may be no more mysterious than the neglect of another prolific writer of genius whom Eurocentric notions of world literature have marginalized: Natsume Sōseki. Surely Machado would be better known if he hadn't been Brazilian and hadn't spent his whole life in Rio de Janeiro—if he were, say, Italian or Russian, or even Portuguese. But the impediment is not simply that Machado was not a European writer. Even more remarkable than his absence from the stage of world literature is that he has been very little known and read in the rest of Latin America—as if it were still hard to digest the fact that the greatest novelist that Latin America has produced wrote in the Portuguese, rather than the Spanish, language. Brazil may be the continent's biggest country (and Rio in the nineteenth century its largest city), but it has always been the outsider country—regarded by the rest of South America, Hispanophone South America, with a good deal of condescension and often in racist terms. A writer from these countries is far likelier to know any of the European literatures or literature in English than to know the literature of Brazil, whereas Brazilian writers are acutely aware of Spanish-American literature. Borges, the other supremely great writer produced on that continent, seems never to have read Machado de Assis. Indeed, Machado is even less well known to Spanish-language readers than to those who read him in English. *The Posthumous Memoirs of Brás Cubas* was finally translated into Spanish only in the 1960s, some eighty years after it was written and a decade after it was translated (twice) into English.

With enough time, enough afterlife, a great book does find its rightful place. And perhaps some books need to be rediscovered again and again. *The Posthumous Memoirs of Brás Cubas* is probably one of those thrillingly original, radically skeptical books that will always impress readers with the force of a private discovery. It hardly seems much of a compliment to say that this novel, written more than a century ago, seems, well . . . modern. Isn't every work that speaks to us with an originality and lucidity we're capable of acknowledging one we want to conscript into what we understand as modernity? Our standards of modernity are a system of flattering illusions, which permit us selectively to colonize the past, as are our ideas of what is provincial, which permit some parts of the world to condescend to all the rest. Being dead may stand for a point of view that cannot be accused of being provincial. Surely *The Posthumous Memoirs of Brás Cubas* is one of the most entertainingly unprovincial books ever written. And to love this book is to become a little less provincial about literature, about literature's possibilities, oneself.

[1990]

A Mind in Mourning

I S LITERARY GREATNESS still possible? Given the implacable devolution of literary ambition, and the concurrent ascendancy of the tepid, the glib, and the senselessly cruel as normative fictional subjects, what would a noble literary enterprise look like now? One of the few answers available to English-language readers is the work of W. G. Sebald.

Vertigo, the third of Sebald's books to be translated into English, is how he began. It appeared in German in 1990, when its author was forty-six; three years later came *The Emigrants*; and two years after that, *The Rings of Saturn*. When *The Emigrants* appeared in English in 1996, the acclaim bordered on awe. Here was a masterly writer, mature, autumnal even, in his persona and themes, who had delivered a book as exotic as it was irrefutable. The language was a wonder—delicate, dense, steeped in thinghood; but there were ample precedents for that in English. What seemed foreign as well as most persuasive was the preternatural authority of Sebald's voice: its gravity, its sinuosity, its precision, its freedom from all-undermining or undignified self-consciousness or irony.

In W. G. Sebald's books, a narrator who, we are reminded occasionally, bears the name W. G. Sebald, travels about registering evidence of the mortality of nature, recoiling from the ravages of modernity, musing over the secrets of obscure lives. On some mission of investigation, triggered by a memory or news from a world irretrievably lost, he remembers, evokes, hallucinates, grieves.

Is the narrator Sebald? Or a fictional character to whom the author has lent his name, and selected elements of his biography? Born in 1944, in a village in Germany he calls "W." in his books (and the dust jacket identifies for us as Wertach im Allgäu), settled in England in his early twenties, and a career academic currently teaching modern German literature at the University of East Anglia, the author includes a scattering of allusions to these bare facts and a few others, as well as, among other self-referring documents reproduced in his books, a grainy picture of himself posed in front of a massive Lebanese cedar in *The Rings of Saturn* and the photo on his new passport in *Vertigo*.

And yet these books ask, rightly, to be considered fiction. Fiction they are, not least because there is good reason to believe that much is invented or altered, just as, surely, some of what he relates really did happen—names, places, dates, and all. Fiction and factuality are, of course, not opposed. One of the founding claims for the novel in English is that it is a true history. What makes a work fiction is not that the story is untrue—it may well be true, in part or in whole—but its use, or extension, of a variety of devices (including false or forged documents) which produce what literary theorists call "the effect of the real." Sebald's fictions—and their accompanying visual illustration— carry the effect of the real to a plangent extreme.

This "real" narrator is an exemplary fictional construction: the *promeneur solitaire* of many generations of romantic literature. A solitary, even when a companion is mentioned (the Clara of the opening paragraph of *The Emigrants*), the narrator is ready to undertake journeys at whim, to follow some flare-up of curiosity about a life that has ended (as, in *The Emigrants*, in the story of Paul, a beloved primary-school teacher, which brings the narrator back for the first time to "the new Germany," and of his Uncle Adelwarth, which brings the narrator to America). Another motive for traveling is proposed in *Vertigo* and *The Rings of Saturn*, where it is clearer that the narrator is also a writer, with a writer's restlessness and a writer's taste for isolation. Often the narrator begins to travel in the wake of some crisis. And usually the journey is a quest, even if the nature of that quest is not immediately apparent.

Here is the beginning of the second of the four narratives in *Vertigo*:

> In October 1980 I traveled from England, where I had then been living for nearly twenty-five years in a county which was almost always under grey skies, to Vienna, hoping that a change of place would help me get over a particularly difficult period in my life. In Vienna, however, I found that the days proved inordinately long, now they were not taken up by my customary routine of writing and gardening tasks, and I literally did not know where to turn. Every morning I would set out and walk without aim or purpose through the streets of the inner city.

This long section, entitled "All' estero" (Abroad), which takes the narrator from Vienna to various places in northern Italy, follows the opening chapter, a brilliant exercise in Brief-Life writing which recounts the biography of the much-traveled Stendhal, and is followed by a brief third chapter relating the Italian journey of another writer, "Dr. K," to some of the sites of Sebald's travels in Italy. The fourth, and last, chapter, as long as the second and complementary to it, is entitled "Il ritorno in patria" (The Return Home). The four narratives of *Vertigo* adumbrate all Sebald's major themes: journeys; the lives of writers, who are also travelers; being haunted and being light. And always, there are visions of destruction. In the first narrative, Stendhal dreams, while recovering from an illness, of the great fire of Moscow; and the last narrative ends with Sebald falling asleep over his Pepys and dreaming of London destroyed by the Great Fire.

The Emigrants uses this same four-part musical structure, in which the fourth narrative is longest and most powerful. Journeys of one kind or another are at the heart of all Sebald's narratives: the narrator's own peregrinations, and the lives, all in some way displaced, that the narrator evokes.

Compare the first sentence of *The Rings of Saturn*:

In August 1992, when the dog days were drawing to an end, I set off to walk the county of Suffolk, in the hope of dispelling the emptiness that takes hold of me whenever I have completed a long stint of work.

The whole of *The Rings of Saturn* is the account of this walking trip undertaken to dispel emptiness. For whereas the traditional tour brought one close to nature, here it measures degrees of devastation, and the opening of the book tells us that the narrator was so overcome by "the traces of destruction" he encountered that, a year to the day after beginning his tour, he was taken to a hospital in Norwich "in a state of almost total immobility."

Travels under the sign of Saturn, emblem of melancholy, are the subject of all three books Sebald wrote in the first half of the 1990s. Destruction is his master theme: of nature (the lament for the trees destroyed by Dutch elm disease and those destroyed in the hurricane of 1987 in the next-to-last section of *The Rings of Saturn*); of cities; of ways of life. *The Emigrants* tells of a trip to Deauville in 1991, in search perhaps of "some remnant of the past," which confirms that "the once legendary resort, like everywhere else that one visits now, regardless of the country or continent, was hopelessly run down and ruined by traffic, shops and boutiques, and the insatiable urge for destruction." And the return home, in the fourth narrative of *Vertigo*, to W., which the narrator says he had not revisited since his childhood, is an extended *recherche du temps perdu*.

The climax of *The Emigrants*, four stories about people who have left their native lands, is the heartrending evocation—purportedly a memoir in manuscript—of an idyllic German-Jewish childhood. The narrator goes on to describe his decision to visit the town, Kissingen, where this life had been lived, to see what traces of it remained. Because it was *The Emigrants* that launched Sebald in English, and because the subject of the last narrative, a famous painter given the name Max Ferber, is a German Jew sent out of Nazi Germany as a child to safety in England—his mother, who perished in the camps with his father, being the author of the memoir—the book was routinely labeled by most of the reviewers (especially, but not only, in America) as an example of Holocaust literature. Ending a book of lament with the ulti-

mate subject of lament, *The Emigrants* may have set up some of Sebald's admirers for a disappointment with the work that followed it in
translation, *The Rings of Saturn*. This book is not divided into distinct
narratives but consists of a chain or progress of stories: one story leads
to another. In *The Rings of Saturn*, the well-stocked mind speculates
whether Sir Thomas Browne, visiting Holland, was present at an
anatomy lesson depicted by Rembrandt; remembers a romantic interlude, during his English exile, in the life of Chateaubriand; recalls
Roger Casement's noble efforts to publicize the infamies of Leopold's
rule in the Congo; and retells the childhood in exile and early adventures at sea of Joseph Conrad—these stories, and many others. With its
cavalcade of erudite and curious anecdotes, and its tender encounters
with bookish people (two lecturers on French literature, one of them a
Flaubert scholar; the translator and poet Michael Hamburger), *The
Rings of Saturn* could seem—after the high excruciation of *The Emigrants*—merely "literary."

It would be a pity if the expectations about Sebald's work created
by *The Emigrants* also influenced the reception of *Vertigo*, which
makes still clearer the nature of his morally accelerated travel narratives—history-minded in their obsessions; fictional in their reach.
Travel frees the mind for the play of associations; for the afflictions
(and erosions) of memory; for the savoring of solitude. The awareness
of the solitary narrator is the true protagonist of Sebald's books, even
when it is doing one of the things it does best: recounting, summing
up, the lives of others.

Vertigo is the book in which the narrator's English life is least in evidence. And, even more than the two succeeding books, this is a self-
portrait of a mind: a restless, chronically dissatisfied mind; a harrowed
mind; a mind prone to hallucinations. Walking in Vienna, he thinks he
recognizes the poet Dante, banished from his hometown on pain of
being burned at the stake. Sitting on the rear bench of a vaporetto in
Venice, he sees Ludwig II of Bavaria; riding on a bus along the shore of
Lake Garda toward Riva, he sees an adolescent boy who looks exactly
like Kafka. This narrator, who defines himself as a foreigner—over-
hearing the babble of some German tourists in a hotel, he wishes he
did not understand them; "that is, that he were the citizen of a better

country, or of no country at all"—is also a mind in mourning. At one moment, the narrator says he does not know whether he is still in the land of the living or already somewhere else.

In fact, he is both: both alive and, if his imagination is the guide, posthumous. A journey is often a revisiting. It is the return to a place for some unfinished business, to retrace a memory, to repeat (or complete) an experience; to offer oneself up—as in the fourth narrative of *The Emigrants*—to the final, most devastating revelations. These heroic acts of remembering and retracing bring with them a price. Part of the power of *Vertigo* is that it dwells more on the cost of this effort. "Vertigo," the word used to translate the playful German title, *Schwindel. Gefühle* (roughly: Giddiness. Feeling), hardly suggests all the kinds of panic and torpor and disorientation described in the book. In *Vertigo*, he relates how, after arriving in Vienna, he walked so far that, he discovered returning to the hotel, his shoes had fallen apart. In *The Rings of Saturn* and, above all, in *The Emigrants*, the mind is less focused on itself; the narrator is more elusive. More than the later books, *Vertigo* is about the narrator's own afflicted consciousness. But the laconically evoked mental distress that edges the narrator's calm, knowledgeable awareness is never solipsistic, as in the literature of lesser concerns.

What anchors the unstable consciousness of the narrator is the spaciousness and acuity of the details. As travel is the generative principle of mental activity in Sebald's books, moving through space gives a kinetic rush to his marvelous descriptions, especially of landscapes. This is a *propelled* narrator.

Where has one heard in English a voice of such confidence and precision, so direct in its expression of feeling, yet so respectfully devoted to recording "the real"? D. H. Lawrence may come to mind, and the Naipaul of *The Enigma of Arrival*. But they have little of the passionate bleakness of Sebald's voice. For this one must look to a German genealogy. Jean Paul, Franz Grillparzer, Adalbert Stifter, Robert Walser, the Hofmannsthal of "The Lord Chandos Letter," Thomas Bernhard are a few of the affiliations of this contemporary master of the literature of lament and of mental restlessness. The consensus about English literature for most of the past century has decreed the relentlessly elegiac and lyrical to be inappropriate for fiction, overblown, pretentious. (Even so great a novel, and exception, as Virginia Woolf's *The Waves* has not escaped these strictures.) Postwar German literature, mindful of how congenial the grandiosity of past art and literature, particularly that of German Romanticism, proved to the work of totalitarian mythmaking, has been suspicious of anything like the romantic or nostalgic relation to the past. But then perhaps only a German writer permanently domiciled abroad, in the precincts of a literature with a modern predilection for the anti-sublime, could indulge in so convincing a noble tone.

Besides the narrator's moral fervency and gifts of compassion (here he parts company with Bernhard), what keeps this writing always fresh, never merely rhetorical, is the saturated naming and visualizing in words; that, and the ever-surprising device of pictorial illustration. Pictures of train tickets or a torn-out leaf from a pocket diary, drawings, a calling card, newspaper clippings, a detail from a painting, and, of course, photographs have the charm and, in many instances, the imperfections of relics. Thus, in *Vertigo*, at one moment the narrator loses his passport; or rather, his hotel loses it for him. And here is the document made out by the police in Riva, with—a touch of mystery—the G in W. G. Sebald inked out. And the new passport, with the photograph issued by the German consulate in Milan. (Yes, this professional foreigner travels on a German passport—at least he did in 1987.) In *The Emigrants* these visual documents seem talismanic. It seems likely that not all of them are genuine. In *The Rings of Saturn* they seem, less interestingly, merely illustrative. If the narrator speaks of Swinburne, there is a small portrait of Swinburne set in the middle of the page; if relating a visit to a cemetery in Suffolk, where his attention is captured by a funerary monument to a woman who died in 1799, which he describes in detail, from fulsome epitaph to the holes bored in the stone on the upper edges of the four sides, we are given a blurry little photograph of the tomb, again in the middle of the page.

In *Vertigo* the documents have a more poignant message. They say, It's true, what I've been telling you—which is hardly what a reader of fiction normally demands. To offer evidence at all is to endow what has been described by words with a mysterious surplus of pathos. The photographs and other relics reproduced on the page become an exquisite index of the pastness of the past.

Sometimes they seem like the squiggles in *Tristram Shandy*; the author is being intimate with us. At other moments, these insistently proffered visual relics seem an insolent challenge to the sufficiency of the verbal. And yet, as Sebald writes in *The Rings of Saturn*, describing a favorite haunt, the Sailors' Reading Room in Southwold, where he pored over entries from the log of a patrol ship anchored off the pier during the autumn of 1914, "Every time I decipher one of these entries I am astounded that a trail that has long since vanished from the air or the water remains visible here on the paper." And, he continues, closing the marbled cover of the logbook, he pondered "the mysterious survival of the written word."

[2000]

The Wisdom Project

A *NOTHER BEAUTY*, a wise, iridescent book by the Polish writer Adam Zagajewski, dips in and out of many genres: coming-of-age memoir, commonplace book, aphoristic musings, vignettes, and defense of poetry—that is, a defense of the idea of literary greatness.

It is, to be sure, something of a misnomer to call Zagajewski a writer: a poet who also writes indispensable prose does not thereby forfeit the better title. Prose being the wordy affair it is, Zagajewski's fills a good many more pages than his poems. But in literature's canonical two-party system, poetry always trumps prose. Poetry stands for literature at its most serious, most improving, most intense, most coveted. "The author and reader always dream of a great poem, of writing it, reading it, living it." Living the poem: being elevated by it; deepened; for a moment, saved.

From a great Polish writer we expect Slavic intensities. (The particular Polish nuance may require a little application.) Literature as soul nourishment has been a Slavic specialty for the last century and a half. It seems hardly surprising that Zagajewski, for all the calm and delicacy of his poet-voice, would hold a view of poetry more akin to that of Shelley than of Ashbery. As it happens, the reality of self-transcendence has even less credibility among younger Polish poets than among those writing in English. And Zagajewski's transposed religious longings—to live, through poetry, on a "higher plane"—are never voiced without a grace note of mild self-deprecation. A recent collection of poems is called, with charming sobriety, *Mysticism for Beginners*. The world (of lyrical feeling, of ecstatic inwardness) to which poetry gives poets and their readers access is one that defective human nature bars us from inhabiting except fleetingly. Poems "don't last," Zagajewski observes wryly, "particularly the short lyric poems that prevail today." All they can offer is "a moment of intense experience." Prose is sturdier, if only because it takes longer to get through.

Another Beauty is Zagajewski's third book of prose to appear in English. The first two are made up of pieces, some essayistic, some memoiristic, with titles. The new book is a flow of untitled (and unnumbered) short and not so short takes. Its mix of narratives, observations, portraits, reflections, reminiscences gives *Another Beauty* a high-velocity variance of mood and attack that we associate more with a volume of poems—lyric poems, anyway—which is a succession of discontinuous intensities, at different pitches of concern.

What kind of intensities? (That is, what kind of prose?) Thoughtful, precise; rhapsodic; rueful; courteous; prone to wonder. Then and now, here and there—the whole book oscillates, vibrates, with contrasts. (This is like this, but that is like that. Or: we expected this, but we got that.) And everything reeks of dissimilarity, savor, message, metaphor. Even the weather:

> The meteorological depressions of Paris have an oceanic feel; the Atlantic dispatches them in the direction of the continent. The winds blow, dark clouds scurry across the city like racecars. The rain falls at a spiteful slant. At times the heavens' face appears, a scrap of blue. Then it's dark again, the Seine becomes a black pavement. The lowlands of Paris seethe with oceanic energy, thunderbolts pop like champagne corks. Whereas a typical Central European depression—centered somewhere above the Carpathians—behaves completely differently: it's subdued and melancholy, one might say philosophical. The clouds barely move. They're shaped differently; they're like an enormous blimp drooping over Kraków's Central Market. The light shifts gradually; the violet glow fades, giving way to yellow spotlights. The sun skulks somewhere behind silken clouds, illuminating the most varied

strata of earth and sky. Some of the clouds resemble deep-sea fishes that have ascended to the surface and swim with mouths wide open, as if startled by the taste of air. This kind of weather can last for several days, the meek climate of Central Europe. And if, after lengthy deliberations, a thunderstorm does strike, it behaves as if it were stuttering. Instead of a sharp, decisive shot, it emits a series of drawn-out sounds, *pa pa pa pa*—an echo instead of a blast. Thunder on the installment plan.

In Zagajewski's rendering, nature turns out to be wittily steeped in the bathos of national histories, with the crisp, bullying weather of Paris flaunting France's indefatigable good fortune and Kraków's tired, melancholy weather summing up Poland's innumerable defeats and other woes. The poet can't escape history, only transmute it sometimes, for purposes of bravura descriptiveness, into magic geography.

ι

MAY YOU BE BORN in interesting times, runs the ancient (or at least proverbial) Chinese curse. Updated for our own hyperinteresting era, it might run: May you be born in an interesting place.

What Czeslaw Milosz calls, mordantly, "the privilege of coming from strange lands where it is difficult to escape history"—think of Poland, Ireland, Israel, Bosnia—prods and pinches, exalts and exhausts a writer like Zagajewski whose standards are set by *world* literature. History means strife. History means tragic impasse—and your friends being jailed or killed. History means perennial challenges to the nation's very right to exist. Poland, of course, had two centuries of history's chokehold—from the First Partition in 1772, which in a few years brought about the end of an autonomous state (not restored until after World War I), to the collapse of the Soviet-style regime in 1989.

Such countries—such histories—make it hard for their writers ever completely to secede from the collective anguish. Here is the testimony of another great writer living in a newer nation condemned to nonstop dread, A. B. Yehoshua:

You are insistently summoned to solidarity, summoned from within yourself rather than by an external compulsion, because you live from one newscast to the next, and it becomes a solidarity that is technical, automatic from the standpoint of its emotional reaction, because by now you are completely built to react that way and live in tension. Your emotional reactions to any piece of news about an Israeli casualty, a plane shot down, are predetermined. Hence the lack of solitude, the inability to be alone in the spiritual sense and to arrive at a life of intellectual creativity.

Yehoshua's terms are identical with those of Zagajewski, whose first prose book in English is a collection of six pieces published in the early 1980s called *Solidarity, Solitude*. Solitude erodes solidarity; solidarity corrupts solitude.

The solitude of a Polish writer is always inflected by a sense of the community formed by the literature itself. Milosz, in his own great defense of poetry, the address that he delivered at the Jagiellonian University in 1989 entitled "With Polish Poetry Against the World," pays homage to Polish poetry for having protected him "from sterile despair in emigration," recalling that "in solitude too difficult and painful to recommend to anyone" there was always "the sense of duty toward my predecessors and successors." For Milosz, born in 1911, a Polish writer may never escape being responsible to others. By this rule, the stellar counterexample of Witold Gombrowicz—in his fiction, in his legendarily egocentric, truculent *Diary*, in his brazen polemic "Against Poetry"—offers evidence, convulsive evidence, of the authority of idealism in Polish literature. History is present even by its absence, Milosz observes in a late book of prose, *Milosz's ABC's*; and the cult of altruism and high-mindedness flourishes, if perversely, in Gombrowicz's denial of responsibility to anything beyond the self's anarchic clamor, his ingenious harangues on behalf of the menial, the immature, the low-minded.

Squeezed right, every life can be construed as embodying exemplary experiences and historical momentousness. Even Gombrowicz could not help but see his life as exemplary, making something didactic—a rebuke to his origins—out of his gentry childhood, his precocious literary notoriety, his fateful, irrevocable emigration. And a writer whose love of literature still entailed, unresentfully, so much piety toward old masters, such eagerness to feed on the magnificent traditions on offer from the past, could hardly help seeing his life—at least his early circumstances—as some kind of representative destiny.

Soon after Zagajewski's birth in October 1945 in the medieval Polish city of Lwów, his family was uprooted in the great displacements (and redrawings of maps) that followed the Yalta agreements of the Three Old Men, which put Lwów in the hands of the Soviet Union; and the poet grew up in the formerly German, now Polish, town of Gliwice, thirty miles from Auschwitz. In *Two Cities*, his second prose book translated into English, Zagajewski writes:

> I spent my childhood in an ugly industrial city; I was brought there when I was barely four months old, and then for many years afterward I was told about the extraordinarily beautiful city that my family had to leave.

The family mythology of an expulsion from paradise may have made him feel, he says, forever homeless. It also seems, on the evidence of his writing, to have made him an expert lover of cities—"beautiful, bewitching Kraków" above all, for which he left unredeemable Gliwice to attend university, and where he remained until he was thirty-seven.

Dates are sparse in *Another Beauty*, and the arrangement of stories-from-a-life is unchronological. But there is, implicitly, always a *where*, with which the poet's heart and senses are in dialogue. Not the traveler, not even the émigré—most of the great Polish poets have gone westward, and Zagajewski is not one of the exceptions—but the continually stimulated city dweller is featured here. There are few living rooms and no bedrooms in *Another Beauty*, but more than a few public squares and libraries and trains. Once he's past his student years, the occasional "we" disappears; there is only an "I." Occasionally he will mention where he is writing: Zagajewski now lives in Paris and teaches one term each year at the University of Houston. "I'm strolling through Paris," one entry begins. "And at this very moment I'm listening to the Seventh Symphony in Houston," notes another. There are always two cities: Lwów and Gliwice, Gliwice and Kraków, Paris and Houston.

More poignant oppositions infuse this book: self and others, youth and age. There are plangent evocations of difficult elderly relatives and cranky professors: this portrait of the poet as a young man is striking for its tenderness toward the old. And the account of the decorous ardors, literary and political, of his student years sets his book quite at odds with the narcissistic purposes, and pointedly indiscreet contents, of most autobiographical writing today. For Zagajewski, autobiography is an occasion to purge oneself of vanity, while advancing the project of self-understanding—call it the wisdom project—which is never completed, however long the life.

To describe oneself as young is to face that one is no longer young. And a pithy acknowledgment that the debilities of age approach, with death in their train, is one of the many observations that cut short a story from Zagajewski's past. Telling the stories discontinuously, as glimpses, secures several good results. It keeps the prose dense, quick. And it invites telling only those stories that lead to some insight, or epiphany. There is a larger lesson in the very way of telling, a lesson in moral tone: how to talk about oneself without complacency. Life, when not a school for heartlessness, is an education in sympathy. The sum of the stories reminds us that in a life of a certain length and spiritual seriousness, change—sometimes not for the worse—is just as real as death.

ALL WRITING IS a species of remembering. If there is anything triumphalist about *Another Beauty* it is that the acts of remembering the book contains seem so frictionless. Imagining—that is, bringing the past to mental life—is there as needed; it never falters; it is by definition a success. The recovery of memory, of course, is an ethical obligation: the obligation to persist in the effort to apprehend the truth. This seems less apparent in America, where the work of memory has been exuberantly identified with the creation of useful or therapeutic fictions, than in Zagajewski's lacerated corner of the world.

To recover a memory—to secure a truth—is a supreme touchstone of value in *Another Beauty*. "I didn't witness the extermination of the Jews," Zagajewski writes:

I was born too late. I bore witness, though, to the gradual process by which Europe recovered its memory. This memory moved slowly, more like a lazy, lowland river than a mountain stream, but it finally, unambiguously condemned the evil of the Holocaust and the Nazis, and the evil of Soviet civilization as well (though in this it was less successful, as if reluctant to admit that two such monstrosities might simultaneously coexist).

That memories are recovered—that is, that the suppressed truths do reemerge—is the basis of whatever hope one can have for justice and a modicum of sanity in the ongoing life of communities.

Once recovered, though, even truth may become complacent and self-flattering. Thus, rather than provide yet one more denunciation of the iniquities and oppressiveness of the regime that was shut down in 1989, Zagajewski chooses to stress the benefits of the struggle against evil that flowed to the idealistic young in his portrayal of the flawed beginnings of his vocation, as a "political poet," and his activities in dissident student and literary circles in the Kraków of the late 1960s and 1970s. (In 1968, Zagajewski was twenty-three years old.) In those heady days, poetry and activism rhymed. Both elevated, heightened; engagement in a just cause, like service to poetry, made you feel larger.

That every generation fears, misunderstands, and condescends to its successor—this, too, is a function of the equivalence of history and memory (history being what it is agreed on, collectively, to remember). Each generation has its distinctive memories, and the elapsing of time, which brings with it a steady accumulation of loss, confers on those memories a normativeness which cannot possibly be honored by the young, who are busy compiling their memories, their benchmarks. One of Zagajewski's most moving portraits of elders is of Stefan Szuman, an illustrious member of the interwar Polish intelligentsia (he had known Stanislaw Witkiewicz and Bruno Schulz) and now a retired professor at the university living in isolation and penury. Its point is Zagajewski's realization, thinking back, that he and his literary friends could only have seemed like fools and savages, "shaped by a postwar education, by new schools, new papers, new radio, new TV," to the defeated, homely, embittered Szuman and his wife. The rule seems to be: each generation looks upon its successor generation as barbarians.

Zagajewski, himself no longer young and now a teacher of American students, is committed to not replicating, in his turn, that kind of despair and incomprehension. Nor is he content to write off an entire older Polish generation of intellectuals and artists, his generation's "enemy"—the true believers and those who just sold out—for turpitude and cowardice: they weren't simply devils, any more than he and his friends were angels. As for those "who began by serving Stalin's civilization" but then changed, Zagajewski writes: "I don't condemn them for their early, youthful intoxication. I'm more inclined to marvel at the generosity of human nature, which offers gifted young people a second chance, the opportunity for a moral comeback."

At the heart of this assessment is the wisdom of the novelist, a professional of empathy, rather than that of a lyric poet. (Zagajewski has written four novels, none as yet translated into English.) The dramatic monologue "Betrayal" in *Two Cities* begins:

> Why did I do that? Why did I do what? Why was I who I was? And who was I? I am already beginning to regret that I agreed to grant you this interview. For years I refused; you must have asked me at a weak moment or in a moment of anxiety . . . What did that world look like? The one you were too late to get to know. The same as this one. Completely different.

That everything is always different . . . and the same: a poet's wisdom. Actually, wisdom *tout court*.

Of course, history should never be thought of with a capital *H*. The governing sense of Zagajewski's memory-work is his awareness of having lived through several historical periods, in the course of which things eventually got better. Modestly, imperfectly—not utopianly—better. The young Zagajewski and his comrades in dissidence had assumed that communism would last another hundred, two hundred years, when, in fact, it had less than two decades to go. Lesson: evil is not immutable. The reality is, everyone outlives an old self, often more than one, in the course of a reasonably long life.

Another Beauty is, in part, a meditation on easing the clamp of history: liberating the self from "the grimaces and caprices" of history. That should not be so hard in the less flagrantly evil public world that has come into being in Poland since 1989. But institutions may be more easily liquidated than a temperament. Zagajewski's temperament (that is, the dialogue he conducts with himself) is rooted in an era when heroism was at least an option, and ethical rigor still something admired and consecrated by the genius of several national literatures. How to negotiate a soft landing onto the new lowland of diminished moral expectations and shabby artistic standards is the problem of all the Central European writers whose tenacities were forged in the bad old days.

The maturing that Zagajewski chronicles can be described as the relaxing of this temperament: the finding of the right openness, the right calmness, the right inwardness. (He says he can only write when he feels happy, peaceful.) Exaltation—and who can gainsay this judgment from a member of the generation of '68?—is viewed with a skeptical eye. Hyperemphatic intensity holds no allure. His end of the religious spectrum does not include any notion of the sacred, which figures centrally in the work of the late Jerzy Grotowski and the theatre center in Gardzienice led by Wlodzimierz Staniewski. While the sacral-ecstatic tradition is still alive in Polish theatre—but then theatre, especially this kind of theatre, is compulsorily collective—it has no place in contemporary Polish literature. *Another Beauty* is suffused with the humility of a spiritual longing that precludes frenzy, and envisages no large gestures of sacrifice. As Zagajewski notes: "The week isn't made up only of Sundays."

Some of his keenest pages are descriptions of happiness, the everyday happiness of a connoisseur of solitary delights: strolling, reading, listening to Beethoven or Schumann. The "I" of *Another Beauty* is scrupulous, vulnerable, earnest—without a jot of self-protective irony. And neither Zagajewski nor this reader would wish it otherwise. Irony would come at the cost of so much pleasure. "Ecstasy and irony rarely meet in the world of art," Zagajewski observes. "When they do it's usually for the purposes of mutual sabotage; they struggle to diminish each other's power." And he is unabashedly on the side of ecstasy.

These descriptions are tributes to what produces happiness, not celebrations of the receptive self. He may simply describe something he loves, or quote a favorite poem: the book is a sampling of appreciations and sympathies. There are penetrating sketches of admired friends such as Adam Michnik, a beacon of resistance to the dictatorship (who while in jail wrote about the poet Zbigniew Herbert, among others, in a book he titled *From the History of Honor in Poland*); there is a reverential salute to the ancient doyen of Polish émigrés in Paris, the painter, writer, and heroic alumnus of Soviet prison camps Józef Czapski. *L'enfer, c'est les autres.* No, it is others who save us, Zagajewski declares in the poem that gives the book its title and serves as its epigraph.

Here is "Another Beauty" in the new version by the book's translator, Clare Cavanagh:

> We find comfort only in
> another beauty, in others'
> music, in the poetry of others.
> Salvation lies with others,
> though solitude may taste like
> opium. Other people aren't hell
> if you glimpse them at dawn, when
> their brows are clean, rinsed by dreams.
> This is why I pause: which word
> to use, you or he. Each he
> betrays some you, but
> calm conversation bides its time
> in others' poems.

And here it is as it appeared in 1985 in *Tremor: Selected Poems*, Zagajewski's first collection of poems in English, translated by Renata Gorczynski, where it is entitled "In the Beauty Created by Others":

> Only in the beauty created
> by others is there consolation,

in the music of others and in others' poems.
Only others save us,
even though solitude tastes like
opium. The others are not hell,
if you see them early, with their
foreheads pure, cleansed by dreams.
That is why I wonder what
word should be used, "he" or "you." Every "he"
is a betrayal of a certain "you" but
in return someone else's poem
offers the fidelity of a sober dialogue.

A defense of poetry *and* a defense of goodness, or, more exactly, of good-naturedness.

Nothing could take the reader in a more contrary direction to today's cult of the excitements of self than to follow Zagajewski as he unspools his seductive praise of serenity, sympathy, forbearance; of "the calm and courage of an ordinary life." To declare "I believe in truth!" and, in another passage, "Goodness does exist!" (those exclamation points!) seems, if not Panglossian—one American reviewer detected a touch of Panglossian uplift in the book—then at least quixotic. This culture offers few current models of masculine sweetness, and those we already possess, from past literature, are associated with naïveté, childlikeness, social innocence: Joe Gargery in *Great Expectations*, Alyosha in *The Brothers Karamazov*. Zagajewski's persona in *Another Beauty* is anything but innocent in that sense. But he has a special gift for conjuring up states of complex innocence, the innocence of genius, as in his heartrending portrait-poem "Franz Schubert: A Press Conference."

THE TITLE MAY MISLEAD. *Another Beauty* makes clear at every turn that, worshipper of greatness in poetry and other arts that he is, Zagajewski is not an aesthete. Poetry is to be judged by standards still higher: "Woe to the writer who values beauty over truth." Poetry must be protected from the temptations to arrogance inherent in its own states of elation.

Of course, both beauty and truth seem like frail guideposts left over from a more innocent past. In the delicate negotiation with the present which Zagajewski conducts on behalf of the endangered verities, nostalgia would count as a deficit of argument. Still, even absent the old certainties and license to perorate, he is pledged to defending the idea of "sublime" or "noble" achievement in literature—assuming, as he does, that we still need the qualities in art that are praised by such now virtually unsayable words. Zagajewski's most eloquent, summative defense is "The Shabby and the Sublime," an address he delivered at a Dutch university in 1998 which posed the pseudo-naïve question: Is literary greatness still possible?

The belief in literary greatness implies that the capacity for admiration is still intact. When admiration is corrupted, that is, made cynical, the question as to whether greatness is possible simply vanishes. Nihilism and admiration compete with each other, sabotage each other, struggle to diminish each other's power. (Like irony and ecstasy.)

Disheartened though he is by "the mutation downward of European literature," Zagajewski declines to speculate about what has given the advantage to subjectivism and the revolt against "greatness." Perhaps those brought up on the fierceness of state-administered mediocrity find it hard to be as indignant as they might be about the extent to which mercantilist values (often sporting the mask of "democratic" or populist values) have sapped the foundations of the sublime. "Soviet civilization," a.k.a. communism, was a great conservative force. The cultural policies of communist regimes embalmed the old, hierarchical notions of achievement, seeking to confer a noble pedigree on propagandistic banalities. In contrast, capitalism has a truly radical relation to culture, dismantling the very notion of greatness in the arts, which is now most successfully dismissed by the ecumenical philistinism of both cultural progressives and cultural reactionaries as an "elitist" presumption.

Zagajewski's protest against the collapse of standards has nothing analytical about it. Yet surely he understands the futility (and indignity) of simply denouncing the collapse. Orphaned pieties overheat sometimes: "Without poetry, we'd hardly be better than the mammals." And many passages assert a familiar dismay, especially when he succumbs to the temptation to see our era as uniquely degraded. What, he inquires rhetorically, would "the great, innocent artists of the past, Giotto or van Eyck, Proust or Apollinaire, have done if some spiteful demon had set them down in our flawed and tawdry world"? Don't know about Giotto or van Eyck; but Proust (d. 1922) and Apollinaire (d. 1918) *innocent*? I should have thought the Europe in which that colossal, senseless slaughter called World War I took place was, if anything, a good deal worse than "flawed and tawdry."

The idea of art as the beleaguered vehicle of spiritual value in a secular age should not have been left unexamined. Nevertheless, Zagajewski's utter absence of rancor and vindictiveness, his generosity of spirit, his awareness of the vulgarity of unremitting complaint and of the self-righteous assumption of one's own cultural superiority, mark off his stance from that of the usual professional mourners of the Death of High Culture, such as the ever portentous George Steiner. (Once in a while he slips into facile assertions of the superiority of the past over the present, but even then he is never grandiose or self-aggrandizing: call it Steinerism with a human face.)

Inveterately prescriptive, occasionally sententious, Zagajewski is too shrewd, too respectful of common or ordinary wisdom, not to see the limits of each of the positions that surround and make sense out of his abiding passions. One *can* be elevated, deepened, improved by works of art. But, Zagajewski cautions, the imagination can become one of its own enemies "if it loses sight of the solid world that cannot be dissolved in art."

Because the book is notational, juxtapositional, it is possible for Zagajewski to entertain quite contradictory assessments. What is valuable is how divided Zagajewski is, as he himself acknowledges. The reflections and the stories in *Another Beauty* show us a subtle, important mind divided between the public world and the claims of art, between solidarity and solitude; between the original "two cities": the Human

City and the City of God. Divided, but not overthrown. There is anguish, but then serenity keeps breaking through. There is desolation and, as well, so many fortifying pleasures supplied by the genius of others. There was scorn, until *caritas* chimed in. There is despair, but there is, just as inexorably, consolation.

[2001]

Writing Itself:
On Roland Barthes

The best poetry will be rhetorical criticism . . .
>   —WALLACE STEVENS (in a journal of 1899)

I rarely lose sight of myself.
>   —PAUL VALÉRY, *Monsieur Teste*

TEACHER, MAN OF LETTERS, moralist, philosopher of culture, connoisseur of strong ideas, protean autobiographer . . . of all the intellectual notables who have emerged since World War II in France, Roland Barthes is the one whose work I am most certain will endure. Barthes was in full flow, incessantly productive, as he had been for over three decades, when he was struck by a van as he started across a street in Paris in early 1980—a death felt by friends and admirers to be excruciatingly untimely. But along with the backward look of grief comes the awareness that confers upon his large, chronically mutating body of writing, as on all major work, its retroactive completeness. The development of Barthes's work now seems logical; more than that, exhaustive. It even begins and falls silent on the same subject—that exemplary instrument in the career of consciousness, the writer's journal. As it happens, the first essay Barthes ever published celebrates the model consciousness he found in the *Journal* of André

Gide, and what turned out to be the last essay published before he died offers Barthes's musings on his own journal-keeping. The symmetry, however adventitious, is an utterly appropriate one, for Barthes's writing, with its prodigious variety of subjects, has finally one great subject: writing itself.

His early themes were those of the freelance partisan of letters, on the occasions afforded by cultural journalism, literary debate, theatre and book reviews. To these were added topics that originated and were recycled in seminars and from the lecture platform, for Barthes's literary career was run concurrently with a (very successful) academic one, and in part *as* an academic one. But the voice was always singular, and self-referring; the achievement is of another, larger order than can be had even by practicing, with thrilling virtuosity, the most lively and many-tracked of academic disciplines. For all his contributions to the would-be science of signs and structures, Barthes's endeavor was the quintessentially literary one: the writer organizing, under a series of doctrinal auspices, the theory of his own mind. And when the current enclosure of his reputation by the labels of semiology and structuralism crumbles, as it must, Barthes will appear, I think, as a rather traditional *promeneur solitaire*, and a greater writer than even his more fervent admirers now claim.

HE ALWAYS WROTE full out, was always concentrated, keen, indefatigable. This dazzling inventiveness seems not just a function of Barthes's extraordinary powers as a mind, as a writer. It seems to have almost the status of a position—as if this is what critical discourse *must* be. "Literature is like phosphorous," he says in his first book, which came out in 1953, *Writing Degree Zero*; "it shines with its maximum brilliance at the moment when it attempts to die." In Barthes's view, literature is already a posthumous affair. His work affirms a standard of vehement brilliance that is indeed one ideal of a cultural moment which believes itself to be having, in several senses, the last word.

Its brilliance aside, Barthes's work has some of the specific traits associated with the style of a late moment in culture—one that presumes an endless discourse anterior to itself, that presumes intellectual sophistication: it is work that, strenuously unwilling to be boring or obvious, favors compact assertion, writing that rapidly covers a great deal of ground. Barthes was an inspired, ingenious practitioner of the essay and the anti-essay—he had a resistance to long forms. Typically, his sentences are complex, comma-ridden and colon-prone, packed with densely worded entailments of ideas deployed as if these were the materials of a supple prose. It is a style of exposition, recognizably French, whose parent tradition is to be found in the tense, idiosyncratic essays published between the two world wars in the *Nouvelle Revue Française*—a perfected version of the *NRF*'s house style which can deliver more ideas per page while retaining the brio of that style, its acuteness of timbre. His vocabulary is large, fastidious, fearlessly mandarin. Even Barthes's less fleet, more jargon-haunted writings—most of them from the 1960s—are full of flavor; he manages to make an exuberant use of neologisms. While exuding straight-ahead energy, his prose constantly reaches for the summative formulation; it is irrepressibly aphoristic. (Indeed, one could go through Barthes's work extracting superb bits—epigrams, maxims—to make a small book, as has been done with Wilde and Proust.) Barthes's strengths as an aphorist suggest a sensibility gifted, before any intervention of theory, for the perception of structure. A method of condensed assertion by means of symmetrically counterposed terms, the aphorism displays the symmetries and complementarities of situations or ideas—their design, their shape. Like a markedly greater feeling for drawings than for paintings, a talent for aphorism is one of the signs of what could be called the formalist temperament.

The formalist temperament is just one variant of a sensibility shared by many who speculate in an era of hypersaturated awareness. What characterizes such a sensibility more generally is its reliance on the criterion of taste, and its proud refusal to propose anything that does not bear the stamp of subjectivity. Confidently assertive, it nevertheless insists that its assertions are no more than provisional. (To do otherwise would be bad taste.) Indeed, adepts of this sensibility usually make a point of claiming and reclaiming amateur status. "In linguistics I have never been anything but an amateur," Barthes told an interviewer in 1975. Throughout his late writings Barthes repeatedly disavows the, as it were, vulgar roles of system-builder, authority, mentor, expert, in order to reserve for himself the privileges and freedoms of delectation: the exercise of taste for Barthes means, usually, to praise. What makes the role a choice one is his unstated commitment to finding something new and unfamiliar to praise (which requires having the right dissonance with established taste); or to praising a familiar work differently.

An early example is his second book—it appeared in 1954—which is on Michelet. Through an inventory of the recurrent metaphors and themes in the great nineteenth-century historian's epic narratives, Barthes discloses a more intimate narration: Michelet's history of his own body and the "lyric resurrection of past bodies." Barthes is always after another meaning, a more eccentric—often utopian—discourse. What pleased him was to show insipid and reactionary works to be quirky and implicitly subversive; to display in the most extravagant projects of the imagination an opposite extreme—in his essay on Sade, a sexual ideal that was really an exercise in delirious rationality; in his essay on Fourier, a rationalist ideal that was really an exercise in sensual delirium. Barthes did take on central figures of the literary canon when he had something polemical to offer: in 1960 he wrote a short book on Racine, which scandalized academic critics (the ensuing controversy ended with Barthes's complete triumph over his detractors); he also wrote on Proust and Flaubert. But more often, armed with his essentially adversary notion of the "text," he applied his ingenuity to the marginal literary subject: an unimportant "work"—say, Balzac's *Sarrasine*, Chateaubriand's *Life of Rancé*—could be a marvelous "text." Considering something as a "text" means for Barthes precisely to suspend conventional evaluations (the difference between major and minor literature), to subvert established classifications (the separation of genres, the distinctions among the arts).

Though work of every form and worth qualifies for citizenship in the great democracy of "texts," the critic will tend to avoid those that everyone has handled, the meaning that everyone knows. The formalist turn in modern criticism—from its pristine phase, as in Shklovsky's idea of defamiliarizing, onward—dictates just this. It charges the critic with the task of discarding worn-out meanings for fresh ones. It is a mandate to scout for new meanings. *Etonne-moi.*

The same mandate is supplied by Barthes's notions of "text" and "textuality." These translate into criticism the modernist ideal of an open-ended, polysemous literature; and thereby make the critic, just like the creators of that literature, the inventor of meaning. (The aim of literature, Barthes asserts, is to put "meaning" into the world but not "a meaning.") To decide that the point of criticism is to alter and to re-locate meaning—adding, subtracting, multiplying it—is in effect to base the critic's exertions on an enterprise of avoidance, and thereby to recommit criticism (if it had ever left) to the dominion of taste. For it is, finally, the exercise of taste which identifies meanings that are famil-iar; a judgment of taste which discriminates against such meanings as too familiar; an ideology of taste which makes of the familiar something vulgar and facile. Barthes's formalism at its most decisive, his ruling that the critic is called on to reconstitute not the "message" of a work but only its "system"—its form, its structure—is perhaps best under-stood thus, as the liberating avoidance of the obvious, as an immense gesture of good taste.

For the modernist—that is, formalist—critic, the work with its re-ceived valuations already exists. Now, what *else* can be said? The canon of great books has been fixed. What can we add or restore to it? The "message" is already understood, or is obsolete. Let's ignore it.

OF A VARIETY of means Barthes possessed for giving himself some-thing to say—he had an exceptionally fluent, ingenious generalizing power—the most elementary was his aphorist's ability to conjure up a vivacious duality: anything could be split either into itself and its oppo-site or into two versions of itself; and one term then fielded against the other to yield an unexpected relation. The point of Voltairean travel, he remarks, is "to manifest an immobility"; Baudelaire "had to protect theatricality from the theatre"; the Eiffel Tower "makes the city into a kind of Nature"—Barthes's writing is seeded with such ostensibly par-adoxical, epigrammatic formulas as these, whose point is to sum some-thing up. It is the nature of aphoristic thinking to be always in a state of concluding; a bid to have the final word is inherent in all powerful phrase-making.

Less elegant, indeed making a point of dogged explicitness, and far more powerful as an instrument for giving himself something to say, are the classifications that Barthes lays out in order to topple himself into a piece of argument—dividing into two, three, even four parts the matter to be considered. Arguments are launched by announcing that there are two main classes and two subclasses of narrative units, two ways in which myth lends itself to history, two facets of Racinean eros, two musics, two ways to read La Rochefoucauld, two kinds of writers, two forms of his own interest in photographs. That there are three types of corrections a writer makes, three Mediterraneans and three tragic sites in Racine, three levels on which to read the plates of the *Encyclopedia*, three areas of spectacle and three types of gesture in Japanese puppet theatre, three attitudes toward speech and writing, equivalent to three vocations: writer, intellectual, and teacher. That there are four kinds of readers, four reasons for keeping a journal . . .

And so on. This is the codifying, frontal style of French intellectual discourse, a branch of the rhetorical tactics that the French call, not quite accurately, Cartesian. Although a few of the classifications Barthes employs are standard, such as semiology's canonical triad of signified, signifier, and sign, many are inventions devised by Barthes in order to *make* an argument, such as his assertion in a late book, *The Pleasure of the Text*, that the modern artist seeks to destroy art, "this effort taking three forms." The aim of this implacable categorizing is not just to map the intellectual territory: Barthes's taxonomies are never static. Often the point is precisely for one category to subvert the other, as do the two forms, which he calls *punctum* and *studium*, of his interest in photographs. Barthes offers classifications to keep matters open—to reserve a place for the uncodified, the enchanted, the intractable, the histrionic. He was fond of bizarre classifications, of classificatory excess (Fourier's, for example), and his boldly physical metaphors for mental life stress not topography but transformation. Drawn to hyperbole, as all aphorists are, Barthes enlists ideas in a drama, often a sensual melodrama or a faintly Gothic one. He speaks of the quiver, thrill, or shudder of meaning, of meanings that themselves vibrate, gather, loosen, disperse, quicken, shine, fold, mutate, delay, slide, separate, that exert pressure, crack, rupture, fissure, are pulverized. Barthes offers something like a poetics of thinking, which identifies the meaning of subjects with the very mobility of meaning, with the kinetics of consciousness itself; and liberates the critic as artist. The uses that binary and triadic thinking had for Barthes's imagination were always provisional, available to correction, destabilization, condensation.

As a writer, he preferred short forms, and had been planning to give a seminar on them; he was particularly drawn to miniature ones, like the haiku and the quotation; and, like all true writers, he was enthralled by "the detail" (his word)—experience's model short form. Even as an essayist, Barthes mostly wrote short, and the books he did write tend to be multiples of short forms rather than "real" books, itineraries of topics rather than unified arguments. His *Michelet*, for example, keys its inventory of the historian's themes to a large number of brief excerpts from Michelet's prolific writings. The most rigorous example of the argument as an itinerary by means of quotation is *S/Z*, published in 1970, his model exegesis of Balzac's *Sarrasine*. From staging the texts of others, he passed inevitably to the staging of his own ideas. And, in the same series on great writers ("Ecrivains de toujours") to which he contributed the Michelet volume, he eventually did one on himself in 1975: that dazzling oddity in the series, *Roland Barthes* by Roland Barthes. The high-velocity arrangements of Barthes's late books dramatize both his fecundity (insatiability *and* lightness) and his desire to subvert all tendencies to system-making.

An animus against the systematizers has been a recurrent feature of intellectual good taste for more than a century; Kierkegaard, Nietzsche, Wittgenstein are among the many voices that proclaim, from a superior if virtually unbearable burden of singularity, the absurdity of systems. In its strong modern form, scorn for systems is one aspect of the protest against Law, against Power itself. An older, milder refusal is lodged in the French skeptic tradition from Montaigne to Gide: writers who are epicures of their own consciousness can be counted on to decry "the sclerosis of systems," a phrase Barthes used in his first essay, on Gide. And along with these refusals a distinctive modern stylistics has evolved, the prototypes of which go back at least to Sterne and the German Romantics—the invention of anti-linear forms of narration: in fiction, the destruction of the "story"; in nonfiction, the abandonment of linear argument. The presumed impossibility (or irrelevance) of producing a continuous systematic argument has led to a remodeling of the standard long forms—the treatise, the long book—and a recasting of the genres of fiction, autobiography, and essay. Of this stylistics Barthes is a particularly inventive practitioner.

The Romantic and post-Romantic sensibility discerns in every book a first-person performance: to write is a dramatic act, subject to dramatic elaboration. One strategy is to use multiple pseudonyms, as Kierkegaard did, concealing and multiplying the figure of the author. When autobiographical, the work invariably includes avowals of reluctance to speak in the first person. One of the conventions of *Roland Barthes* is for the autobiographer to refer to himself sometimes as "I," sometimes as "he." All this, Barthes announces on the first page of this book about himself, "must be considered as if spoken by a character in a novel." Under the meta-category of performance, not only the line between autobiography and fiction is muted, but that between essay and fiction as well. "Let the essay avow itself almost a novel," he says in *Roland Barthes.* Writing registers new forms of dramatic stress, of a self-referring kind: writing becomes the record of compulsions and of resistances to write. (In the further extension of this view, writing itself becomes the writer's subject.)

For the purpose of achieving an ideal digressiveness and an ideal intensity, two strategies have been widely adopted. One is to abolish some or all of the conventional demarcations or separations of discourse, such as chapters, paragraphing, even punctuation, whatever is regarded as impeding formally the continuous production of (the writer's) voice—the run-on method favored by writers of philosophical fictions such as Hermann Broch, Joyce, Stein, Beckett. The other strategy is the opposite one: to multiply the ways in which discourse is segmented, to invent further ways of breaking it up. Joyce and Stein used this method, too; Viktor Shklovsky in his best books, from the 1920s, writes in one-sentence paragraphs. The multiple openings and closures produced by the start-and-stop method permit discourse to become as differentiated, as polyphonous, as possible. Its most common shape in expository discourse is that of short, one- or two-paragraph units separated by spaces. "Notes on . . ." is the usual literary title—a form Barthes uses in the essay on Gide, and returns to often in his later work. Much of his writing proceeds by techniques of interruption, sometimes in the form of an excerpt alternating with a disjunctive commentary, as in *Michelet* and *S/Z*. To write in fragments or sequences or "notes" entails new, serial (rather than linear) forms of arrangement. These sequences may be staged in some arbitrary way. For example, they may be numbered—a method practiced with great refinement by Wittgenstein. Or they may be given headings, sometimes ironic or overemphatic—Barthes's strategy in *Roland Barthes*. Headings allow an additional possibility: for the elements to be arranged alphabetically, to emphasize further the arbitrary character of their sequence—the method of *A Lover's Discourse* (1977), whose real title evokes the notion of the fragment; it is *Fragments d'un discours amoureux*.

Barthes's late writing is his boldest formally: all major work was organized in a serial rather than linear form. Straight essay writing was reserved for the literary good deed (prefaces, for example, of which Barthes wrote many) or journalistic whim. However, these strong forms of the late writing only bring forward a desire implicit in all of his work—Barthes's wish to have a superior relation to assertion: the relation that art has, of pleasure. Such a conception of writing excludes the fear of contradiction. (In Wilde's phrase: "A truth in art is that whose contradiction is also true.") Barthes repeatedly compared teaching to play, reading to eros, writing to seduction. His voice became more and more personal, more full of grain, as he called it; his intellectual art more openly a performance, like that of the other great antisystematizers. But whereas Nietzsche addresses the reader in many tones, mostly aggressive—exulting, berating, coaxing, prodding, taunting, inviting complicity—Barthes invariably performs in an affable register. There are no rude or prophetic claims, no pleadings with the reader, and no efforts *not* to be understood. This is seduction as play, never violation. All of Barthes's work is an exploration of the histrionic or ludic; in many ingenious modes, a plea for savor, for a festive (rather than dogmatic or credulous) relation to ideas. For Barthes, as for

Nietzsche, the point is not to teach us something in particular. The point is to make us bold, agile, subtle, intelligent, detached. And to give pleasure.

WRITING IS BARTHES'S perennial subject—indeed, perhaps no one since Flaubert (in his letters) has thought as brilliantly, as passionately as Barthes has about what writing is. Much of his work is devoted to portraits of the vocation of the writer: from the early debunking studies included in *Mythologies* (1957) of the writer as seen by others, that is, the writer as fraud, such as "The Writer on Holiday," to more ambitious essays on writers writing, that is, the writer as hero and martyr, such as "Flaubert and the Sentence," about the writer's "agony of style." Barthes's wonderful essays on writers must be considered as different versions of his great apologia for the vocation of the writer. For all his admiration for the self-punishing standards of integrity set by Flaubert, he dares to conceive of writing as a kind of happiness: the point of his essay on Voltaire ("The Last Happy Writer"), and of his portrait of Fourier, unvexed by the sense of evil. In his late work he speaks directly of his own practice, scruples, bliss.

Barthes construes writing as an ideally complex form of consciousness: a way of being both passive and active, social and asocial, present and absent in one's own life. His idea of the writer's vocation excludes the sequestration that Flaubert thought inevitable, would appear to deny any conflict between the writer's necessary inwardness and the pleasures of worldliness. It is, so to speak, Flaubert strongly amended by Gide: a more well bred, casual rigor, an avid, guileful relation to ideas that excludes fanaticism. Indeed, the ideal self-portrait—the portrait of the self as writer—that Barthes sketched throughout his work is virtually complete in the first essay, on Gide's "work of egoism," his *Journal.* Gide supplied Barthes with the patrician model for the writer who is supple, multiple; never strident or vulgarly indignant; generous but also properly egotistical; incapable of being deeply influenced. He notes how little Gide was altered by his vast reading ("so many self-recognitions"), how his "discoveries" were never "denials." And he praises the profusion of Gide's scruples, observing that Gide's "situation at the intersection of great contradictory currents has nothing facile about it . . ." Barthes subscribes as well to Gide's idea of writing that is elusive, willing to be minor. His relation to politics also recalls Gide's: a willingness in times of ideological mobilization to take the right stands, to be political—but, finally, not: and thereby, perhaps, to tell the truth that hardly anybody else is telling. (See the short essay Barthes wrote after a trip to China in 1974.) Barthes had many affinities with Gide, and much of what he says of Gide applies unaltered to himself. How remarkable to find it all laid out—including the program of "perpetual self-correction"—well before he embarked on his career. (Barthes was twenty-seven, a patient in a sanatorium for tubercular students, when he wrote this essay in 1942 for the sanatorium's magazine; he did not enter the Paris literary arena for another five years.)

When Barthes, who began under the aegis of Gide's doctrine of psychic and moral availability, started writing regularly, Gide's important work was long over, his influence already negligible (he died in 1951); and Barthes put on the armor of postwar debate about the responsibility of literature, the terms of which were set up by Sartre—the demand that the writer be in a militant relation to virtue, which Sartre described by the tautological notion of "commitment." Gide and Sartre were, of course, the two most influential writer-moralists of this century in France, and the work of these two sons of French Protestant culture suggests quite opposed moral and aesthetic choices. But it is just this kind of polarization that Barthes, another Protestant in revolt against Protestant moralism, seeks to avoid. Supple Gidean that he is, Barthes is eager to acknowledge the model of Sartre as well. While a quarrel with Sartre's view of literature lies at the heart of his first book, *Writing Degree Zero* (Sartre is never mentioned by name), an agreement with Sartre's view of the imagination, and its obsessional energies, surfaces in Barthes's last book, *Camera Lucida* (written "in homage" to the early Sartre, the author of *L'Imaginaire*). Even in the first book, Barthes concedes a good deal to Sartre's view of literature and language—for example, putting poetry with the other "arts" and identifying literature with prose, with argument. Barthes's view of literature in his subsequent writing was more complex. Though he never wrote on poetry, his standards for literature approached those of the poet: language that has undergone an upheaval, has been displaced, liberated from ungrateful contexts; that, so to speak, lives on its own. Although Barthes agrees with Sartre that the writer's vocation has an ethical imperative, he insists on its complexity and ambiguity. Sartre appeals to the morality of ends. Barthes invokes "the morality of form"—what makes literature a problem rather than a solution; what makes literature.

To conceive of literature as successful "communication" and position-taking, however, is a sentiment that must inevitably become conformist. The instrumental view expounded in Sartre's *What Is Literature?* (1948) makes of literature something perpetually obsolete, a vain—and misplaced—struggle between ethical good soldiers and literary purists, that is, modernists. (Contrast the latent philistinism of this view of literature with the subtlety and acuity of what Sartre had to say about visual images.) Riven by his love of literature (the love recounted in his one perfect book, *The Words*) and an evangelical contempt for literature, one of the century's great *littérateurs* spent the last years of his life insulting literature and himself with that indigent idea, "the neurosis of literature." His defense of the writer's project of commitment is no more convincing. Accused of thereby reducing literature (to politics), Sartre protested that it would be more correct to accuse him of overestimating it. "If literature isn't *everything*, it's not worth a single hour of someone's trouble," he declared in an interview in 1960. "That's what I mean by 'commitment.' " But Sartre's inflation of literature to "everything" is another brand of depreciation.

Barthes, too, might be charged with overestimating literature—with treating literature as "everything"—but at least he made a good case for doing so. For Barthes understood (as Sartre did not) that literature is first of all, last of all, language. It is language that is everything. Which is to say that all of reality is presented in the form of language— the poet's wisdom, and also the structuralist's. And Barthes takes for granted (as Sartre, with his notion of writing as communication, did not) what he calls the "radical exploration of writing" undertaken by Mallarmé, Joyce, Proust, and their successors. That no venture is valuable unless it can be conceived as a species of radicalism, radicalism thereby unhinged from any distinctive content, is perhaps the essence of what we call modernism. Barthes's work belongs to the sensibility of modernism in the extent to which it assumes the necessity of the adversary stance: literature conceived by modernist standards but not necessarily a modernist literature. Rather, all varieties of counterposition are available to it.

Perhaps the most striking difference between Sartre and Barthes is the deep one, of temperament. Sartre has an intellectually brutal, *bon enfant* view of the world, a view that wills simplicity, resolution, transparence; Barthes's view is irrevocably complex, self-conscious, refined, irresolute. Sartre was eager, too eager, to seek confrontation, and the tragedy of this great career, of the use he made of his stupendous intellect, was just his willingness to simplify himself. Barthes preferred to avoid confrontation, to evade polarization. He defines the writer as "the watcher who stands at the crossroads of all other discourses"— the opposite of an activist or a purveyor of doctrine.

Barthes's utopia of literature has an ethical character almost the opposite of Sartre's. It emerges in the connections he makes between desire and reading, desire and writing—his insistence that his own writing is, more than anything, the product of appetite. The words "pleasure," "bliss," "happiness" recur in his work with a weight, reminiscent of Gide, that is both voluptuous and subversive. As a moralist—Puritan or anti-Puritan—might solemnly distinguish sex for procreation from sex for pleasure, Barthes divides writers into those who write *something* (what Sartre meant by a writer) and the real writers, who do not write something but, rather, *write*. This intransitive sense of the verb "to write" Barthes endorses as not only the source of the writer's felicity but the model of freedom. For Barthes, it is not the commitment that writing makes to something outside of itself (to a social or moral goal) that makes literature an instrument of opposition and subversion but a certain practice of writing itself: excessive, playful, intricate, subtle, sensuous—language which can never be that of power.

Barthes's praise of writing as a gratuitous, free activity is, in one sense, a political view. He conceives of literature as a perpetual renewal of the right of individual assertion; and all rights are, finally, political ones. Still, Barthes has an evasive relation to politics, and he is one of the great modern refusers of history. Barthes started publishing and mattering in the aftermath of World War II, which, astonishingly, he never mentions; indeed, in all his writings he never, as far as I recall, mentions the word "war." Barthes's friendly way of understanding subjects domesticates them, in the best sense. He lacks anything like Walter Benjamin's tragic awareness that every work of civilization is also a work of barbarism. The ethical burden for Benjamin was a kind of martyrdom; he could not help connecting it with politics. Barthes regards politics as a kind of constriction of the human (and intellectual) subject which has to be outwitted; in *Roland Barthes* he declares that he likes political positions "lightly held." Hence, perhaps, he was never gripped by the project that is central for Benjamin, as for all true modernists: to try to fathom the nature of "the modern." Barthes, who was not tormented by the catastrophes of modernity or tempted by its revolutionary illusions, had a post-tragic sensibility. He refers to the present literary era as "a moment of gentle apocalypse." Happy indeed the writer who can utter such a phrase.

MUCH OF BARTHES'S WORK is devoted to the repertoire of pleasure—"the great adventure of desire," as he calls it in the essay on Brillat-Savarin's *Physiology of Taste*. Collecting a model of felicity from each thing he examines, he assimilates intellectual practice itself to the erotic. Barthes called the life of the mind desire, and was concerned to defend "the plurality of desire." Meaning is never monogamous. His joyful wisdom or gay science offers the ideal of a free yet capacious, satisfied consciousness; of a condition in which one does not have to choose between good and bad, true and false, in which it is not necessary to justify. The texts and enterprises that engaged Barthes tend to be those in which he could read a defiance of these antitheses. For example, this is how Barthes construes fashion: as a domain, like eros, where contraries do not exist ("Fashion seeks equivalences, validities—not verities"); where one can allow oneself to be gratified; where meaning—and pleasure—is profuse.

To construe in this way, Barthes requires a master category through which everything can be refracted, which makes possible the maximum number of intellectual moves. That most inclusive category is language, the widest sense of language—meaning form itself. Thus, the subject of *Système de la mode* (1967) is not fashion but the language of fashion. Barthes assumes, of course, that the language of fashion *is* fashion; that, as he said in an interview, "fashion exists only through the discourse on it." Assumptions of this sort (myth is a language, fashion is a language) have become a leading, often reductive convention of contemporary intellectual endeavor. In Barthes's work the assumption is less a reductive one than it is proliferative—embarrassment of riches for the critic as artist. To stipulate that there is no understanding outside of language is to assert that there is meaning *everywhere*.

By so extending the reach of meaning, Barthes takes the notion over the top, to arrive at such triumphant paradoxes as the empty subject that contains everything, the empty sign to which all meaning can be attributed. With this euphoric sense of how meaning proliferates, Barthes reads that "zero degree of the monument," the Eiffel Tower, as "this pure—virtually empty—sign" that (his italics) "*means everything.*" (The characteristic point of Barthes's arguments-by-paradox is to vindicate subjects untrammeled by utility: it is the uselessness of the Eiffel Tower that makes it infinitely useful as a sign, just as the uselessness of genuine literature is what makes it morally useful.) Barthes found a world of such liberating absences of meaning, both modernist and simply non-Western, in Japan; Japan, he noted, was full of empty signs. In place of moralistic antitheses—true versus false, good versus bad—Barthes offers complementary extremes. "Its form is empty but present, its meaning absent but full," he writes about myth in an essay in the 1950s. Arguments about many subjects have this identical climax: that absence is really presence, emptiness repletion, impersonality the highest achievement of the personal.

Like that euphoric register of religious understanding which discerns treasures of meaning in the most banal and meaningless, which designates as the richest carrier of meaning one vacant of meaning, the brilliant descriptions in Barthes's work bespeak an ecstatic experience of understanding; and ecstasy—whether religious, aesthetic, or sexual—has perennially been described by the metaphors of being empty and being full, the zero state and the state of maximal plenitude: their alternation, their equivalence. The very transposing of subjects into the discourse about them is the same kind of move: emptying subjects out to fill them up again. It is a method of understanding that, presuming ecstasy, fosters detachment. And his very idea of language also supports both aspects of Barthes's sensibility: while endorsing a profusion of meaning, the Saussurean theory—that language *is* form (rather than substance)—is wonderfully congruent with a taste for elegant, that is, reticent, discourse. Creating meaning through the intellectual equivalent of negative space, Barthes's method has one never talking about subjects in themselves: fashion is the language of fashion, a country is "the empire of signs"—the ultimate accolade. For reality to exist *as* signs conforms to a maximum idea of decorum: all meaning is deferred, indirect, elegant.

Barthes's ideals of impersonality, of reticence, of elegance, are set forth most beautifully in his appreciation of Japanese culture in the book called *Empire of Signs* (1970) and in his essay on the Bunraku puppets. This essay, "Lesson in Writing," recalls Kleist's "On the Puppet Theatre," which similarly celebrates the tranquillity, lightness, and grace of beings free of thinking, of meaning—free of "the disorders of consciousness." Like the puppets in Kleist's essay, the Bunraku puppets are seen as incarnating an ideal "impassivity, clarity, agility, subtlety." To be both impassive and fantastic, inane and profound, unselfconscious and supremely sensuous—these qualities that Barthes discerned in various facets of Japanese civilization project an ideal of taste and deportment, the ideal of the aesthete in its larger meaning that has been in general circulation since the dandies of the late eighteenth century. Barthes was hardly the first Western observer for whom Japan has been an aesthete's utopia, the place where one finds aesthete views everywhere and exercises one's own at liberty. The culture where aesthete goals are central—not, as in the West, eccentric—was bound to elicit a strong response. (Japan is mentioned in the Gide essay written in 1942.)

Of the available models of the aesthetic way of looking at the world, perhaps the most eloquent are French and Japanese. In France it has largely been a literary tradition, though with annexes in two popular arts, gastronomy and fashion. Barthes did take up the subject of food as ideology, as classification, as taste—he talks often of savoring; and it seems inevitable that he would find the subject of fashion congenial. Writers from Baudelaire to Cocteau have taken fashion seriously, and one of the founding figures of literary modernism, Mallarmé, edited a fashion magazine. French culture, where aesthete ideals have been more explicit and influential than in any other European culture, allows a link between ideas of vanguard art and of fashion. (The French have never shared the Anglo-American conviction that makes the fashionable the opposite of the serious.) In Japan, aesthete standards appear to imbue the whole culture, and long predate the modern ironies; they were formulated as early as the late tenth century, in Sei Shōnagon's *Pillow Book*, that breviary of consummate dandy attitudes, written in what appears to us an astonishingly modern, disjunctive form—notes, anecdotes, and lists. Barthes's interest in Japan expresses the attraction to a less defensive, more innocent, and far more elaborated version of the aesthete sensibility: emptier and prettier than the French, more straightforward (no beauty in ugliness, as in Baudelaire); pre-apocalyptic, refined, serene.

In Western culture, where it remains marginal, the dandy attitude has the character of an exaggeration. In one form, the older one, the aesthete is a willful exclusionist of taste, holding attitudes that make it possible to like, to be comfortable with, to give one's assent to the smallest number of things; reducing things to the smallest expression of them. (When taste distributes its plusses and minuses, it favors diminutive adjectives, such as—for praise—"happy," "amusing," "charming," "agreeable," "suitable.") Elegance equals the largest amount of refusal. As language, this attitude finds its consummate expression in the rueful quip, the disdainful one-liner. In the other form, the aesthete sustains standards that make it possible to be pleased with the largest number of things; annexing new, unconventional, even illicit sources of pleasure. The literary device that best projects this attitude is the list (*Roland Barthes* has many)—the whimsical aesthete polyphony that juxtaposes things and experiences of a starkly different, often incongruous nature, turning them all, by this technique, into artifacts, aesthetic objects. Here elegance equals the wittiest acceptances. The aesthete's posture alternates between *never* being satisfied and *always* finding a way of being satisfied, being pleased with virtually everything.*

Although both directions of dandy taste presuppose detachment, the exclusivist version is cooler. The inclusivist version can be enthusiastic, even effusive; the adjectives used for praise tend to be over- rather than understatements. Barthes, who had much of the high exclusivist taste of the dandy, was more inclined to its modern, democratizing form: aesthete leveling—hence his willingness to find charm, amusement, happiness, pleasure in so many things. His account of Fourier, for example, is finally an aesthete's appraisal. Of the "little details" that, he says, make up the "whole of Fourier," Barthes writes: "I am carried away, dazzled, convinced by a sort of charm of expressions . . . Fourier is swarming with these felicities . . . I cannot resist these pleasures; they seem 'true' to me." Similarly: what another *flâneur*, less committed to finding pleasure everywhere, might experience as the oppressive overcrowdedness of streets in Tokyo signifies for Barthes "the transformation of quality by quantity," a new relation that is "a source of endless jubilation."

Many of Barthes's judgments and interests are implicitly affirmations of the aesthete's standards. His early essays championing the fiction of Robbe-Grillet, which gave Barthes the misleading reputation as an advocate of literary modernism, were in effect aesthete polemics. The "objective," the "literal"—these austere, minimalist ideas of literature are in fact Barthes's ingenious recycling of one of the aesthete's principal theses: that surface is as telling as depth. What Barthes discerned in Robbe-Grillet in the 1950s was a new, high-tech version of the dandy writer; what he hailed in Robbe-Grillet was the desire "to establish the novel on the surface," thereby frustrating our desire to "fall back on a psychology." The idea that depths are obfuscating, demagogic, that no human essence stirs at the bottom of things, and that

---

*The version of the aesthete sensibility I once tried to include under the name "camp" can be regarded as a technique of taste for making the aesthete appreciations less exclusionary (a way of liking more than one really wants to like) and as part of the democratizing of dandy attitudes. Camp taste, however, still presupposes the older, high standards of discrimination— in contrast to the taste incarnated by, say, Andy Warhol, the franchiser and mass marketer of the dandyism of leveling.

freedom lies in staying on the surface, the large glass on which desire circulates—this is the central argument of the modern aesthete position, in the various exemplary forms it has taken over the last hundred years. (Baudelaire. Wilde. Duchamp. Cage.)

Barthes is constantly making an argument against depth, against the idea that the most real is latent, submerged. Bunraku is seen as refusing the antinomy of matter and soul, inner and outer. *"Myth hides nothing,"* he declares in "Myth Today" (1956). The aesthete position not only regards the notion of depths, of hiddenness, as a mystification, a lie, but opposes the very idea of antitheses. Of course, to speak of depths and surfaces is already to misrepresent the aesthetic view of the world—to reiterate a duality, like that of form and content, it precisely denies. The largest statement of this position was made by Nietzsche, whose work constitutes a criticism of fixed antitheses (good versus evil, right versus wrong, true versus false).

But while Nietzsche scorned "depths," he exalted "heights." In the post-Nietzschean tradition, there are neither depths nor heights; there are only various kinds of surface, of spectacle. Nietzsche said that every profound nature needs a mask, and spoke—profoundly—in praise of intellectual ruse; but he was making the gloomiest prediction when he said that the coming century, ours, would be the age of the actor. An ideal of seriousness, of sincerity, underlies all of Nietzsche's work, which makes the overlap of his ideas and those of a true aesthete (like Wilde, like Barthes) so problematic. Nietzsche was a histrionic thinker but not a lover of the histrionic. His ambivalence toward spectacle (after all, his criticism of Wagner's music was finally that it was a seduction), his insistence on the authenticity of spectacle, mean that criteria other than the histrionic are at work. In the aesthete's position, the notions of reality and spectacle precisely reinforce and infuse each other, and seduction is always something positive. In this respect, Barthes's ideas have an exemplary coherence. Notions of the theatre inform, directly or indirectly, all his work. (Divulging the secret, late, he declares in *Roland Barthes* that there was no single text of his "which did not treat of a certain theatre, and the spectacle is the universal category through whose forms the world is seen.") Barthes explains Robbe-Grillet's empty, "anthological" description as a technique of theatrical distancing (presenting an object "as if it were in itself a spectacle"). Fashion is, of course, another casebook of the theatrical. So is Barthes's interest in photography, which he treats as a realm of pure haunted spectatorship. In the account of photography given in *Camera Lucida* there are hardly any photographers—the subject is photographs (treated virtually as found objects) and those who are fascinated by them: as objects of erotic reverie, as *memento mori*.

What he wrote about Brecht, whom he discovered in 1954 (when the Berliner Ensemble visited Paris with their production of *Mother Courage*) and helped make known in France, says less about the theatrical than his treatment of many subjects as *forms* of the theatrical. In his frequent use of Brecht in seminars of the 1970s, he cited the prose writings, which he took as a model of critical acuity; it was not Brecht the maker of didactic spectacles but Brecht the didactic intellectual who finally mattered to Barthes. In contrast, with Bunraku what Barthes valued was the element of theatricality as such. In Barthes's early work, the theatrical is the domain of liberty, the place where identities are only roles and one can *change* roles, a zone where meaning itself may be refused. (Barthes speaks of Bunraku's privileged "exemption from meaning.") Barthes's talk about the theatrical, like his evangelism of pleasure, is a way of proselytizing for the attenuating, lightening, baffling of the Logos, of meaning itself.

To affirm the notion of the spectacle is the triumph of the aesthete's position: the promulgation of the ludic, the refusal of the tragic. All of Barthes's intellectual moves have the effect of voiding work of its "content," the tragic of its finality. That is the sense in which his work is genuinely subversive, liberating—playful. It is outlaw discourse in the great aesthete tradition, which often assumes the liberty of rejecting the "substance" of discourse in order better to appreciate its "form": outlaw discourse turned respectable, as it were, with the help of various theories known as varieties of formalism. In numerous accounts of his intellectual evolution, Barthes describes himself as the perpetual disciple—but the point that he really wants to make is that he remains, finally, untouched. He spoke of his having worked under the aegis of a succession of theories and masters. In fact, Barthes's work has altogether more coherence, and ambivalence. For all his connection with tutelary doctrines, Barthes's submission to doctrine was superficial. In the end, it was necessary that all intellectual gadgetry be discarded. His last books are a kind of unraveling of his ideas. *Roland Barthes*, he says, is the book of his resistance to his ideas, the dismantling of his own power. And in the inaugural lecture that marked his acceding to a position of the highest eminence—the Chair of Literary Semiology at the Collège de France in 1977—Barthes chooses, characteristically enough, to argue for a soft intellectual authority. He praises teaching as a permissive, not a coercive, space where one can be relaxed, disarmed, floating.

Language itself, which Barthes called a "utopia" in the euphoric formulation that ends *Writing Degree Zero*, now comes under attack, as another form of "power," and his very effort to convey his sensitivity to the ways in which language is "power" gives rise to that instantly notorious hyperbole in his Collège de France lecture: the power of language is "quite simply fascist." To assume that society is ruled by monolithic ideologies and repressive mystifications is necessary to Barthes's advocacy of egoism, post-revolutionary but nevertheless antinomian: his notion that the affirmation of the unremittingly personal is a subversive act. This is a classic extension of the aesthete attitude, in which it becomes a politics: a politics of radical individuality. Pleasure is largely identified with unauthorized pleasure, and the right of individual assertion with the sanctity of the asocial self. In the late writings, the theme of protest against power takes the form of an increasingly private definition of experience (as fetishized involvement) and a ludic definition of thought. "The great problem," Barthes says in a late interview, "is to outplay the signified, to outplay law, to outplay the father, to outplay the repressed—I do not say to explode it, but to outplay it." The aesthete's ideal of detachment, of the selfishness of detachment, allows for avowals of passionate, obsessed involvement: the selfishness of ardor, of fascination. (Wilde speaks of his "curious mixture of ardour and of indifference . . . I would go to the stake for a sensation and be a sceptic to the last.") Barthes has to keep affirming the aesthete's detachment, and undermining it—with passions.

Like all great aesthetes, Barthes was an expert at having it both ways. Thus, he identifies writing both with a generous relation to the world (writing as "perpetual production") and with a defiant relation (writing as "a perpetual revolution of language," outside the bounds of power). He wants a politics and an anti-politics, a critical relation to the world and one free of moral considerations. The aesthete's radicalism is the radicalism of a privileged, even a replete, consciousness—but a genuine radicalism nonetheless. All genuine moral views are founded on a notion of refusal, and the aesthete's view, which can be conformist, does provide certain potentially powerful, not just elegant, grounds for a great refusal.

The aesthete's radicalism: to be multiple, to make multiple identifications; to assume fully the privilege of the personal. Barthes's work—he avows that he writes by obsessions—consists of continuities and detours; the accumulation of points of view; finally, their disburdenment: a mixture of progress and caprice. For Barthes, liberty is a state that consists in remaining plural, fluid, vibrating with doctrine; whose price is being indecisive, apprehensive, fearful of being taken for an impostor. The writer's freedom that Barthes describes is, in part, flight. The writer is the deputy of his own ego—of that self in perpetual flight before what is fixed by writing, as the mind is in perpetual flight from doctrine. "Who *speaks* is not who *writes*, and who *writes* is not who *is*." Barthes wants to move on—that is one of the imperatives of the aesthete's sensibility.

THROUGHOUT HIS WORK Barthes projects himself into his subject. He is Fourier: unvexed by the sense of evil, aloof from politics, "that necessary purge"; he "vomits it up." He is the Bunraku puppet: impersonal, subtle. He is Gide: the writer who is ageless (always young, always mature); the writer as egoist—a triumphant species of "simultaneous being" or plural desire. He is the subject of all the subjects that he praises. (That he must, characteristically, praise may be connected with his project of defining, creating standards for himself.) In this sense, much of what Barthes wrote now appears autobiographical.

Eventually, it became autobiographical in the literal sense. A brave meditation on the personal, on the self, is at the center of his late writ-

ings and seminars. Much of Barthes's work, especially the last three books with their poignant themes of loss, constitutes a candid defense of his sensuality (as well as his sexuality)—his flavor, his way of tasting the world. The books are also artfully anti-confessional. *Camera Lucida* is a meta-book: a meditation on the even more personal autobiographical book that he planned to write about photographs of his mother, who died in 1978, and then put aside. Barthes starts from the modernist model of writing that is superior to any idea of intention or mere expressiveness; a mask. "The work," Valéry insists, "should not give the person it affects anything that can be reduced to an idea of the author's person and thinking."* But this commitment to impersonality does not preclude the avowal of the self; it is only another variation on the project of self-examination: the noblest project of French literature. Valéry offers one ideal of self-absorption—impersonal, disinterested. Rousseau offers another ideal—passionate, avowing vulnerability. Many themes of Barthes's work lie in the classic discourse of French literary culture: its taste for elegant abstraction, in particular for the formal analysis of the sentiments; its disdain for mere psychology; and its coquetry about the impersonal (Flaubert declaring *"Madame Bovary, c'est moi,"* but also insisting in letters on his novel's "impersonality," its lack of connection with himself).

Barthes is the latest major participant in the great national literary project, inaugurated by Montaigne: the self as vocation, life as a reading of the self. The enterprise construes the self as the locus of all possibilities, avid, unafraid of contradiction (nothing need be lost, everything may be gained), and the exercise of consciousness as a life's highest aim, because only through becoming fully conscious may one be free. The distinctive French utopian tradition is this vision of reality redeemed, recovered, transcended by consciousness; a vision of the life of the mind as a life of desire, of full intelligence and pleasure—so dif-

---

*This modernist dictum that writing is, ideally, a form of impersonality or absence underlies Barthes's move to eliminate the "author" when considering a book. (The method of his *S/Z*: an exemplary reading of a Balzac novella as virtually an authorless text.) One of the things Barthes does as a critic is to formulate the mandate for one kind of writer's modernism (Flaubert, Valéry, Eliot) as a general program for *readers*. Another is to contravene that mandate in practice—for most of Barthes's writing is precisely devoted to personal singularity.

ferent from, say, the traditions of high moral seriousness of German
and of Russian literature.

Inevitably, Barthes's work had to end in autobiography. "One
must choose between being a terrorist and being an egoist," he once
observed in a seminar. The options seem very French. Intellectual ter-
rorism is a central, respectable form of intellectual practice in France—
tolerated, humored, rewarded: the "Jacobin" tradition of ruthless
assertion and shameless ideological about-faces; the mandate of incessant judgment, opinion, anathematizing, overpraising; the taste for extreme positions, then casually reversed, and for deliberate provocation.
Alongside this, how modest egoism is!

Barthes's voice became steadily more intimate, his subjects more inward. An affirmation of his own idiosyncrasy (which he does not "decipher") is the main theme of *Roland Barthes*. He writes about the
body, taste, love; solitude; erotic desolation; finally, death, or rather desire and death: the twin subjects of the book on photography. As in the
Platonic dialogues, the thinker (writer, reader, teacher) and the lover—
the two main figures of the Barthesian self—are joined. Barthes, of
course, means his erotics of literature more literally, as literally as he
can. (The text *enters*, *fills*, it *grants* euphoria.) But finally he seems
fairly Platonic after all. The monologue of *A Lover's Discourse*, which
obviously draws on a story of disappointment in love, ends in a spiritual vision in the classic Platonic way, in which lower loves are trans-
muted into higher, more inclusive ones. Barthes avows that he "wants
to unmask, no longer to interpret, but to make of consciousness itself a
drug, and thus accede to a vision of irreducible reality, to the great
drama of clarity, to prophetic love."

As he divested himself of theories, he gave less weight to the modernist standard of the intricate. He does not want, he says, to place any
obstacles between himself and the reader. The last book is part memoir
(of his mother), part meditation on eros, part treatise on the photographic image, part invocation of death—a book of piety, resignation,
desire; a certain brilliance is being renounced, and the view itself is of
the simplest. The subject of photography provided the great exemption, perhaps release, from the exactions of formalist taste. In choosing
to write about photography, Barthes takes the occasion to adopt the

warmest kind of realism: photographs fascinate because of what they are about. And they may awaken a desire for a further divestment of the self. ("Looking at certain photographs," he writes in *Camera Lucida*, "I wanted to be a primitive, without culture.") The Socratic sweetness and charm become more plaintive, more desperate: writing is an embrace, a being embraced; every idea is an idea reaching out. There is a sense of disaggregation of his ideas, and of himself—represented by his increasing fascination with what he calls "the detail." In the preface to *Sade/Fourier/Loyola*, Barthes writes: "Were I a writer, and dead, how pleased I would be if my life, through the efforts of some friendly and detached biographer, were to reduce itself to a few details, a few preferences, a few inflections, let us say: to 'biographemes' whose distinction and mobility might travel beyond the limits of any fate, and come to touch, like Epicurean atoms, some future body, destined to the same dispersion." The need to touch, even in the perspective of his own mortality.

Barthes's late work is filled with signals that he had come to the end of something—the enterprise of the critic as artist—and was seeking to become another kind of writer. (He announced his intention to write a novel.) There were exalted avowals of vulnerability, of being forlorn. Barthes more and more entertained an idea of writing which resembles the mystical idea of *kenosis*, emptying out. He acknowledged that not only systems—his ideas were in a state of melt—but the "I" as well had to be dismantled. (True knowledge, says Barthes, depends on the "unmasking of the 'I.' ") The aesthetics of absence—the empty sign, the empty subject, the exemption from meaning—were all intimations of the great project of depersonalization which is the aesthete's highest gesture of good taste. Toward the close of Barthes's work, this ideal took on another inflection. A spiritual ideal of depersonalization—that is perhaps the characteristic terminus of every serious aesthete's position. (Think of Wilde, of Valéry.) It is the point at which the aesthete's view self-destructs: what follows is either silence—or transformation.

Barthes harbored spiritual strivings that could not be supported by his aesthete's position. It was inevitable that he pass beyond it, as he did in his very last work and teaching. At the end, he had done with the aesthetics of absence, and now spoke of literature as the embrace of subject and object. There was an emergence of a vision of "wisdom" of the Platonic sort—tempered, to be sure, by wisdom of a worldly kind: skeptical of dogmatisms, conscientious about gratification, wistfully attached to utopian ideals. Barthes's temperament, style, sensibility, had run their course. And from this vantage point his work now appears to unfold, with more grace and poignancy and with far greater intellectual power than that of any of his contemporaries, the considerable truths vouchsafed to the aesthete's sensibility, to a commitment to intellectual adventure, to the talent for contradiction and inversion— those "late" ways of experiencing, evaluating, reading the world; and surviving in it, drawing energy, finding consolation (but finally not), taking pleasure, expressing love.

[1982]

Walser's Voice

R OBERT WALSER IS one of the important German-language
writers of the twentieth century—a major writer, both for his
four novels that have survived (my favorite is the third, written in 1908,
Jakob von Gunten) and for his short prose, where the musicality and
free fall of his writing are less impeded by plot. Anyone seeking to
bring Walser to a public that has yet to discover him has at hand a
whole arsenal of glorious comparisons. A Paul Klee in prose—as delicate, as sly, as haunted. A cross between Stevie Smith and Beckett: a
good-humored, sweet Beckett. And, as literature's present inevitably
remakes its past, so we cannot help but see Walser as the missing link
between Kleist and Kafka, who admired him greatly. (At the time, it
was more likely to be Kafka who was seen through the prism of Walser.
Robert Musil, another admirer among Walser's contemporaries, after
first reading Kafka pronounced him "a peculiar case of the Walser
type.") I get a similar rush of pleasure from Walser's single-voiced
short prose as I do from Leopardi's dialogues and playlets, that great
writer's triumphant short prose form. And the variety of mental
weather in Walser's stories and sketches, their elegance and their un-
predictable lengths remind me of the free, first-person forms that
abound in classical Japanese literature: pillow book, poetic diary, "essays in idleness." But any true lover of Walser will want to disregard
the net of comparisons that one can throw over his work.

In long as in short prose Walser is a miniaturist, promulgating the claims of the anti-heroic, the limited, the humble, the small—as if in response to his acute feeling for the interminable. Walser's life illustrates the restlessness of one kind of depressive temperament; he had the depressive's fascination with stasis, and with the way time distends, is consumed, and spent much of his life obsessively turning time into space: his walks. His work plays with the depressive's appalled vision of endlessness: it is all voice—musing, conversing, rambling, running on. The important is redeemed as a species of the unimportant, wisdom as a kind of shy, valiant loquacity.

The moral core of Walser's art is the refusal of power, of domination. I'm ordinary—that is, nobody—declares the characteristic Walser persona. In "Flower Days" (1911), Walser evokes the race of "odd people, who lack character," who don't want to do anything. The recurrent "I" of Walser's prose is the opposite of the egotist's: it is that of someone "drowning in obedience." One knows about the repugnance Walser felt for success—the prodigious spread of failure that was his life. In "Kienast" (1917), Walser describes "a man who wanted nothing to do with anything." This non-doer was, of course, a proud, stupendously productive writer who secreted work, much of it written in his astonishing micro-script, without pause. What Walser says about inaction, renunciation of effort, effortlessness, is a program, an anti-romantic one, of the artist's activity. In "A Little Ramble" (1914), he observes: "We don't need to see anything out of the ordinary. We already see so much."

Walser often writes, from the point of view of a casualty, of the romantic visionary imagination. "Kleist in Thun" (1913), both self-portrait and authoritative tour of the mental landscape of suicide-destined romantic genius, depicts the precipice on the edge of which Walser lived. The last paragraph, with its excruciating modulations, seals an account of mental ruin as grand as anything I know in literature. But most of his stories and sketches bring consciousness back from the brink. He is just having his "gentle and courteous bit of fun," Walser can assure us, in "Nervous" (1916), speaking in the first person. "Grouches, grouches, one must have them, and one must have the courage to live with them. That's the nicest way to live. Nobody should be afraid of his little bit of weirdness." The longest of the stories, "The Walk" (1917), identifies walking with a lyrical mobility and detachment of temperament, with the "raptures of freedom"; darkness arrives only at the end. Walser's art assumes depression and terror, in order (mostly) to accept it—ironize over it, lighten it. These are gleeful as well as somber soliloquies about the relation to gravity, in both senses, physical and characterological: anti-gravity writing, in praise of movement and sloughing off, weightlessness; portraits of consciousness walking about in the world, enjoying its "morsel of life," radiant with despair.

In Walser's fictions one is (as in so much of modern art) always inside a head, but this universe—and this despair—is anything but solipsistic. It is charged with compassion: awareness of the creatureliness of life, of the fellowship of sadness. "What kind of people am I thinking of?" Walser's voice asks in "A Sort of Speech" (1925). "Of me, of you, of all our theatrical little dominations, of the freedoms that are none, of the un-freedoms that are not taken seriously, of these destroyers who never pass up a chance for a joke, of the people who are desolate?" That question mark at the end of the answer is a typical Walser courtesy. Walser's virtues are those of the most mature, most civilized art. He is a truly wonderful, heartbreaking writer.

[1982]

Danilo Kiš

T HE DEATH OF Danilo Kiš on October 15, 1989, at the age
of fifty-four, wrenchingly cut short one of the most important
journeys in literature made by any writer during the second half of the
twentieth century. Born on the rim of the Yugoslav cauldron (in Subo-
tica, near the frontier with Hungary) a few years before World War II
to a Hungarian Jewish father (Kiš is a Hungarian name) who perished
in Auschwitz and a Serb Orthodox mother from rural Montenegro,
raised mostly in Hungary and in Montenegro, a graduate in literature
of the university in Belgrade, where he made his debut as a writer,
eventually a part-time expatriate, doing some teaching in France, and
finally a full-time one, in Paris, where he lived his last ten years, Kiš had
a life span that matched, from start to finish, what might have been
thought the worst the century had to offer his part of Europe: Nazi
conquest and the genocide of the Jews, followed by Soviet takeover.

Nineteen eighty-nine, the year Kiš died of cancer, was, of course,
the annus mirabilis in which Soviet-style totalitarian rule ended in Central Europe. By mid-October, the collapse of what had seemed immutable was clearly under way; three weeks later, the Berlin Wall was
torn down. It is comforting to think that he died knowing only the
good news. Happily—it is the only thing about his premature death
which gives some consolation—he didn't live to see the collapse of the
multi-confessional, multi-ethnic state of which he was a citizen (his

"mixed" origin made Kiš very much a Yugoslav), and the return, on European soil, in his own country, of concentration camps and geno-cide. An ardent foe of nationalist vanities, he would have loathed Serb ethnic fascism even more than he loathed the neo-Bolshevik official culture of the Second Yugoslavia it has replaced. It is hard to imagine that, if he were still alive, he could have borne the destruction of Bosnia.

The amount of history, or horror, a writer is obliged to endure does not make him or her a great writer. But geography is destiny. For Kiš there was no retreating from an exalted sense of the writer's place and of the writer's responsibility that, literally, came with the territory. Kiš was from a small country where writers are for better and for worse im-portant, with the most gifted becoming moral, and sometimes even po-litical, legislators. Perhaps more often for worse: it was eminent Belgrade writers who provided the ideological underpinning of the Serbian genocidal project known as ethnic cleansing. The complicity of most Serb writers and artists not in exile in the current triumph of Greater Serbian imperialism suggests that the anti-nationalist voices, of which Kiš was the bravest and most eloquent, have always been in the minority. Much as by temperament and exquisitely cosmopolitan literary culture he would have preferred a less embattled course, in which literature was kept separate from politics, Kiš was always under attack and therefore, necessarily, on the attack. The first fight was against provincialism. This was the provincialism not so much of a small literature (for the former Yugoslavia produced at least two world-class prose writers, Ivo Andrić and Miroslav Krleža) as of a state-supported, state-rewarded literature. It could be fought simply by his being the utterly independent, artistically ambitious writer he was, almost from the beginning. But worse attacks were to come.

One of those writers who are first of all readers, who prefer dawdling and grazing and blissing out in the Great Library and surren-der to their vocation only when the urge to write becomes unbearable, Kiš was not what would be called prolific. In his lifetime he published nine books, seven of them in the fourteen years between 1962, when he was twenty-seven, and 1976, when he was forty-one. First came a pair of short novels, *The Attic* and *Psalm 44* (published in 1962; not yet translated into English). The second book, *Garden, Ashes* (1965), was a novel. The third, *Early Sorrows* (1968), was a book of stories. The fourth, *Hourglass* (1972), was a novel. The fifth and sixth were two collections of essays, *Po-etika* (1972) and *Po-etika II* (1974). The seventh, *A Tomb for Boris Davidovich* (1976), was a collection of thematically linked stories that his publishers chose to call a novel. He wrote it while an instructor in Serbo-Croatian at the University of Bordeaux, as he'd written *Garden, Ashes* when he taught at Strasbourg.

By this time, Kiš was spending more and more time abroad, though he did not consider himself to be in exile, any more than he would have said he was a "dissident writer": it was too clear to him that writing worthy of the name of literature had to be unofficial. With this seventh book, a suite of fictional case histories of the Stalinist Terror, Kiš's work finally attracted the international attention it deserved. *A Tomb for Boris Davidovich* also attracted a seven-month-long campaign of negative attention back home in Belgrade. The campaign, which reeked of anti-Semitism, centered on an accusation—that the book was a web of plagiarisms from an arcane bibliography—to which Kiš had no choice but to respond. The result was his eighth book, *The Anatomy Lesson* (1978). Defending *A Tomb for Boris Davidovich* against these scurrilous charges, Kiš mounted a full-scale exposition of his literary genealogy (that is, his literary tastes), a post- or proto-modernist poetics of the novel, and a portrait of what a writer's honor could be. During the next ten years, he published only one more book, *The Encyclopedia of the Dead* (1984), a collection of unlinked stories.

The Western European, and eventually North American, acclaim for *A Tomb for Boris Davidovich*—typically confining it within the literature of dissidence from "the other Europe"—had brought about translations of the earlier books into the major foreign languages, and Kiš started to be invited to first-rank literary conferences, to win prizes, and to seem a plausible Nobel candidate. Becoming an internationally famous writer meant becoming a much interviewed writer. Asked to pronounce on literary matters and, invariably, to comment on the infamies back home, he did so with grave, always incisive combativeness—he gave splendidly substantive interviews. He was also asked to contribute short pieces to newspapers and magazines—treating no literary solicitation as ever less than an occasion for intensity. Recalling that Kiš published only one book of fiction in the last decade of his life, one can't but regret that he gave as many interviews, wrote as many essays and prefaces, as he did. A poet in prose as well as a prince of indignation, Kiš surely was not best employed in these discursive forms. No great writer of fiction is. And unlike Italo Calvino and Thomas Bernhard, who were also lost to literature in the late 1980s, Kiš had probably not yet done the best of what he was capable in fiction. But the novels and stories he did write still assure him a place alongside these two somewhat older, far more prolific contemporaries—which is to say that Kiš is one of the handful of incontestably major writers of the second half of the century.

Kiš had a complicated literary genealogy, which he was undoubtedly simplifying when he declared himself, as he often did, a child of Borges and of Bruno Schulz. But to marry the cosmopolitan Argentine to the immured small-town Polish Jew sounds the right note. Most obviously, he was claiming foreign relatives over his descendance from his native Serbo-Croatian literary family. Specifically, by yoking together the serenely, speculatively erudite Borges and the inward-looking, hyperdescriptive Schulz, he was pointing to the principal double strand in his own work. Odd mixtures were very much to Kiš's taste. His "mixed" literary methods—most fully realized in *Hourglass* (historical fiction) and *A Tomb for Boris Davidovich* (fictional history)—gave him exactly the right freedoms to advance the cause of both truth and art. Finally: one can, in literature, choose one's own parents. But nobody obliges a writer to declare his or her parentage. Kiš, however, had to proclaim his. Like every writer who is a great reader, he was an inveterate enthusiast about the work of others. His talent for admiration also made him an extremely collegial writer, which he expressed best in his numerous translations of contemporary writers he undertook from French, Hungarian, Russian, and English into Serbo-Croatian. In expatriation he was still really back home, in his head and in all his work—despite his lived estrangement from the literary world of his native country. He had never forsaken them, though they had betrayed him.

When Kiš died in Paris in 1989, the Belgrade press went into national mourning. The renegade star of Yugoslav literature had been extinguished. Safely dead, he could be eulogized by the mediocrities who had always envied him and had engineered his literary excommunication, and who would then proceed—as Yugoslavia fell apart—to become official writers of the new post-communist, national chauvinist order. Kiš is, of course, admired by everyone who genuinely cares about literature, in Belgrade as elsewhere. The place in the former Yugoslavia where he was and is perhaps most ardently admired is Sarajevo. Literary people there did not exactly ply me with questions about American literature when I went to Sarajevo for the first time in April 1993, but they were extremely impressed that I'd had the privilege of being a friend of Danilo Kiš. In besieged Sarajevo people think a lot about Kiš. His fervent screed against nationalism, incorporated into *The Anatomy Lesson*, is one of the two prophetic texts—the other is a story by Andrić, "A Letter from 1920"—that one hears most often cited. As secular, multi-ethnic Bosnia—Yugoslavia's Yugoslavia—is crushed under the new imperative of one ethnicity / one state, Kiš is more present than ever. He deserves to be a hero in Sarajevo, whose struggle to survive embodies the honor of Europe.

Unfortunately, the honor of Europe has been lost at Sarajevo. Kiš and like-minded writers who spoke up against nationalism and fomented-from-the-top ethnic hatreds could not save Europe's honor, Europe's better idea. But it is not true that, to paraphrase Auden, a great writer does not make anything happen. At the end of the century, which is the end of many things, literature, too, is besieged. The work of Danilo Kiš preserves the honor of literature.

[1994]

Gombrowicz's *Ferdydurke*

S TART WITH the title. Which means . . . nothing. There is no character in the novel called Ferdydurke. And this is only a foretaste of insolence to come.

Published in late 1937, when its author was thirty-three, *Ferdydurke* is the great Polish writer's second book. The title of his first, *Memoirs of a Time of Immaturity* (1933), would have served beautifully for the novel. Perhaps this is why Gombrowicz opted for jabberwocky.

That first book, whose title was pounced on by the Warsaw review-ers as if Gombrowicz had made a shaming confession inadvertently, was a collection of stories (he'd been publishing them in magazines since 1926); over the next two years more stories appeared, including a pair ("The Child Runs Deep in Filidor" and "The Child Runs Deep in Filibert") that he would use, with chapter-long mock prefaces, as inter-ludes in *Ferdydurke*, as well as a first play, *Princess Ivona*; then, in early 1935, he embarked on a novel. Had the title of his volume of fanciful stories seemed—his word—"ill-chosen"? Now he would *really* pro-voke. He would write an epic in defense of immaturity. As he declared toward the end of his life: "Immaturity—what a compromising, dis-agreeable word!—became my war cry."

"Immaturity" (not "youth") is the word Gombrowicz insists on, in-sists on because it represents something unattractive, something, to use another of his key words, *inferior.* The longing his novel describes, and endorses, is not, Faust-like, to relive the glory days of youth. What happens to the thirty-year-old who, waking up one morning roiled in the conviction of the futility of his life and all his projects, is abducted by a teacher and returned to the world of callow schoolboys is a humiliation, a fall.

From the start, Gombrowicz was to write, he had chosen to adopt a "fantastic, eccentric, and bizarre tone" bordering on "mania, folly, absurdity." To irritate, Gombrowicz might have said, is to conquer. I think, therefore I contradict. A young aspirant to glory in 1930s literary Warsaw, Gombrowicz had already become legendary in the writers' cafés for his madcap grimaces and poses. On the page, he sought an equally vehement relation to the reader. Grandiose and goofy, this is a work of unrelenting address.

Still, it seems likely that Gombrowicz did not know where he was going when he began the novel. "I can well remember," Gombrowicz declared in 1968, a year before he died (did he remember? or was he massaging his legend?),

> that, when I started *Ferdydurke*, I wanted to write no more than a biting satire that would put me in a superior position over my enemies. But my words were soon whirled away in a violent dance, they took the bit between their teeth and galloped towards a grotesque lunacy with such speed that I had to rewrite the first part of the book in order to give it the same grotesque intensity.

But the problem was less (I suspect) that the first chapters needed a further infusion of lunatic energies than that Gombrowicz did not anticipate the freight of argument—about the nature of eros, about culture (particularly Polish culture), about ideals—his tale would carry.

Ferdydurke starts with a dream-like abduction to an absurd world in which the big become small and the small monstrously big: those great buttocks in the sky. In contrast to the landscape Lewis Carroll conjured up for a prepubescent girl, Gombrowicz's wonderland of shape-shiftings and resizings seethes with lust:

Everything was expanding in blackness. Inflating and widening, yet at the same time shrinking and straining, evading something, and some kind of winnowing, general and particular, a coagulating tension and a tensing coagulation, a dangling by a fine thread, as well as transformation into something, transmutation, and furthermore—a falling into some cumulative, towering system, and as if on a narrow little plank raised six stories up, together with the excitement of all organs. And tickling.

In Alice's story, a child falls into an asexual underworld governed by a new, fantastic but implacable logic. In *Ferdydurke*, the grownup who is turned into a schoolboy discovers new, puerile freedoms for giving offense and owning up to disreputable desire.

Starts with an abduction; ends with an abduction. The first (by Professor Pimko) returns the protagonist to the scene of true, that is, unmanageable, feeling and desire. The second abduction shows the protagonist making a provisional flight back into so-called maturity:

If someone were to spot me in the hallway, in the darkness, how would I explain this escapade? How do we find ourselves on these tortuous and abnormal roads? Normality is a tightrope-walker above the abyss of abnormality. How much potential madness is contained in the everyday order of things—you never know when and how the course of events will lead you to kidnap a farmhand and take to the fields. It's Zosia that I should be kidnapping. If anyone, it should be Zosia, kidnapping Zosia from a country manor would be the normal and correct thing to do, if anyone it was Zosia, and not this stupid, idiotic farmhand . . .

Ferdydurke is one of the most bracing, direct books ever written about sexual desire—this without a single scene of sexual union. To be sure, the cards are stacked from the start in favor of eros. Who would not concur in the silencing of *this* social babble by the clamor of rumps, thighs, calves? The head commands, or wishes to. The buttocks reign.

Later, Gombrowicz referred to his novel as a pamphlet. He also called it a parody of a philosophical tale in the manner of Voltaire. Gombrowicz is one of the super-arguers of the twentieth century—"*To contradict*, even on little matters," he declared, "is the supreme necessity of art today"—and *Ferdydurke* is a dazzling novel of ideas. These ideas give the novel both weight and wings.

Gombrowicz capers and thunders, hectors and mocks, but he is also entirely serious about his project of transvaluation, his critique of high "ideals." *Ferdydurke* is one of the few novels I know that could be called Nietzschean; certainly it is the only comic novel that could be so described. (The affecting fantasia of Hesse's *Steppenwolf* seems, in comparison, riddled with sentimentality.) Nietzsche deplored the ascendancy of slave values sponsored by Christianity, and called for the overthrowing of corrupt ideals and for new forms of masterfulness. Gombrowicz, affirming the "human" need for imperfection, incompleteness, youth, proclaims himself a specialist in inferiority. Swinish adolescence may seem a drastic antidote to smug maturity, but this is exactly what Gombrowicz has in mind. "Degradation became my ideal forever. I worshipped the slave." It is still a Nietzschean project of unmasking, of exposing, with a merry satyr-dance of dualisms: mature versus immature, wholes versus parts, clothed versus naked, heterosexuality versus homosexuality, complete versus incomplete.

Gombrowicz gaily deploys many of the devices of high literary modernism, lately relabeled "post-modern," which tweak the traditional decorums of novel writing: notably, that of a garrulous, intrusive narrator awash in his own contradictory emotional states. Burlesque slides into pathos. When not preening, he is abject; when not clowning, he is vulnerable and self-pitying.

An immature narrator is some sort of candid narrator; even one who flaunts what is usually hidden. What he is not is a "sincere" narrator, sincerity being one of those ideals that make no sense in the world of candor and provocation. "In literature sincerity leads nowhere . . . the more artificial we are, the closer we come to frankness. Artificiality allows the artist to approach shameful truths." As for his celebrated *Diary*, Gombrowicz says:

Have you ever read a "sincere" diary? The "sincere" diary is the most mendacious diary . . . And, in the long run, what a bore sincerity is! It is ineffectual.

Then what? My diary had to be sincere, but it could not be sincere. How could I solve the problem? The word, the loose, spoken word, has this consoling particularity: it is close to sincerity, not in what it confesses but in what it claims to be and in what it pursues.

So I had to avoid turning my diary into a confession. I had to show myself "in action," in my intention of imposing myself on the reader in a certain way, in my desire to create myself with everyone looking on. "This is how I would like to be for you," and not "This is how I am."

Still, however fanciful the plot of *Ferdydurke*, no reader will regard the protagonist and his longings as anything other than a transposition of the author's own personality and pathology. By making Joey Kowalski (as the Polish name of the protagonist-narrator is rendered in English) a writer—and the author of an unsuccessful, much derided book of stories entitled, yes, *Memoirs of a Time of Immaturity*—Gombrowicz dares the reader *not* to think about the man who wrote the novel.

A WRITER WHO REVELS in the fantasy of renouncing his identity and its privileges. A writer who imagines a flight into youth, represented as a kidnapping; a discarding of the destiny expected of an adult, represented as a subtraction from the world in which one is known.

And then the fantasy came true. (Few writers' lives have so clearly taken the shape of a destiny.) At the age of thirty-five, a few days short of the fateful date of September 1, 1939, Gombrowicz was dropped into unexpected exile, far from Europe, in the "immature" New World. It was as brutal a change in his real life as the imagined turning of a thirty-year-old man into a schoolboy. Stranded, without any means of support, where nothing was expected of him because nothing was known about him, he was offered the divine opportunity to lose himself. In Poland, he was well-born Witold Gombrowicz, a prominent "vanguard" writer who had written a book many (including his friend, the other great Polish writer of the same period, Bruno Schulz) considered a masterpiece. In Argentina, he writes, "I was nothing, so I could do anything."

It is impossible to imagine Gombrowicz without his twenty-four years in Argentina (much of which was spent in penury), an Argentina he made to suit his own fantasies, his daring, his pride. He left Poland a relatively young man; he returned to Europe (but never to Poland) when he was nearing sixty, and died six years later in the south of France. Separation from Europe was not the making of Gombrowicz as a writer: the man who published *Ferdydurke* two years earlier was already fully formed as a literary artist. It was, rather, the most providential confirmation of everything his novel knows, and gave direction and bite to the marvelous writings still to come.

The ordeal of emigration—and for Gombrowicz it was an ordeal—sharpened his cultural combativeness, as we know from the *Diary*. The *Diary*—in three volumes in English, and anything but a "personal" diary—can be read as a kind of free-form fiction, post-modern *avant la lettre*; that is, animated by a program of violating decorum similar to that of *Ferdydurke*. Claims for the staggering genius and intellectual acuity of the author vie with a running account of his insecurities, imperfections, and embarrassments, and a defiant avowal of barbaric, yokel prejudices. Considering himself slighted by, and therefore eager to reject, the lively literary milieu of late-1930s Buenos Aires, and aware that it harbored one indisputably great writer, Gombrowicz declared himself "at opposite poles" from Borges. "He is deeply rooted in literature, I in life. To tell the truth I am anti-literature."

As if in agreement, shallow agreement, with Gombrowicz's entirely self-serving quarrel with the idea of literature, many now regard the *Diary* instead of *Ferdydurke* as his greatest work.

No one can forget the notorious opening of the *Diary*:

> *Monday*
> *Me.*
> *Tuesday*
> *Me.*

Wednesday
Me.
Thursday
Me.

Having got *that* straight, Gombrowicz devoted Friday's entry to a subtle reflection on some material he had been reading in the Polish press.

Gombrowicz expected to offend with his egocentricity: a writer must continually defend his borders. But a writer is also someone who must abandon borders, and egotism, so Gombrowicz argued, is the precondition of spiritual and intellectual freedom. In the "me . . . me . . . me . . . me" one hears the solitary émigré thumbing his nose at "we . . . we . . . we . . . we." Gombrowicz never stopped arguing with Polish culture, with its intractable collectivism of spirit (usually called romanticism) and the obsession of its writers with the national martyrdom, the national identity. The relentless intelligence and energy of his observations on cultural and artistic matters, the pertinence of his challenge to Polish pieties, his bravura contentiousness, ended by making him the most influential prose writer of the past half century in his native country.

The Polish sense of being marginal to European culture, and to Western European concern while enduring generations of foreign occupation, had prepared the hapless émigré better than he might have wished to endure being sentenced to many years of near-total isolation as a writer. Courageously, he embarked on the enterprise of making deep, liberating sense out of the unprotectedness of his situation in Argentina. Exile tested his vocation and expanded it. Strengthening his disaffection from nationalist pieties and self-congratulation, it made him a consummate citizen of world literature.

MORE THAN SIXTY YEARS after *Ferdydurke* was written, little remains of the specifically Polish targets of Gombrowicz's scorn. These have vanished along with the Poland in which he was reared and came of age—destroyed by the multiple blows of war, Nazi occupation, Soviet dominance (which prevented him from ever returning), and the post-1989 ethos of consumerism. Almost as dated is his assumption that adults always claim to be mature:

> In our relations with other people we want to be cultivated, superior, mature, so we use the language of maturity and we talk about, for instance, Beauty, Goodness, Truth . . . But, within our own confidential, intimate reality, we feel nothing but inadequacy, immaturity . . .

The declaration seems from another world. How unlikely it would be now for whatever embarrassing inadequacies people feel to be covered over with hifalutin absolutes such as Beauty, Goodness, Truth. The European-style ideals of maturity, cultivation, wisdom have given way steadily to American-style celebrations of the Forever Young. The discrediting of literature and other expressions of "high" culture as elitist or anti-life is a staple of the new culture ruled by entertainment values. Indiscretion about one's unconventional sexual feelings is now a routine, if not mandatory, contribution to public entertainment. Anyone now who would claim to love "the inferior" would argue that it is not inferior at all; that actually it is superior. Hardly any of the cherished opinions against which Gombrowicz contended are still cherished.

Then can *Ferdydurke* still offend? Still seem outrageous? Exception made for the novel's acidic misogyny, probably not. Does it still seem extravagant, brilliant, disturbing, brave, funny . . . wonderful? Yes.

A zealous administrator of his own legend, Gombrowicz was both telling and not telling the truth when he claimed to have successfully avoided all forms of greatness. But whatever he thought, or wanted us to think he thought, there are certain unavoidable consequences if one has produced a masterpiece, and it eventually comes to be acknowledged as such. In the late 1950s *Ferdydurke* was finally translated (under auspicious sponsorship) into French, and Gombrowicz was, at last, "discovered." He had wanted nothing more than this success; this triumph over his adversaries and detractors, real and imagined. But the writer who counseled his readers to try to avoid all expressions of themselves, to guard against all their beliefs, and to mistrust their feelings, above all, to stop identifying themselves with what defines them, could hardly fail to insist that he, Gombrowicz, was not *that book*. Indeed, he has to be inferior to it. "The work, transformed into culture, hovered in the sky, while I remained below." Like the great backside that hovers high above the protagonist's halfhearted flight into normality at the end of the novel, *Ferdydurke* has floated upward to the literary empyrean. Long live its sublime mockery of all attempts to normalize desire . . . and the reach of great literature.

[2000]

Pedro Páramo

"**I CAME TO COMALA** because I had been told that my father, a man named Pedro Páramo, lived there. It was my mother who told me. And I had promised her that after she died I would go see him. I squeezed her hands as a sign I would do it. She was near death, and I would have promised her anything . . ." With the opening sentences of Juan Rulfo's *Pedro Páramo*, as with the beginnings of Kleist's novella *Michael Kohlhaas* and Joseph Roth's novel *The Radetzky March*, we know we are in the hands of a master storyteller. These sentences, of a bewitching concision and directness that pull the reader into the book, have a burnished, already-told quality, like the beginning of a fairy tale.

But the limpid opening of the book is only its first move. In fact, *Pedro Páramo* is a far more complex narrative than its beginning suggests. The novel's premise—a dead mother sending her son out into the world, a son's quest for his father—mutates into a multi-voiced sojourn in hell. The narrative takes place in two worlds: the Comala of the present, to which Juan Preciado, the "I" of the first sentences, is journeying; and the Comala of the past, the village of his mother's memories and of Pedro Páramo's youth. The narrative switches back and forth between first person and third person, present and past. (The great stories are not only told in the past tense, they are about the past.) The Comala of the past is a village of the living. The Comala of the

106

present is inhabited by the dead, and the encounters that Juan Preciado will have when he reaches Comala are with ghosts. *Páramo* means in Spanish barren plain, wasteland. Not only is the father he seeks dead, but so is everyone else in the village. Being dead, they have nothing to express except their essence.

"In my life there are many silences," Rulfo once said. "In my writing, too."

Rulfo has said that he carried *Pedro Páramo* inside him for many years before he knew how to write it. Rather, he was writing hundreds of pages, then discarding them—he once called the novel an exercise in elimination. "The practice of writing the short stories disciplined me," he said, "and made me see the need to disappear and to leave my characters the freedom to talk at will, which provoked, it would seem, a lack of structure. Yes, there is a structure in *Pedro Páramo*, but it is a structure made of silences, of hanging threads, of cut scenes, where everything occurs in a simultaneous time which is a no-time."

Pedro Páramo is a legendary book by a writer who became a legend, too, in his lifetime. Rulfo was born in 1918 in a village in the state of Jalisco, went to Mexico City when he was fifteen, studied law at the university, and began writing, but not publishing, in the late 1930s. His first stories appeared in magazines in the 1940s, and a collection of stories came out in 1953. It was called *El llano en llamas*, which has been translated into English under the title *The Burning Plain and Other Stories*. *Pedro Páramo* appeared two years later. The two books established him as a voice of unprecedented originality and authority in Mexican literature. Quiet (or taciturn), courteous, fastidious, learned, and utterly without pretensions, Rulfo was a kind of invisible man who earned his living in ways entirely unconnected with literature (for years he was a tire salesman), who married and had children, and who spent most nights of his life reading ("I travel in books") and listening to music. He also was extremely famous, and revered by his fellow writers. It is rare for a writer to publish his first books when he is already in his mid-forties, even rarer for first books to be immediately acknowledged as masterpieces. And rarer still for such a writer never to publish another book. A novel called *La Cordillera* was announced as forthcoming by Rulfo's publisher for many years, starting in the late 1960s—

and announced by the author as destroyed, a few years before his death in 1986.

Everyone asked Rulfo why he did not publish another book, as if the point of a writer's life were to go on writing and publishing. In fact, the point of a writer's life is to produce a great book—that is, a book which will last—and this is what Rulfo did. No book is worth reading once if it is not worth reading many times. García Márquez has said that after he discovered *Pedro Páramo* (with Kafka's *Metamorphosis*, the most important reading of his early writing years), he could recite from memory long passages and eventually knew the whole book by heart, so much did he admire it and want to be saturated by it.

Rulfo's novel is not only one of the masterpieces of twentieth-century world literature but one of the most influential of the century's books; indeed, it would be hard to overestimate its impact on literature in Spanish in the last forty years. *Pedro Páramo* is a classic in the truest sense. It is a book that seems, in retrospect, as if it had to be written. It is a book that has profoundly affected the making of literature and continues to resonate in other books. The translation by Margaret Jill Costa, which fulfills the promise I made to Juan Rulfo when we met in Buenos Aires shortly before his death that *Pedro Páramo* would appear in an accurate and uncut English version, is an important literary event.

[1994]

DQ

H E "SO BURIED HIMSELF in his books that he spent the nights reading from twilight to daybreak and the days from dawn till dark; and so from little sleep and much reading, his brain dried up and he lost his mind."

Don Quixote, like *Madame Bovary*, is about the tragedy of reading. But Flaubert's novel is a piece of realism: Emma's imagination is corrupted by the kind of books she reads, vulgar tales of romantic satisfaction. With Don Quixote, a hero of excess, the problem is not so much that the books are bad; it is the sheer quantity of his reading. Reading has not merely deformed his imagination; it has kidnapped it. He thinks the world is the inside of a book. (According to Cervantes, everything Don Quixote thought, saw, or imagined followed the pattern of his reading.) Bookishness makes him, in contrast to Emma Bovary, beyond compromise or corruption. It makes him mad; it makes him profound, heroic, genuinely noble.

Not only the hero of the novel but also the narrator is someone besotted by reading. The narrator of *Don Quixote* reports that he has a taste for reading even torn papers lying in the streets. But whereas the result of Don Quixote's excessive reading is madness, the result of the narrator's is authorship.

The first and greatest epic about addiction, *Don Quixote* is both a denunciation of the establishment of literature and a rhapsodic call to literature. *Don Quixote* is an inexhaustible book, whose subject is everything (the whole world) and nothing (the inside of someone's head—that is, madness). Relentless, verbose, self-cannibalizing, reflexive, playful, irresponsible, accretive, self-replicating—Cervantes's book is the very image of that glorious *mise-en-abîme* which is literature, and of that fragile delirium which is authorship, its manic expansiveness.

A writer is first of all a reader—a reader gone berserk; a rogue reader; an impertinent reader who claims to be able to do it *better*. Yet, justly, when the greatest living author composed his definitive fable about the writer's vocation, he invented an early-twentieth-century writer who had chosen as his most ambitious work to write (parts of) *Don Quixote*. Once again. Exactly as is (was). For *Don Quixote*, more than any book ever written, *is* literature.

[1985]

A Letter to Borges

June 13, 1996
New York

Dear Borges,

Since your literature was always placed under the sign of eternity, it doesn't seem *too* odd to be addressing a letter to you. (Borges, it's ten years!) If ever a contemporary seemed destined for literary immortality, it was you. You were very much the product of your time, your culture, and yet you knew how to transcend your time, your culture, in ways that seem quite magical. This had something to do with the openness and generosity of your attention. You were the least egocentric, the most transparent of writers, as well as the most artful. It also had something to do with a natural purity of spirit. Though you lived among us for a rather long time, you perfected practices of fastidiousness and of detachment that made you an expert mental traveler to other eras as well. You had a sense of time that was different from other people's. The ordinary ideas of past, present, and future seemed banal under your gaze. You liked to say that every moment of time contains the past and the future, quoting (as I remember) the poet Browning, who wrote something like "the present is the instant in which the future crumbles into the past." That, of course, was part of your modesty: your taste for finding your ideas in the ideas of other writers.

Your modesty was part of the sureness of your presence. You were a discoverer of new joys. A pessimism as profound, as serene, as yours did not need to be indignant. It had, rather, to be inventive—and you were, above all, inventive. The serenity and the transcendence of self that you found are to me exemplary. You showed that it is not necessary to be unhappy, even while one is clear-eyed and undeluded about how terrible everything is. Somewhere you said that a writer—delicately you added: all persons—must think that whatever happens to him or her is a *resource*. (You were speaking of your blindness.)

You have been a great resource, for other writers. In 1982—that is, four years before you died—I said in an interview, "There is no writer living today who matters more to other writers than Borges. Many people would say he is the greatest living writer . . . Very few writers of today have not learned from him or imitated him." That is still true. We are still learning from you. We are still imitating you. You gave people new ways of imagining, while proclaiming over and over our indebtedness to the past, above all, to literature. You said that we owe literature almost everything we are and what we have been. If books disappear, history will disappear, and human beings will also disappear. I am sure you are right. Books are not only the arbitrary sum of our dreams, and our memory. They also give us the model of self-transcendence. Some people think of reading only as a kind of escape: an escape from the "real" everyday world to an imaginary world, the world of books. Books are much more. They are a way of being fully human.

I'm sorry to have to tell you that books are now considered an endangered species. By books, I also mean the conditions of reading that make possible literature and its soul effects. Soon, we are told, we will call up on "bookscreens" any "text" on demand, and will be able to change its appearance, ask questions of it, "interact" with it. When books become "texts" that we "interact" with according to criteria of utility, the written word will have become simply another aspect of our advertising-driven televisual reality. This is the glorious future being created, and promised to us, as something more "democratic." Of course, it means nothing less than the death of inwardness—and of the book.

This time around, there will be no need for a great conflagration. The barbarians don't have to burn the books. The tiger is in the library. Dear Borges, please understand that it gives me no satisfaction to complain. But to whom could such complaints about the fate of books—of reading itself—be better addressed than to you? (Borges, it's ten years!) All I mean to say is that we miss you. *I* miss you. You continue to make a difference. The era we are entering now, this twenty-first century, will test the soul in new ways. But, you can be sure, some of us are not going to abandon the Great Library. And you will continue to be our patron and our hero.

SUSAN

SEEING

A Century of Cinema

CINEMA'S HUNDRED YEARS appear to have the shape of a life cycle: an inevitable birth, the steady accumulation of glories, and the onset in the last decade of an ignominious, irreversible decline. This doesn't mean that there won't be any more new films one can admire. But such films will not simply be exceptions; that's true of great achievement in any art. They will have to be heroic violations of the norms and practices which now govern moviemaking everywhere in the capitalist and would-be capitalist world—which is to say, everywhere. And ordinary films, films made purely for entertainment (that is, commercial) purposes, will continue to be astonishingly witless; already the vast majority fail resoundingly to appeal to their cynically targeted audiences. While the point of a great film is now, more than ever, to be a one-of-a-kind achievement, the commercial cinema has settled for a policy of bloated, derivative filmmaking, a brazen combinatory or re-combinatory art, in the hope of reproducing past successes. Every film that hopes to reach the largest possible audience is designed as some kind of remake. Cinema, once heralded as *the* art of the twentieth century, seems now, as the century closes numerically, to be a decadent art.

Perhaps it is not cinema which has ended but only cinephilia—the name of the distinctive kind of love that cinema inspired. Each art breeds its fanatics. The love movies aroused was more imperial. It was born of the conviction that cinema was an art unlike any other: quintessentially modern; distinctively accessible; poetic and mysterious and erotic and moral—all at the same time. Cinema had apostles (it was like religion). Cinema was a crusade. Cinema was a world view. Lovers of poetry or opera or dance don't think there is *only* poetry or opera or dance. But lovers of cinema could think there was only cinema. That the movies encapsulated everything—and they did. It was both the book of art and the book of life.

As many have noted, the start of moviemaking a hundred years ago was, conveniently, a double start. In that first year, 1895, two kinds of films were made, proposing two modes of what cinema could be: cinema as the transcription of real, unstaged life (the Lumière brothers) and cinema as invention, artifice, illusion, fantasy (Méliès). But this was never a true opposition. For those first audiences watching the Lumière brothers' *The Arrival of a Train at La Ciotat Station*, the camera's transmission of a banal sight was a fantastic experience. Cinema began in wonder, the wonder that reality can be transcribed with such magical immediacy. All of cinema is an attempt to perpetuate and to reinvent that sense of wonder.

Everything begins with that moment, one hundred years ago, when the train pulled into the station. People took movies into themselves, just as the public cried out with excitement, actually ducked, as the train seemed to move toward *them*. Until the advent of television emptied the movie theatres, it was from a weekly visit to the cinema that you learned (or tried to learn) how to strut, to smoke, to kiss, to fight, to grieve. Movies gave you tips about how to be attractive, such as . . . it looks good to wear a raincoat even when it isn't raining. But whatever you took home from the movies was only a part of the larger experience of losing yourself in faces, in lives that were *not* yours—which is the more inclusive form of desire embodied in the movie experience. The strongest experience was simply to surrender to, to be transported by, what was on the screen. You wanted to be kidnapped by the movie.

The prerequisite of being kidnapped was to be overwhelmed by the physical presence of the image. And the conditions of "going to the movies" secured that experience. To see a great film only on television isn't to have really seen that film. (This is equally true of those made for

TV, like Fassbinder's *Berlin Alexanderplatz* and the two *Heimat* films of Edgar Reitz.) It's not only the difference of dimensions: the superiority of the larger-than-you image in the theatre to the little image on the box at home. The conditions of paying attention in a domestic space are radically disrespectful of film. Since film no longer has a standard size, home screens can be as big as living room or bedroom walls. But you are still in a living room or a bedroom, alone or with familiars. To be kidnapped, you have to be in a movie theatre, seated in the dark among anonymous strangers.

No amount of mourning will revive the vanished rituals—erotic, ruminative—of the darkened theatre. The reduction of cinema to assaultive images, and the unprincipled manipulation of images (faster and faster cutting) to be more attention-grabbing, have produced a disincarnated, lightweight cinema that doesn't demand anyone's full attention. Images now appear in any size and on a variety of surfaces: on a screen in a theatre, on home screens as small as the palm of your hand or as big as a wall, on disco walls and mega-screens hanging above sports arenas and the outsides of tall public buildings. The sheer ubiquity of moving images has steadily undermined the standards people once had both for cinema as art at its most serious and for cinema as popular entertainment.

In the first years there was, essentially, no difference between cinema as art and cinema as entertainment. And *all* films of the silent era—from the masterpieces of Feuillade, D. W. Griffith, Dziga Vertov, Pabst, Murnau, King Vidor to the most formula-ridden melodramas and comedies—look, are, better than most of what was to follow. With the coming of sound, the image-making lost much of its brilliance and poetry, and commercial standards tightened. This way of making movies—the Hollywood system—dominated filmmaking for about twenty-five years (roughly from 1930 to 1955). The most original directors, like Erich von Stroheim and Orson Welles, were defeated by the system and eventually went into artistic exile in Europe—where more or less the same quality-defeating system was in place with lower budgets; only in France were a large number of superb films produced throughout this period. Then, in the mid-1950s, vanguard ideas took hold again, rooted in the idea of cinema as a craft pioneered by the

Italian films of the early postwar era. A dazzling number of original, passionate films of the highest seriousness got made with new actors and tiny crews, went to film festivals (of which there were more and more), and from there, garlanded with festival prizes, into movie theatres around the world. This golden age actually lasted as long as twenty years.

It was at this specific moment in the hundred-year history of cinema that going to movies, thinking about movies, talking about movies became a passion among university students and other young people. You fell in love not just with actors but with cinema itself. Cinephilia had first become visible in the 1950s in France: its forum was the legendary film magazine *Cahiers du Cinéma* (followed by similarly fervent magazines in Germany, Italy, Great Britain, Sweden, the United States, Canada). Its temples, as it spread throughout Europe and the Americas, were the cinematheques and film clubs specializing in films from the past and directors' retrospectives. The 1960s and early 1970s were the age of feverish moviegoing, with the full-time cinephile always hoping to find a seat as close as possible to the big screen, ideally the third row center. "One can't live without Rossellini," declares a character in Bertolucci's *Before the Revolution* (1964)—and means it.

Cinephilia—a source of exultation in the films of Godard and Truffaut and the early Bertolucci and Syberberg; a morose lament in the recent films of Nanni Moretti—was mostly a Western European affair. The great directors of "the other Europe" (Zanussi in Poland, Angelopoulos in Greece, Tarkovsky and Sokurov in Russia, Jancsó and Tarr in Hungary) and the great Japanese directors (Ozu, Mizoguchi, Kurosawa, Naruse, Oshima, Imamura) have tended not to be cinephiles, perhaps because in Budapest or Moscow or Tokyo or Warsaw or Athens there wasn't a chance to get a cinematheque education. The distinctive thing about cinephile taste was that it embraced both "art" films and popular films. Thus, European cinephilia had a romantic relation to the films of certain directors in Hollywood at the apogee of the studio system: Godard for Howard Hawks, Fassbinder for Douglas Sirk. Of course, this moment—when cinephilia emerged—was also the moment when the Hollywood studio system was breaking up. It seemed that moviemaking had re-won the right to experiment;

cinephiles could *afford* to be passionate (or sentimental) about the old Hollywood genre films. A host of new people came into cinema, including a generation of young film critics from *Cahiers du Cinéma*; the towering figure of that generation, indeed of several decades of filmmaking anywhere, was Jean-Luc Godard. A few writers turned out to be wildly talented filmmakers: Alexander Kluge in Germany, Pier Paolo Pasolini in Italy. (The model for the writer who turns to filmmaking actually emerged earlier, in France, with Pagnol in the 1930s and Cocteau in the 1940s; but it was not until the 1960s that this seemed, at least in Europe, normal.) Cinema appeared to be reborn.

For some fifteen years there was a profusion of masterpieces, and one allowed oneself to imagine that this would go on forever. To be sure, there was always a conflict between cinema as an industry and cinema as an art, cinema as routine and cinema as experiment. But the conflict was not such as to make impossible the making of wonderful films, sometimes within and sometimes outside of mainstream cinema. Now the balance has tipped decisively in favor of cinema as an industry. The great cinema of the 1960s and 1970s has been thoroughly repudiated. Already in the 1970s Hollywood was plagiarizing and banalizing the innovations in narrative method and editing of successful new European and ever-marginal independent American films. Then came the catastrophic rise in production costs in the 1980s, which secured the worldwide reimposition of industry standards of making and distributing films on a far more coercive, this time truly global, scale. The result can be seen in the melancholy fate of some of the greatest directors of the last decades. What place is there today for a maverick like Hans Jürgen Syberberg, who has stopped making films altogether, or for the great Godard, who now makes films about the history of film on video? Consider some other cases. The internationalizing of financing and therefore of casts was a disaster for Andrei Tarkovsky in the last two films of his stupendous, tragically abbreviated career. And these conditions for making films have proved to be as much an artistic disaster for two of the most valuable directors still working: Krzysztof Zanussi (*The Structure of Crystals, Illumination, Spiral, Contract*) and Theo Angelopoulos (*Reconstruction, Days of '36, The Travelling Players*). And what will happen now to Béla Tarr (*Damnation, Satantango*)? And how will Aleksandr Sokurov (*Save and Protect*, *Days of Eclipse*, *The Second Circle*, *Stone*, *Whispering Pages*) find the money to go on making films, his sublime films, under the rude conditions of Russian capitalism?

Predictably, the love of cinema has waned. People still like going to the movies, and some people still care about and expect something special, necessary from a film. And wonderful films are still being made: Mike Leigh's *Naked*, Gianni Amelio's *Lamerica*, Hou Hsiao-hsien's *Goodbye South, Goodbye*, and Abbas Kiarostami's *Close-Up* and Koker trilogy. But one hardly finds anymore, at least among the young, the distinctive cinephilic love of movies, which is not simply love of but a certain *taste* in films (grounded in a vast appetite for seeing and re-seeing as much as possible of cinema's glorious past). Cinephilia itself has come under attack, as something quaint, outmoded, snobbish. For cinephilia implies that films are unique, unrepeatable, magic experiences. Cinephilia tells us that the Hollywood remake of Godard's *Breathless* cannot be as good as the original. Cinephilia has no role in the era of hyperindustrial films. For by the very range and eclecticism of its passions, cinephilia cannot help but sponsor the idea of the film as, first of all, a poetic object; and cannot help but incite those outside the movie industry, like painters and writers, to want to make films, too. It is precisely this that must be defeated. That has been defeated.

If cinephilia is dead, then movies are dead . . . no matter how many movies, even very good ones, go on being made. If cinema can be resurrected, it will only be through the birth of a new kind of cine-love.

[1995]

Novel into Film:
Fassbinder's *Berlin Alexanderplatz*

W E **TAKE IT** for granted that film directors are, if they so wish, in the game of recycling. Adapting novels is one of the most respectable of movie projects, while a book that calls itself the novelization of a film seems, rightly, barbarous. Being a hybrid art as well as a late one, film has always been in a dialogue with other narrative genres. Movies were first seen as an exceptionally potent kind of illusionist theatre, the rectangle of the screen corresponding to the proscenium of a stage, on which appear—actors. Starting in the early silent period, plays were regularly "turned into" films. But filming plays did not encourage the evolution of what truly was distinctive about a movie: the intervention of the camera—its mobility of vision. As a source of plot, character, and dialogue, the novel, being a form of narrative art that (like movies) ranges freely in time and space, seemed more suitable. Many early successes of cinema (*The Birth of a Nation, The Four Horsemen of the Apocalypse, Ramona, Stella Dallas, It*) were adaptations of popular novels. The 1930s and 1940s, when movies attained their largest audience and had an unprecedented monopoly on entertainment, were probably the heyday of novel-into-film projects— the sleek Hollywood classic-comics of the novels by the Brontë sisters or Tolstoy being no more or less ambitious, as films, than those adapted from such bestsellers as *Gone With the Wind*, *Lost Horizon*, *Rebecca*, *The Good Earth*, *Gentleman's Agreement*. The presumption was that it was the destiny of a novel to "become" a film.

Since the film that is a transcription of a novel is riding piggyback on the reputation and interest of the novel, comparisons are inevitable. And now that movies have ceased to have a monopoly of entertainment, standards have risen. Who can see the films made from *Lolita* or *Oblomov* or *The Trial* without asking if the film is adequate to the novel—the making of invariably invidious comparisons depending on whether or not the novel belongs to literature. Even a minor novel, like Klaus Mann's *Mephisto*, turns out to be far richer than the film. It seems almost in the nature of film—regardless of the film's quality—to abridge, dilute, and simplify any good novel that it adapts. In fact, far more good movies have been made from good plays than from good novels—despite the view that such films tend to be static and thereby go against the grain of what is distinctly cinematic.

Directors of the 1930s and 1940s like Wyler, Stevens, Lean, and Autant-Lara were particularly drawn to good-novel-into-movie projects—as have been, more recently, Visconti, Losey, and Schlöndorff. But the failure rate has been so spectacular that since the 1960s the venture has been considered suspect in certain quarters. Godard, Resnais, and Truffaut declared their preference for subliterary genres—crime and adventure novels, science fiction. Classics seemed cursed: it became a dictum that cinema was better nourished by pulp fiction than by literature. A minor novel could serve as a pretext, a repertoire of themes with which the director is free to play. With a good novel there is the problem of being "faithful" to it. Visconti's first film, *Ossessione*—adapted from James M. Cain's *The Postman Always Rings Twice*—is a far nobler achievement than his handsome, respectful transcription of *The Leopard* or his stiff, rather absent version of Camus's *The Stranger*. Cain's melodrama did not have to be "followed."

There is also the obstacle posed by the length of the work of fiction, not just by its quality as literature. Until this past winter I had seen only one film adaptation of a literary work I thought entirely admirable: a Russian film, *The Lady with the Dog*, made from a short story by Chekhov. The standard, and arbitrary, length of feature films is approximately the time in which one can render a short story or a play. But not a novel—whose nature is expansiveness. To do justice to a novel requires a film that is not just somewhat longer but radically long —one that breaks with the conventions of length set by theatregoing. This was surely the conviction of Erich von Stroheim when he attempted his legendary, aborted adaptation of *McTeague*, called *Greed*. Stroheim, who wanted to film all of Frank Norris's novel, had made a film of ten hours, which the studio reedited and eventually reduced to two hours and forty-five minutes (ten reels out of Stroheim's forty-two); the negative of the thirty-two reels of discarded footage was destroyed. The version of *Greed* that survived this butchery is one of the most admired of films. But movie lovers will be forever in mourning for the loss of the ten-hour *Greed* that Stroheim edited.

FASSBINDER SUCCEEDS WHERE Stroheim was thwarted—he has filmed virtually all of a novel. More: he has made a great film of, and one faithful to, a great novel—although if in some Platonic heaven, or haven, of judgments there is a list of the, say, ten greatest novels of the twentieth century, probably the least familiar title on it is *Berlin Alexanderplatz* by Alfred Döblin (1878–1957). Stroheim was not allowed to make a film of ten hours. Fassbinder, thanks to the possibility of showing a film in parts, on television, was allowed to make a film of fifteen hours and twenty-one minutes. Inordinate length could hardly assure the successful transposition of a great novel into a great film. But though not a sufficient condition, it is probably a necessary one.

Berlin Alexanderplatz is Fassbinder's *Greed* not only in the sense that Fassbinder succeeded in making *the* long film, the great film of a novel, but also because of the many striking parallels between the plot of *Berlin Alexanderplatz* and the plot of *Greed*. For, indeed, the American novel, published in 1899, tells a primitive version of the story related in the German novel, published thirty years later, which has a much thicker texture and greater range. Writing in San Francisco at the end of the last century, the youthful Frank Norris had Zola as a model of a dispassionate "naturalism." The far more sophisticated Döblin, already in midcareer (he was fifty-one when *Berlin Alexander-*

platz was published) and writing in the century's single most creative decade in the arts, had the inspiration (it is said) of Joyce's *Ulysses*, as well as the expressive hypernaturalist tendencies in German theatre, film, painting, and photography with which he was familiar. (In 1929, the same year that *Berlin Alexanderplatz* appeared, Döblin wrote an elegant essay on photography as the preface to a volume of work by the great August Sander.)

A burly, sentimental, naïve, violent man, both innocent and brute, is the protagonist of both novels. Franz Biberkopf is already a murderer when *Berlin Alexanderplatz* starts—he has just finished serving a sentence of four years for killing the prostitute with whom he lived, Ida. The protagonist of *McTeague* eventually kills a woman, his wife, Trina. Both novels are anatomies of a city, or part of it: San Francisco's shoddy Polk Street in Norris's novel and the Berlin district of workers, whores, and petty criminals in Döblin's novel are far more than mere background to the hero's misfortunes. Both novels open with a depiction of the unmated hero afoot and alone in the city—McTeague following his Sunday routine of solitary walk, dinner, and beer; Biberkopf, just discharged from prison, wandering in a daze about the Alexanderplatz. A former car boy in a mine, McTeague has managed to set himself up in San Francisco as a dentist; by the middle of the novel he is forbidden to practice. The ex-pimp Biberkopf tries to earn his living honestly in a series of menial jobs, but when he can no longer work (he loses his right arm), the woman he loves goes on the street to support them.

In both novels, the downfall of the protagonist is not just bad luck or circumstantial, but is engineered by his former best friend—Marcus in *McTeague*, Reinhold in *Berlin Alexanderplatz*. And both pairs of friends are studies in contrasts. McTeague is inarticulate; Marcus is hyperverbal—a budding political boss, spouting the clichés of reactionary populism. Biberkopf, who has vowed, on coming out of prison, to go straight, is not inarticulate; Reinhold belongs to a gang of thieves and is a stutterer. The gullible hero is obtusely devoted to the secretly malevolent friend. In Norris's novel, McTeague inherits—with Marcus's permission—the girl Marcus has been courting and marries her just as she wins a large sum of money in a lottery; Marcus vows revenge. In *Berlin Alexanderplatz*, Biberkopf inherits—on Reinhold's urging—a number of Reinhold's women, and it is when he refuses to discard one ex-girl of Reinhold's as the next is ready to be passed on to him that Reinhold turns treacherous. It is Marcus who has McTeague deprived of his livelihood and fragile respectability: he reports him to the city authorities for practicing dentistry without having a diploma, and the result is not only destitution but the ruin of his relationship with his already deranged, pathetic wife. It is Reinhold who puts an atrocious end to Biberkopf's valiant efforts to stay honest, first tricking him into taking part in a burglary and then, during the getaway, pushing him out of the van into the path of a car—but Biberkopf, after the amputation of his arm, is strangely without desire for revenge. When his protector and former lover Eva brings the crippled Biberkopf out of his despair by finding him a woman, Mieze, with whom he falls in love, Reinhold, unable to endure Biberkopf's happiness, seduces and murders Mieze. Marcus is motivated by envy; Reinhold by an ultimately motiveless malignity. (Fassbinder calls Biberkopf's forbearance toward Reinhold a kind of "pure," that is, motiveless, love.)

In *McTeague* the fatal bond that unites McTeague and Marcus is depicted more summarily. Toward the end of the novel Norris removes his characters from San Francisco: the two men find each other in the desert, the landscape that is the city's opposite. The last paragraph has McTeague accidentally handcuffed to Marcus (whom he has just killed, in self-defense), in the middle of Death Valley, "stupidly looking around him," doomed to await death beside the corpse of his enemy/friend. The ending of *McTeague* is merely dramatic, though wonderfully so. *Berlin Alexanderplatz* ends as a series of arias on grief, pain, death, and survival. Biberkopf does not kill Reinhold, nor does he die himself. He goes mad after the murder of his beloved Mieze (the most lacerating description of grief I know in literature), is confined to a mental hospital, and when released, a burnt-out case, finally lands his respectable job, as night watchman in a factory. When Reinhold is eventually brought to trial for Mieze's murder, Biberkopf refuses to testify against him.

Both McTeague and Biberkopf go on savage, character-altering alcoholic binges—McTeague because he feels too little, Biberkopf because he feels too much (remorse, grief, dread). The naïve, virile Biberkopf, not stupid but oddly docile, is capable of tenderness and generosity toward, as well as real love for, Mieze; in contrast to what McTeague can feel for Trina: abject fascination, succeeded by the stupor of habit. Norris denies hulking, pitiable, semi-retarded McTeague a soul; he is repeatedly described as animal-like or primitive. Döblin does not condescend to his hero—who is part Woyzeck, part Job. Biberkopf has a rich, convulsive inner life; indeed, in the course of the novel he acquires more and more understanding, although this is never adequate to events, to the depth or the gruesome specificity of suffering. Döblin's novel is an educational novel, and a modern *Inferno*.

In *McTeague* there is one point of view, one dispassionate voice—selective, summarizing, compressive, photographic. Filming *Greed*, Stroheim is said to have followed Norris's novel paragraph by paragraph—one can see how. *Berlin Alexanderplatz* is as much (or more) for the ear as for the eye. It has a complex method of narration: free-form, encyclopedic, with many layers of narrative, anecdote, and commentary. Döblin cuts from one kind of material to another, often within the same paragraph: documentary evidence, myths, moral tales, literary allusions—in the same way that he shifts between slang and a stylized lyrical language. The principal voice, that of the all-knowing author, is exalted, urgent, anything but dispassionate.

The style of *Greed* is anti-artificial. Stroheim refused to shoot anything in the studio, insisting on making all of *Greed* in "natural" locations. More than a half century later, Fassbinder has no need to make a point about realism or about veracity. And it would hardly have been possible to film in the Alexanderplatz, which was annihilated in the bombing of Berlin during World War II. Most of *Berlin Alexanderplatz* looks as if it were shot in a studio. Fassbinder chooses a broad, familiar stylization: illuminating the principal location, Biberkopf's room, by a flashing neon sign on the street; shooting often through windows and in mirrors. The extreme of artificiality, or theatricality, is reached in the sequences in the circus-like street of whores, and in most of the two-hour epilogue.

Berlin Alexanderplatz has the distension of a novel, but it is also very theatrical, as are most of Fassbinder's best films. Fassbinder's genius was in his eclecticism, his extraordinary freedom as an artist: he was not looking for the specifically cinematic, and borrowed freely from theatre. He began as the director of a theatre group in Munich; he directed almost as many plays as movies, and some of his best films are filmed plays, like his own *The Bitter Tears of Petra von Kant* and *Bremen Freedom*, or take place mostly in one interior, such as *Chinese Roulette* and *Satan's Brew*. In a 1974 interview Fassbinder described his first years of activity thus: "I produced theatre as if it were film, and directed film as if it were theatre, and did this quite stubbornly." Where other directors, adapting a novel to a film, would have thought to abridge a scene because it went on too long, and thereby became (as they might fear) static, Fassbinder would persist, and insist. The theatrical-looking style that Fassbinder devised helps him stay close to Döblin's book.

Apart from the invention of one new character—an all-forgiving mother figure, Biberkopf's landlady Frau Bast—most of the changes Fassbinder has made in the story simply render the action more compact visually. In the novel Biberkopf does not always live in the same one-room apartment, as he does in the film, and Fassbinder sets events there that in the novel take place elsewhere. For example, in the novel Franz kills Ida at her sister's place; in the film, the gruesome battering—which we see in repeated, hallucinatory flashback—takes place in Biberkopf's room, witnessed by Frau Bast. In the novel, Biberkopf doesn't live with all the women with whom he takes up; in the film each of them, one by one, moves into his place, reinforcing the film's visual unity, but also making the relationships that precede Biberkopf's union with Mieze perhaps a bit too cozy. The women seem more whores-with-hearts-of-gold than they do in the book. One last invention: it is hard not to suspect that the canary in a cage Mieze gives Biberkopf (such a gift is just mentioned, once, in Döblin's novel), which we see Biberkopf doting on, and is often in the shot in scenes that take place in Biberkopf's room, is a reincarnation of the canary that is McTeague's most cherished possession, the only thing he salvages from his wrecked domestic felicity, and still by his side "in its little gilt prison" when his doom is sealed in the desert.

Fassbinder's cinema is full of Biberkopfs—victims of false consciousness. And the material of *Berlin Alexanderplatz* is prefigured throughout his films, whose recurrent subject is damaged lives and marginal existences—petty criminals, prostitutes, transvestites, immigrant workers, depressed housewives, and overweight workers at the end of their tether. More specifically, the harrowing slaughterhouse scenes in *Berlin Alexanderplatz* are anticipated by the slaughterhouse sequence in *Jail Bait* and *In a Year of 13 Moons*. But *Berlin Alexanderplatz* is more than a compendium of his main themes. It was the fulfillment—and the origin.

In an article he wrote in March 1980, toward the end of the ten months it took to film *Berlin Alexanderplatz*, Fassbinder declared that he had first read Döblin's novel when he was fourteen or fifteen, and had dreamed of making it into a film from the beginning of his career. It was the novel of his life—he described how his own fantasies had been impregnated by the novel—and its protagonist was Fassbinder's elected alter ego. Several heroes of his films were called Franz; and he gave the name Franz Biberkopf to the protagonist of *Fox and His Friends*, a role he played himself. It is said that Fassbinder would have liked to play Biberkopf. He did not; but he did something equally appropriate. He became Döblin: his is the voice of the narrator. Döblin is omnipresent in his book, commenting and lamenting. And the film has a recurrent voiceover, the voice of the novel, so to speak—and Fassbinder's. Thus we hear many of the parallel stories, such as the sacrifice of Isaac, related in the novel. Fassbinder preserves the novel's extravagant ruminating energy without breaking the narrative stride. The ruminating voice is used not as an anti-narrative device, as in Godard's films, but to intensify the narrative; not to distance us but to make us feel more. The story continues to evolve, in the most direct, affecting way.

Berlin Alexanderplatz is not a meta-film, like Hans Jürgen Syberberg's *Hitler*; Fassbinder has nothing of Syberberg's aesthetic of the grandiose, for all the length of *Berlin Alexanderplatz*, or his reverence for high culture. It is a narrative film, but one that is *that* long: a film that tells a story, in decors of the period (the late 1920s), with more than a hundred actors (many roles are taken by actors from Fassbinder's regular troupe) and thousands of extras. A fifty-three-year-old theatre actor who has had minor roles in a few of Fassbinder's films, Günter Lamprecht, plays Franz Biberkopf. Splendid as are all the actors, particularly Barbara Sukowa as Mieze and Hanna Schygulla as Eva, Lamprecht's Biberkopf overshadows the others—an intensely moving, expressive, brilliantly varied performance, as good as anything done by Emil Jannings or by Raimu.

Though made possible by television—it is a co-production of German and Italian TV—*Berlin Alexanderplatz* is not a TV series. A TV series is constructed in "episodes," which are *designed* to be seen at an interval—one week being the convention, like the old Saturday afternoon movie serials (*Fantômas*, *The Perils of Pauline*, *Flash Gordon*). The parts of *Berlin Alexanderplatz* are not really episodes, strictly speaking, since the film is diminished when seen in this way, spaced out over fourteen weeks (as I saw it for the first time, on Italian TV). Presentation in a movie theatre—five segments of approximately three hours each, over five consecutive weeks—is certainly a better way to see it. Seeing it over three or four days would be far better. The more one can watch over the shortest time works best, exactly as one reads a long novel with maximum pleasure and intensity. In *Berlin Alexanderplatz*, cinema, that hybrid art, has at last achieved some of the dilatory, open form and accumulative power of the novel by being longer than any film has dared to be—and by being theatrical.

[1983]

A Note on Bunraku

Art is something which lies in the slender margin
between the real and the unreal . . . it is unreal, and
yet it is not unreal; it is real, and yet it is not real.
> —CHIKAMATSU MONZAEMON
> (1653–1725)

IN BUNRAKU THE PLAY is identified, first of all, as a physical object: a text. And the text is sacred—that is, generative. Hence, the grave ceremony that opens each performance: the chief reader holds out the text and bows to it, before setting it down on the low lectern and beginning to read. Bunraku is a theatre that transcends the actor, by multiplying and displacing the sources of dramatic pathos.

The play is acted; that is to say, recited; that is, read. The text (declaimed, sung, chanted, wailed) is punctuated or italicized by music produced by a string instrument, the shamisen. It is also, simultaneously, enacted by piercingly expressive large puppets, half or two-thirds life-size. The enacting of the drama occupies the stage proper, in front of the audience: the wide rectangular space where figures—the puppets and their handlers—move. But the source of the words and the music—the one or more reciters and musicians who sit to the right of the stage on a rostrum—constitutes a parallel performance. The dialogue is not "off," as in a certain kind of narrative film, but off-center—displaced, given its own expressive and corporeal autonomy.

The drama has a double displacement of emotion, a double scale, a double physical and emotional gait. On the stage proper the leading principle is a kind of anti-hysteria. There is the muteness of the protagonists—who, instead of being living actors, are puppets; there is the impassivity and omnipresence of the humans who make them move. To the *joruri* reciter, who is not only off-center (from the audience's point of view) but physically immobile, is given the task of maximal expressiveness. Most of the texts, which consist of narrative and commentary as well as dialogue, are floridly emotional, and the narration may modulate into a lengthy crescendo of sobs and gasps. The figure of the reciter, who acts, as it were, by proxy, on behalf of the puppets, is just one of the devices whereby Bunraku isolates—decomposes, illustrates, transcends, intensifies—what acting is.

The puppet is, in prototype, a supple doll operated by a single person. The invention, in 1734, of a puppet to be operated by three persons brought the puppet's emotional and gestural potency to a point never equaled before or since. The Japanese puppet can roll its eyes, raise its eyebrows, smile, clench its fists; it can languish, dress itself, run, convincingly take its own life. No string puppet or hand puppet can perform such complex and detailed actions; and the Bunraku puppets have an ability to move audiences, move them to tears, unmatched in any other puppet tradition.

But apart from widening the emotional range and expressiveness of the puppet (a gain we may or may not choose to identify with "realism"), the fact of multiplying the operators—and, of necessity, putting them onstage with the puppets—decisively shapes and transforms the emotional register of puppet drama. The puppet is literally outnumbered, beleaguered, surrounded. The presence of three outsized handlers endows the puppet's movements and efforts with a sheen of pathos. The puppets seem helpless, childlike, vulnerable. Yet they also seem sovereign, imperious, in their very smallness and precision and elegance.

Bunraku works on two scales of relatedness in space. The often elaborate decor is constructed to the puppets' measurements. The operators are giants, interlopers. Alongside each delicate puppet head are the three large heads of the operators. The operators look at the puppet as they manipulate it. The audience watches the operators observing the puppet, primal spectators to the drama they animate. The three operators sum up the essence of what it is to be a god. To be seen, and impassive: one has his face bared. And to be hidden: the other two wear black hoods. The puppet gestures. The operators move together, as one giant body, animating the different parts of the puppet body, in a perfected division of labor. What the audience sees is that to act is to be moved. (And, simultaneously, observed.) What is enacted is the submission to a fate. That one operator's face is exposed and two are veiled is another device making Bunraku's characteristic double statement: hyperbole and discretion, presence and absence of the dramatic substance.

This relation between the operators and the puppet is not simply an efficient relation; it is the cruel mystery which is at the center of the Bunraku drama. Handing the puppet a comb, rushing the puppet to its doom—some moments the operators seem like the puppet's servants, at other moments its captors. Sometimes the puppet seems to be reposing solidly on the operators or to be borne placidly aloft by them; other times to be in perpetual, hapless flight. There are constant shifts of scale, to delight the senses and wring the emotions. Sometimes the shadowy manipulators shrink and the puppets swell into a normal scale. Then the operators loom once more and the puppets re-become fragile, persecuted Lilliputians.

The situation we call art characteristically requires us both to look very attentively and to look "beyond" (or "through") what is understood as an impediment, distraction, irrelevance. At an opera performance, we look past or over the orchestra to concentrate on the stage. But in Bunraku we are not supposed to look past the shadowy, black-garbed puppeteers. The presence of the operators is what gives Bunraku its elevated, mythic impersonality and heightened, purified emotionality. In order to make the art of the puppets competitive with the art of living actors, says Chikamatsu, the text must be "charged with feeling." But, he adds, "I take pathos to be entirely a matter of restraint." Compare Balanchine, who brought the naïvely emotive classical ballet tradition to its apex by developing the sense in which dancers are co-sharers, with ideal puppets, in the sublimity of the impersonal:

"Silence, placidity, and immobility are perhaps the most powerful forces. They are as impressive, even more so, than rage, delirium, or ecstasy."

In the most profound Western meditation on puppet theatre (and, by extension, on the dance), Kleist wrote that the very inanimateness of the puppet was the precondition for expressing an ideal state of the spirit. Kleist's speculative fantasy—he was writing in 1810, about string puppets—is incarnated and fulfilled in Bunraku.

[1983]

A Place for Fantasy

G ARDEN HISTORY IS an enthralling branch of art history, opening onto the history of outdoor spectacles (the masque, fireworks, pageants), of architecture, of urban planning—and of literary history as well. Once mainly a European subject (its scholars were French, English, German), it now flourishes in this country, too. One center of activity is the Dumbarton Oaks Research Library in Washington, D.C., which possesses superb materials on garden history.

The principal tradition of Western garden art is inclusive rather than exclusionary, putting human-made constructions—of marble, brick, tufa, stucco, wood—among the trees and plants. And of the many constructions that recur in gardens (statuary, fountains, follies, bridges), none is more fascinating or complex in its history and associations than the grotto. It is a space that is, literally, profound. The human-made recess or subterranean space that is called a grotto is, usually, a space already tamed. Other, less reassuring names for the same kind of space are "cave," "underground vault," "crypt." The grotto in the garden is the domesticated version of a space that is often scary, even repulsive, and yet exercises on some people, of whom I am one, a very strong attraction. I have always been fascinated by grottoes and have gone out of my way to look at them and at constructions that echo them. This curiosity is perhaps no more than dread mastered—

but then the grotto seems no more, or less, than a playfulness with morbid feelings.

For grottoes to enter the garden, a place conceived as a haven and a site of recreation, their original functions had to be secularized or miniaturized. Grottoes, mostly real grottoes, were first of all sacred places. The sibyl's or oracle's lair, the hermit's retreat, the sect's sanctuary, the resting place of the bones of holy men and revered ancestors—we are never far, in our imaginations, from being reminded of the cell and the grave. And grottoes that were artificial had, to begin with, severely practical purposes: like the marvelous vaults the Romans built as part of hydraulic projects. Artificial caves first appear as an element in the garden program in the late Roman Republic. From the latter part of the first century B.C., artificial grottoes, and rooms fitted out to resemble grottoes, became common features of the gardens of the villas of Roman patricians. These caverns, ornamented spaces that alluded gracefully to the old sacred spaces and their mysteries, were partly practical constructions for pleasures and entertainments conducted outdoors—for example, as the backdrop of satyr plays and for banquets. Perhaps the most famous and grandiose, though hardly typical, of the villas whose ruins survive from the ancient world was Hadrian's villa in Tivoli near Rome, which had a number of grottoes.

Christianity gave the grotto new associations and succeeded in monopolizing grotto imagery for more than a thousand years. Supposedly natural but in fact thoroughly stylized grottoes figure in paintings of the Christian narratives—the cave of the Nativity, the sepulchre of the Entombment—and in the lives of saints like Jerome and Anthony, who are often depicted as praying or being assailed at the mouth of their hermit's grotto. The revival of the garden grotto—that is, the reconnecting of the grotto with the garden—had to wait for the Renaissance, when the grotto could be divested of its principally Christian associations and infused with new, eclectic symbolism (Neo-Platonist, humanist). Although the gardens and grottoes of the classical villas had long since been leveled, descriptions of them—for example, by Ovid and Livy—had been preserved, and were admired. The elaboration of the garden grotto, a principal feature of the new heights attained by the garden in the Renaissance, produced such triumphs as the Grotta Grande in the Medici's Boboli Gardens in Florence and the many grottoes and hydraulic marvels of Pratolino, so admired by Montaigne and other foreign visitors. The use of the grottoes of ancient villas as banquet sites protected from the sun was replaced in the Renaissance by their employment as backdrops for theatrical spectacles.

The distinctive, complex idea of the garden as a work of art, which has been most prevalent in Western culture—the garden as an "ideal" landscape, including an anthology of architectural elements, and featuring waterworks of various spectacular contrivance—is defined in the Renaissance. Though only one element of the garden program, which in the West has mostly been heterogeneous, the grotto has a privileged place: it is an intensification, in miniature, of the whole garden-world. It is also the garden's inversion. The essence of the garden is that it is outdoors, open, light, spacious, natural, while the grotto is the quintessence of what is indoors, hidden, dim, artificial, decorated. The grotto is characteristically a space that is adorned—with frescoes, painted stuccos, mosaics, or (the association with water remaining paramount) shells.

In the garden history that starts in the Renaissance, the grotto reflected all the turns of taste, all the ideas of the theatre. The grotto as artificial ruin. The grotto as a place for foolery and escapades. (A modern, degraded form of this survives in the fairground's papier-mâché Tunnel of Love.) The grotto as showcase. The grotto is, as it were, the innately decadent element of the garden ensemble, the one that is most impure, and most ambiguous. It is a space that is complex and accumulative, dimly lit, thickly ornamented. (An appeal to fantasy, and a likely site for the elaboration of bad taste.) At first it was thought to be the most intensively "rustic" space—the imitation of a cave, as in some Roman villas. Eventually it became an elaborately theatrical, encrusted space. The roof and walls of the famous grotto built by Alexander Pope at Twickenham in the 1720s and 1730s were studded with shards of mirror interspersed with shells. (The grotto as *camera obscura*, in Pope's phrase.) In the eighteenth century, many grottoes were built by shell collectors principally as a setting to display their treasures. One of the last private grottoes, the Venus Grotto built by Ludwig II of

Bavaria at Linderhof in 1876–1877, was itself a theatrical space, the setting of several scenes from Wagner's *Tannhäuser*. Le Palais Idéal du Facteur Cheval, in a small village in central France, could be regarded as the great garden grotto of the beginning of this century—and perhaps the last of the breed. The crypt-like ground level of this astonishing building has the characteristic encrustedness of the grotto interior, the didacticism, and the reach for the sublime. Its builder's aim is nothing less than to miniaturize, and thereby to possess, the sublime. There are inscriptions, labels, declarations, adages incised throughout on the walls—the whole structure being designed, with something like genius, by the inspired autodidactic village postman who built it single-handedly between 1879 and 1912, as an anthology of world spiritual wisdom. However different in materials and sensibility, Ferdinand Cheval's grotto-labyrinth belongs to the same family as the grotto of Pope.

Grottoes are places of fantasy, but the greatest grotto buildings are, and always have been, functional: from the *cryptoportici* of the Roman villas (underground passageways one could take from one building to another to avoid the heat of the day), or that stupendous achievement of Roman engineering, the *emissarium* of Lake Albano (the subject of one of Piranesi's most haunting books of engravings), to such modern fantasy lands as the limestone caves, over six hundred feet long, that house the operations of the Brunson Instrument Company in Kansas City, Missouri; or the miles of underground shopping streets in Osaka; or the vast caverns dug in the mountain behind the National Museum in Taipei that store the innumerable art treasures that Chiang Kai-shek made off with when he fled from China to Taiwan in 1949; or the Louvre Métro station in Paris, several stations of the Stockholm subway system, and, above all, the justly celebrated Moscow subway, especially the Mayakovsky and Dynamo stations. Modern technology has made it possible to build below ground on a scale never before feasible: the great subterranean installations are bound to multiply. Grottoes of art, grottoes of industry, grottoes of shopkeeping, grottoes of war—all these are functional and yet seem the epitome of the poetry of space. In grottoes the functional and the fantastic are anything but incompatible. Perhaps that is why the museum for his art collection that

Philip Johnson put underground next to his Glass House in New Canaan, Connecticut, seems like the famous house's twin—a house with glass walls demands one that is sunk beneath the ground—but is not convincing as an example of the grotto in the garden: it is too purely functional, stripped down.

Many tourist-worn sites can supply the grotto experience. The Carlsbad Caverns in New Mexico, the Postojna Caves in Slovenia (near Ljubljana), the Grotte d'Arcy near Vézelay, south of Paris, the Grotte di Nettuno near Alghero on the western coast of Sardinia—such natural caves admired by grotto-buffs like myself serve as well the function of artificial grottoes. For there is no natural cave open to tourists that (if only because of the requirements of safety) has not been turned into a stage set, or museum, with guides pointing out zoomorphic forms and organ pipes in stalagmites and stalactites with their flashlights to the visitors lined up on the stairs and walkways. (In Postojna, one traverses part of the caves by miniature railroad.) The cemetery is a garden with—generally inaccessible—grottoes. But some cemeteries, particularly in Latin countries, have mausoleums and aboveground crypts with grilles instead of doors, into which one can peer. Visits to the Etruscan tombs excavated at Cerveteri, near Rome—such as the Tomba Bella, with its relief-encrusted walls—resemble visits to grottoes, as do visits to the catacombs of Palermo and of Guanajuato, whose walls are decorated with upright mummies or artful piles of bones instead of shells.

The garden grotto is not extinct, but it is not to be found in gardens anymore. And it is above ground more than below. While the dominant architectural tradition for half a century was the machine phase of the Bauhaus style, much of the building that contradicted, dissented from, or simply ignored the hyperrational Bauhaus aesthetic precisely tended to have a "grotto" look: the curving line, the encrusted wall surface, the underground mood, in buildings as different as Antoni Gaudí's Casa Milá and Parque Güell (indeed most of Gaudí's work), Kurt Schwitters's *Merzbau* (with its Nibelungen and Goethe grottoes), Frederick Kiesler's "Endless House" (he designed a "Grotto for Meditation"), the Rudolf Steiner Goetheanum in Switzerland, and Eero Saarinen's TWA terminal at Kennedy Airport. One of the more flamboyant recent versions is the design developed by John Portman for the Hyatt Hotels. In the first of the hotels, in Atlanta, one goes through an oddly small, unprepossessing entrance to receive the full shock of unexpected height in an enclosed space. The Portman atrium—overdecorated, cluttered, and centered on water, usually a waterfall—is a deliberately coarse transposition of some garden-grotto motifs.

Grottoes affirm the element of fantasy, of frivolity, of excess in architecture and feeling. Garden grottoes may be, in the sense projected in garden history writing, obsolete. But one can predict an interminable future for this kind of space, for it is a permanent part of our imagination.

A grotto is both a hiding place and a kind of ruin; it is on the border between the scary and the safe, the sublime and the decrepit. It is also a permanent part of our reality. And added to the archaic fears and apprehensions embodied in the grotto is a specific modern scariness. In the 1950s there was considerable pressure on all American house owners to build grottoes in their gardens. They were called bomb shelters.

[1983]

The Pleasure of the Image

A S SATISFYINGLY ELATED as I become roaming among
the transfiguring masterpieces in the Mauritshuis collection, I
still need to succumb to the spell exercised by some indisputably
minor paintings: those that depict the interiors of churches. Among the
pleasures these images offer, there is first of all a generic pleasure I associate particularly with Dutch painting (I first consciously experienced it before a skating scene by Brueghel) of falling forward into . . .
a world. And that flicker of an out-of-body, into-the-picture sensation
I'm granted in the course of scrutinizing the renderings of these large,
impersonal spaces populated with very small figures has proved, over
decades of museum-going, to be addictive.

So, demagnetizing myself with difficulty from the Rembrandts and
the Vermeers, I might drift off to, say, *The Tomb of William the Silent
in the Nieuwe Kerk in Delft*, painted in 1651 by Gerard Houckgeest, a
petit maître who was an almost exact contemporary of Rembrandt's,
for some less individualizing pleasures.

The public space chosen for depiction here is one consecrated by
two notions of elevated feeling: religious feeling (it is a church) and national feeling (it houses the tomb of the martyred founder of the House
of Orange). But the painting's title supplies the pretext, not the subject.
The Tomb of William the Silent is dominated not by the monument, of
which only part is visible, but by the strong verticals of the columns

and by the happy light. The subject is an architecture (in which the monument has its place) and, to our incorrigibly modern eyes, a way of presenting space.

All renderings of the large, populated by the small, which disclose the meticulously precise, invite this imagined entry. Of course, savoring the miniaturizing of a public space both deep and wide in a painting is a far more complex pleasure than, say, daydreaming in historical museums over tabletop models of the scenography of the past. Transcription through miniaturization in three dimensions gives us a thing whose aim is that of an inventory, completeness, and which enchants by being replete with unexpected detail—as true of a model railroad or a doll's house as of a diorama. The painting's surface gives us a view, which is shaped by preexisting formal notions of the visually appropriate (such as perspective), and which delights by what it excludes as much as by what it selects. And much of the pleasure of *The Tomb of William the Silent* comes from how bold its exclusions are.

To start with, the painting is not just the view of something but (like a photograph) something as viewed. Houckgeest made other portraits of the interior of the Nieuwe Kerk, including a wider-angle picture of the same site, now in the Hamburg Kunsthalle, and presumed to be earlier than the Mauritshuis picture. But this is surely his most original account of the space, not least because of the features it shares with a photographic way of seeing. For in addition to its illusionist method— that it records the site, with considerable accuracy, from a real viewpoint—there is the unconventionally tight framing, which brings the base of the column looming in the center almost to the picture's bottom edge. And while the Hamburg version shows three windows, the main sources of light in the Mauritshuis painting are "off." We see only a dull bit of high window, just below the arched top border of the panel; the potent light which strikes the columns comes from a window beyond the picture's right edge. In contrast to the panoramic view usually sought by painters documenting an architecture (or a landscape), which takes in more than could be seen by a single viewer, and whose norm is a space that appears comprehensive, unabridged (if indoors, self-contained, wall-to-wall), the space depicted here is one framed and lit so as to refuse visual closure. The very nearness of Houckgeest's viewpoint is a way of referring to, making the viewer aware of, the much larger space that continues beyond the space depicted within the borders of the picture. This is the method central to the aesthetics of photography (both still photography and film): to make what is not visible, what lies just outside the visual field, a constituent—dramatically, logically—of what we see.

THE CLOSE POINT OF VIEW, which is the most immediately engaging feature of Houckgeest's painting, produces an allied impression: of an unusual fullness of the space. Traditionally, church interiors are rendered as relatively empty, the better to achieve the impression of vastness, which was thought to be the church's most eloquent visual aspect. Architecture was depicted as framing, rather than filling, this deep space, and the lighting ensured that structures looked plausibly three-dimensional; without dramatic lighting, the architectural details tended to flatten out. In Houckgeest's painting, the foreshortened view—not the light, which is benign rather than dramatic—brings out the three-dimensionality of the architecture. By being so close, and making the architecture so palpable, Houckgeest has forfeited the look that seems redolent of inwardness, aura, emotion, spirituality, as it is found in paintings by his contemporary Pieter Jansz Saenredam, most admired of all the Dutch painters of church interiors, or by an almost equally admired architectural painter of the succeeding generation, Emanuel de Witte. By the standard associated with the "poetic" emptiness of such paintings as Saenredam's *Interior of the Cunerakerk, Rhenen* (1655) and de Witte's *Interior of an Imaginary Catholic Church* (1668), also in the Mauritshuis, Houckgeest's painting may seem underevocative, perversely literal. Saenredam's achievement was to combine the atmospherics of remoteness with accuracy of depiction, depiction of a real church from a real viewpoint, though never from a near one—the eccentric choice Houckgeest has made in *The Tomb of William the Silent*.

Masking a portion of the real or nominal subject by architectural bulk, or interposing a screen or lattice or other grid-like barrier between viewer and subject, is a perennial strategy of photographic framing, and it is worth noting that Houckgeest, who has chosen an angle for his view that leaves a good part of the sepulchre behind the column in the center foreground, could have made his framing even more proto-photographic. For the next column to the right, the column that looms largest in the Hamburg version, should still be partly visible in the cropped composition of the Mauritshuis picture—both are painted from the same angle—and would, if it were there, further block our view of the monument. Houckgeest has preferred to be inaccurate, and leave the right side of the picture's space more open.

To this space, more fully than usual inhabited by its architectural elements, are added a few inhabitants in the normal sense: eight chunky, bundled-up people with covered heads, two of whom are children; one animal; and an allegorical statue on a pedestal, the farthest forward element of the partially obscured monument. We contemplate the space Houckgeest has rendered, which includes, inside the space, these diminutive figures, coming to see or already in position for seeing. In an architecture, looking at an architecture. Giving the measure of an architecture.

Although the people in Houckgeest's painting are larger (we are closer) and more detailed than the tiny staffage figures that classical landscape painters added to their panoramic views, they function in a comparable way, establishing the architecture's heroic scale. By setting scale, human figures also, almost inadvertently, create mood: they look dwarfed by the spaces they inhabit and are, usually, but few. In contrast to three-dimensional model worlds, whose miniaturized representations seem most satisfying when a large number of tiny figures are deployed on the landscape, architectural space as a subject of painting is characteristically, if unrealistically, underpopulated. Indeed, a public space thronged with people is now a signature subject of the "naïve" painter, who, by putting in lots of tiny figures, appears to be making, as it were, a genre mistake. What seems professional in the depiction of the interior of grandiose buildings or of outdoor space enclosed by buildings is that the space, which always looks somewhat stage-like, be sparsely populated. This is the involuntary pathos of many portraits of architecture that are not laden with obvious affect, like *The Tomb of William the Silent*. All church interiors, even this one, become "metaphysical" interiors in de Chirico's sense; that is, they speak of a necessary *absence* of the human. They cannot help but suggest this pathos, this sense of enigma.

THE PRESENCE OF PEOPLE, if just one person, makes this not only a space but a moment of stopped time. Of course, tableaux in which people are depicted in the throes of some ceremony or way of being busy project a different feeling from those in which they're resting or gazing or explaining. As befits a church, the mood is calm—but perhaps more than calm: becalmed, indolent, though not suggestive of introspection. We are far from the visions of alienation relished by the mid-eighteenth century, when sublimity was identified with the *decay* of the grandiose architecture of the past, and staffage was turned into a population of spindly dejected figures stationed among the ruins, lost in reverie. The full-bodied figures in Houckgeest's painting have a status, not just a size: they are citizens, townspeople. Where they are is where they belong.

Public space, whether rendered in two dimensions or three, is usually shown being used in a variety of representative or stereotypically contrasting ways. In the Dutch paintings of church interiors, the use of the church is often, as it is here, wholly secular. The people in the Nieuwe Kerk we are shown are spectators, visitors, not worshippers. Except for the pair of men entering the picture at the left, they have their backs to us, the viewers, but their mood seems clear. The father in the family group in the foreground with one hand raised, his head partly turned to his wife, seems to be in a posture of explaining. The two men on the far side of the barrier enclosing the sepulchre (one of whom, having turned to speak to his companion, is seen full face) and the child with the dog seem to be just loitering. This most un-Hebraic mode of Christianity does not require the continual re-performing of the separateness of the sacred; space designed for devoutness is fully open to the irreverent accents and mixtures of daily life.

Sacred space that is mildly profaned, grandiose space that is domesticated, made tender—children and dogs (often a child paired with a dog) are characteristic presences in the Dutch paintings of church interiors: emblems of creatureliness amid the marmoreal splendors. Compare the modest number of such emblems Houckgeest settles for (one dog, two children), having chosen to treat the site at close range, with the variety offered in a conventional wide-angle view, such as de Witte's *Interior of the Oude Kerk, Amsterdam* (1659), which has four dogs, one of them urinating at the base of the pillar on the left, and two children, one an infant at its mother's breast. Graffiti are a related if less regular presence—they, too, would invariably be read as the trace of small children. The most legible of the drawings in red that Houckgeest has recorded on the warm, whitish column in the center is a stick man with a hat (the same hat worn by all six males in the painting), the stereotype of the human figure as drawn by a child. And below, scrawled in the same red chalk or ink, is the painter's monogram and the date. As if he, too, were an artless vandal.

Devising ingenious locations for the signature or monogram is a strong Northern tradition, of which Dürer was a master, and the Dutch painters of church interiors play a witty variant of the game. In Saenredam's *Interior of the Cunerakerk, Rhenen*, the painter's name, the name of the church, and the date of the painting are to be deciphered, foreground center, as the inscription incised on the tombstone set in the floor. And in several other church interiors Saenredam inserts this information on a column on which there are some crude drawings. A brilliant example is the *Interior of the Mariakerk, Utrecht* (1641), in the Rijksmuseum in Amsterdam, where Saenredam's inscription (name of church, date of painting, painter's name) appears on a pillar at far right in three colors, as if these were graffiti made by three different hands, along with several drawings of human figures in the same three inks or chalks. Saenredam's *Interior of the Buurkerk, Utrecht* (1644), in the National Gallery in London, is notable because he shows us, standing before the pillar on the far right which has an amusing drawing in red of four figures astride a horse (below which, in another color, is Saenredam's artfully printed signature), a child, arm raised, who is starting another drawing. (Beside him is a seated child playing with a dog.) One imagines him, far from being engaged in a surreptitious defacing, embarking on a happy exercise of immature prowess, in the mood of the grinning child displaying his stick-figure drawing in a painting done around 1520, *Portrait of a Boy with Drawing* by Giovanni Francesco Caroto, in the Museo del Castelvecchio in Verona—one of the other rare, premodern representations of children's art. Houckgeest's graffiti-plus-signature in *The Tomb of William the Silent* is not, then, original. But it is unusual because of its placement—the center of the picture, not on a pillar to the side—and its simplicity, its lack of informativeness. It is just a self-effacing monogram, barely distinguishable from the child's drawings.

THE GRAFFITI HOUCKGEEST has put on the central column signify childishness but are pieces of visual wit. Two spaces are being described. Two notions of presence. A child has made an inscription on the column; the painter has drawn on the panel—two spaces, logically, that can only be depicted as one space, physically. And two temporal relations of painter to church: as a vandalizing presence in the church anterior to the painting; and as the faithful documentarist of the church who, after recording the architecture as is, signs the document.

Hindsight instructs us that the ironic paralleling of the signature of a painter with the scribbling of a child on a public surface is potentially a very rich conceit, which was to have a long career in the visual arts and has perhaps never been so generative as in recent decades. But this could not begin to happen as long as graffiti were defined only privatively—as immature, embryonic, unskilled. Graffiti have to be seen as an assertion of something, a criticism of public reality. Not until the mid-nineteenth century were graffiti discovered to be "interesting"— the key word that signals the advent of modern taste—by such pioneers of modern taste as Grandville and Baudelaire. A self-portrait Grandville did in 1844 showing himself drawing alongside a small child on a graffiti-covered wall makes a far bigger point than Houckgeest's paralleling of two kinds of inscription, which are here only *traces* (their perpetrators are absent).

Houckgeest's painting describes a world in which the abstract order of the State, of collective life (represented by gigantic space) is so assumed, so successful, that it can be played with, by miniature elements that represent the incursion of the personal, the creaturely. Public order can be relaxed, can even be mildly defaced. The sacred and solemn can tolerate a bit of profaning. The imposing main column in his portrait of the Nieuwe Kerk is not really damaged by the graffiti, any more than the less centrally located column in de Witte's painting is ruined by the dog's peeing on it. Reality is sturdy, not fragile. Graffiti are an element of charm in the majestic visual environment, with not even the slightest foretaste of the menace carried by the tide of indecipherable signatures of mutinous adolescents which has washed over and bitten into the façades of monuments and the surfaces of public vehicles in the city where I live—graffiti as an assertion of disrespect, yes, but most of all simply an assertion: the powerless saying, I'm here, too. The graffiti recorded in the Dutch paintings of church interiors are mute; they do not express anything, other than their own naïveté, the endearing lack of skill of their perpetrators. The drawing on the column in Houckgeest's painting is not directed at anyone; it is, so to speak, intransitive. Even that red "GH" seems barely directed at anyone.

What this painting shows is a friendly space, a space without discord, without aggression. The grandiose before, innocent of, the invention of melancholy space. Church interiors are the opposite of ruins, which is where the sublimity of space was to be most eloquently located in the following century. The ruin says, This is our past. The church interior says, This is our present. (It is because the beauty of the church was a matter of local pride that these paintings were commissioned, bought, hung.) Now—whether the churches have survived intact, as has the Nieuwe Kerk in Delft, or not—the church interior also says, This is our past. Still, even installed in those temples of melancholy that are the great museums of Old Master paintings like the Mauritshuis, they do not lend themselves to elegiac reverie. Attached as I am to the melancholy registers of space, as found in the architectural portraits done in Italy in the eighteenth century, particularly of Roman ruins, and in images of great natural ruins (volcanoes) and of space as labyrinth (grottoes), I also crave the relief offered by these robust, unsoulful renderings in miniature of grandiose public space that were painted a century earlier in Holland. Who could fail to take pleasure in the thought of a world in which trespass is not a threat, perfection is not an ideal, and nostalgia is not a compulsion?

[1987]

About Hodgkin

1

DEVOLVING NOW, the modernist tasks and liberties have stirred up a canny diffidence among painters of the largest accomplishment when pressed to talk about their art. It appears unseemly, or naïve, to have much to say about the pictures or to attach to them any explicit "program." No more theories expounding an ideal way of painting. And, as statements wither and with them counterstatements, hardly anything in the way of provocation, either. Decorum suggests that artists sound somewhat trapped when being drawn out, and venturing a few cagey glimpses of intention. Complementing that venerable fortress of modernist taste, the white wall of the gallery, is a final redoubt of modernism under siege, the white mind of the painter. And the thoughtful—as distinct from the inarticulate—may have good reason to be wary, anxious, at a loss (for words).

2

EARLIER IN THE CENTURY, it was the most responsive writers who might begin their setting of the encounter with a much admired body of pictures to words by paying tribute to painting as a form of the *unsayable*.

As Paul Valéry wrote in 1932 (it's the first sentence of "About Corot"): "One must always apologize for talking about painting."

From the summoning of each art to what its means only could enact, it follows that nothing can be paraphrased or transposed into another medium. Painting, like music and dance, does not signify in the verbal sense; what you see is what you get. "A work of art, if it does not leave us mute, is of little value" (Valéry again). Of course, we don't *stay* mute.

But there is a further incentive to be self-conscious about what can be said now, as the aim and justification of art after modernism becomes precisely to generate talk—about what is not art. A mighty repudiation of the idea of art pursued out of reverence for art has overwhelmed art-making and critical discourse in the last decade. It has centered on the equating of aesthetic purposes, and their unforgivingly "high" standards, with illegitimate or indefensible forms of social privilege. For those whose principal interest is neither to come clean about adventures in selfhood nor to speak on behalf of fervent communities but rather to perpetuate the old, semi-opaque continuities of admiring, emulating, and surpassing, prudence may suggest saying less rather than more.

3

THE ATTACK ON ART—for being, just, art—has to have been abetted by modernism's peculiar, reductive way of affirming the autonomy of art, which derived much of its energy by denying the idea of hierarchy among kinds of art. Shorn of the support of received ways of discriminating among subjects and destinations, the nature of pictures was inexorably subjectivized; and archly plebeianized.

There are two leading assertions in this reduced field of saying for the painter. The painter asserts that the pictures don't need to be "explained." The painter explains that the pictures should, properly, be regarded as "things."

4

THERE'S ONE JUST AHEAD ... or nearby ... or over there ...
And perhaps not in the obvious place, such as a museum or the collector's living room; it may be on the wall of a restaurant or a hotel lobby.

But wherever we see it, we know *what* it is. We may not know *which* one. But we know, even from far across the room, *who* did it.

In contrast to the painting of earlier eras, this is one of the regulating aspects of the experience—and making—of art in this century. Each artist is responsible for creating his or her unique "vision"—a signature style, of which each work is an example. A style is equivalent to a pictorial language of maximum distinctiveness: what declares itself as *that* artist's language, and nobody else's. To use again and again the same gestures and forms is not deemed a failure of imagination in a painter (or choreographer), as it might be in a writer. Repetitiveness seems like intensity. Like purity. Like strength.

5

A FIRST OBSERVATION about Howard Hodgkin's work: the extent to which everything by Hodgkin looks so unmistakably by him.

That the pictures are done on wood seems to heighten their rectangularity—and their "thingness." Usually modest in size by current standards, they seem boxy, blunt, even heavy sometimes because of the proportions of frame to interior of the picture, with something like the form, if not the scale, of a window, displaying a ballet of plump shapes which either are enclosed within thickly emphatic brush strokes that frame (or shield) or are painted out to the edge of the raised frame. The pictures are packed with cunning design and thick, luscious color. (Hodgkin's green is as excruciating as de Kooning's pink and Tiepolo's blue.) Having renounced painting's other primary resource, drawing, Hodgkin has fielded the most inventive, sensuously affecting color repertory of any contemporary painter—as if, in taking up the ancient quarrel between *disegno* and *colore*, he had wanted to give *colore* its most sumptuous exclusive victory.

6

"MY PICTURES TEND TO destroy each other when they are hung too closely together," Hodgkin has remarked. No wonder. Each picture is, ideally, a maximum seduction. Harder for the picture to make its case if, at the distance from which it is best seen, one is unable to exclude some adjacent solicitations. But the viewer may be tempted to solve the problem, abandoning the proper distance from which all the picture's charms may be appreciated to zero in for immersion in sheer color-bliss—what Hodgkin's pictures can always be counted on to provide.

7

TOO CLOSE A VIEW of the picture will not only yield a new round of voluptuous sensation (say, the streaks of salmon-pink now visible beneath what reads ten feet away as cobalt blue). It will also remind the viewer of what is written beside or below: its title.

Leaves, Interior with Figures, After Dinner, The Terrace, Delhi, Venice/Shadows, Clean Sheets, Red Bermudas, Mr. and Mrs. James Kirkman, After Corot . . . titles like these indicate a pleasingly large range of familiar subjects: the still life, the *plein-air* scene, the intimate interior, the portrait, the art history homage.

Sometimes the title corresponds to something that can be discerned.

More often, it doesn't. This is most obviously true of the portraits—that is, the pictures whose titles are someone's name; usually two names, a couple. (The names, those of friends and collectors, will be unfamiliar to viewers.)

Some titles that are phrases, such as *Like an Open Book, Haven't We Met?, Counting the Days*, seem to be drawn from the history of a love life. *In Central Park, Egypt, On the Riviera, Venice Evening*—many titles evoke a very specific world, the world known through tours of seeing and savoring. (We hear about quite a lot of meals.) Some titles hint at a submerged story, which we can be sure we're not going to hear—like the glimpses, in several of the pictures, of the form of a body on a bed. But there's as much an impulse to play down as to reveal the charge of some of the pictures. Thus, one of the largest of Hodgkin's recent pictures, and one of the most glorious and emotionally affecting, has the title *Snapshot*. While offering a shrewd spread of signals, from the diaristically offhand, like *Coming Up from the Beach* and *Cafeteria at the Grand Palais*, to the bluntly plaintive, like *Passion*, *Jealousy*, and *Love Letter*, the majority of the titles are casually nominative or slightly ironic, which makes them nicely at variance with the pictures' proud exuberance of feeling, their buoyant, ecstatic palette.

Of course, the fact that a person or place is named does not mean it is depicted.

In the Bay of Naples, Still Life in a Restaurant, In a Hot Country— the "in" in a fair number of titles carries a dual meaning. It signifies that the artist has been "in" these places, on these fortunate holidays. (We don't expect a Hodgkin title that tells us we are "in" a dungeon.) And that, whether the space named is outdoors or indoors, the picture itself is a kind of interior. One looks into the picture, to something which is both disclosed and hidden.

Some titles—*Lovers*, for instance—confirm the suggestiveness of certain enlacing shapes. A few titles—like *Egyptian Night* and *House near Venice*—succeed in making the pictures seem representational in the conventional sense. But, exception made for such bravura performances as *Venetian Glass*, Hodgkin is not offering the *look* of the world, an impression. (An emotion is not an impression.) Hardly any of Hodgkin's paintings harbor mimetically distinct shapes, and only a few have shapes which would seem even allusively distinct without the clue supplied by the title. The subjectivism of these pictures is the opposite of the one associated with Impressionism: to preserve the visual freshness of the first fleeting moment that something is seen. Hodgkin aims to reinvent the sight of something after it has been seen, when it has acquired the heavy trappings of inner necessity.

8

OPERATING ON A BORDER very much of his own devising between figuration and abstraction, Hodgkin has made a sturdy case for regarding his choreography of spots, stripes, discs, arcs, swaths, lozenges, arrows, and wavy bands as always representational.

"I am a representational painter, but not a painter of appearances" is how he puts it. "I paint representational pictures of emotional situations." Note that Hodgkin says "emotional situations," not "emotions"; he is not licensing the attempt to read a specific emotion from a given picture, as if *that* were what the picture was "about."

Hodgkin's formula is as elegantly withholding as it is incisive and alert.

Whose emotional situations? The artist's?

Obviously, titles like *After Visiting David Hockney* or *Dinner in Palazzo Albrizzi* or *Indian Sky* would seem to be deceptions if the painter had never met David Hockney, had never visited Italy or India. One has to assume that, in this sense, all the pictures are autobiographical, though only some of the titles make this explicit. Still, few of them are self-referential in the narrow sense. What's on display is not the emotional state of the artist. And the pictures offer the most earnest, emphatic tribute to the world outside, its treasurable objects and beauties and opportunities. Indeed, the sublimity of the color in Hodgkin's pictures can be thought of as, first of all, expressive of gratitude—for the world that resists and survives the ego and its discontents. Two passions which we associate with this painter, traveling and collecting, are both expressions of ardent, deferential feeling for what is *not* oneself.

9

SO MANY OF the pictures refer to "abroad," as it used to be called. To sites of dalliance already consecrated by great painters of the past, which one never tires of revisiting: India, Italy, France, Morocco, Egypt. Seasons in their foreign plumage: fruit, palm trees, a searingly colored sky. And home pleasures consumed on foreign premises. (*In Bed in Venice*, not in bed in London; the painter is not traveling alone.) There is lovemaking and dining and looking at art and shopping and gazing out over water. The sites bespeak an avid eye, and a taste for the domesticated; gardens and terraces, not forests and mountains. The evocation of sensuous, congenial tourism—dinner parties, nocturnal promenades, cherished art, memorable visits—boldly affirms the idea of pleasure.

But the titles also intimate another relation to pleasure, with their naming of weather and seasons and times of day. The most common weather is rain; the season is invariably autumn; if a time of day is cited, it's usually sunset—which, apart from being the biggest color story in the daily existence of most people, has a large place in the thesaurus of melancholy.

All those titles with "sunset," "autumn," "rain," "after . . . ," "goodbye to . . . ," "the last time . . ." suggest the pensive shadow cast on all pleasures when they are framed, theatricalized even, as acts of memory.

Hodgkin may often be *en voyage*, but not as a beholder (the Impressionist project). In place of a beholder, there is a rememberer. Both pursuits, that of the traveler and that of the collector, are steeped in elegiac feeling.

10

AFTER THE SHOP HAD CLOSED, *The Last Time I Saw Paris*, *When Did We Go to Morocco?*, *Goodbye to the Bay of Naples* . . . many titles focus on time ("after"), on the awareness of finalities.

Art made out of a sense of difference, a sense of triumph, a sense of regret.

If there are so many pictures which offer homage to the feelings and sensations that Venice inspires, it is because that city is now, as it could never have been for Turner, a quintessential evoker of the sentiment of loss.

11

IT'S NOT THAT the exotic, or the southern, is required to release the impulse of this "northern" sensibility to paint.

But it may be that this painter needs to travel.

A trip is an intensifier, license to the avid eye (and other senses). You need the separation from home. And then you need the return home, to consider what you have stored up.

In principle, the painter could make pictures out of everything he has lived through and done and seen. This creates an unbearably acute pressure to paint, and an equally acute feeling of anxiety.

Travel, the impression that one has ventured outside oneself, can be used as a filter and goad. It organizes the desire to paint. It gives it a rhythm, and the right kind of delay.

It is important not to see *too much*. (And there is nothing to reproduce.) Hence, Hodgkin doesn't sketch, doesn't take photographs, doesn't do anything obvious to commit to memory the scene or an interior or a view or a face—instead trusting what will happen when the sight of something has burrowed itself deep down in memory, when it has accumulated emotional and pictorial gravity.

A way of feeling is a way of seeing.

What is worth painting is what remains in, and is transformed by, memory. And what survives the test of long-term deliberation and countless acts of re-vision. Pictures result from the accretion of many decisions (or layers, or brush strokes); some are worked on for years, to find the exact thickness of a feeling.

12

LOOKING CLOSELY at what the swipes and plunges of Hodgkin's brush have deposited on a surface is to feel, sometimes, that one has divined the brush's itinerary, starting from the first, generative surge of feelings. The distinctive shapes in Hodgkin's pictures read like a vocabulary of signals for the circulation, collision, and rerouting of desire.

Sometimes it feels as if the flooding or brimming has spilled over onto the frame. Sometimes it is the frame that has moved inward, thickened, doubled, as if to contain what cannot be contained. (The fat verticals of *Snapshot*, like the sides of a proscenium stage or a gate; the thick oval frame of *Love Letter* that squeezes, crowds the heart of what lies pulsing in the center.)

Framing hems in, keeps one from falling off the edge of the world. And framing gives permission to emote.

It makes possible the ambitiousness of Hodgkin's work, and its tight, cunningly judged compactness of statement. Hodgkin has understood that if the pictures are dense enough, they can go in two directions, doing justice to intimate textures as well as to emotions of a large expressiveness. (Vuillard *and* opera, so to speak.)

13

VENICE: ONCE, AGAIN. Imagining the imagined. When you want to see Venice again, and you have seen it many times, rising out of the sea, in winter perhaps, semi-deserted, what you appreciate is that it will not have changed at all.

Or you stand at the railing of the boat going up the Nile, a day's journey from Luxor, and it's sunset. You're just looking. There are no words you are impelled to write down; you don't make a sketch or take a photograph. You look, and sometimes your eyes feel tired, and you look again, and you feel saturated, and happy, and terribly anxious.

There is a price to be paid for stubbornly continuing to make love with one's eyes to these famous tourist-weary old places. For not letting go: of ruined grandeur, of the imperative of bliss. For continuing to work on behalf of, in praise of, beauty. It's not that one hasn't noticed that this is an activity which people rather condescend to now.

Indeed, one might spend a lifetime apologizing for having found so many ways of acceding to ecstasy.

14

THE IDEA IS to put as much as possible, of color, of feeling, in each picture. It's as if the pictures need their broad border to contain so much feeling. As if they need to be painted on something hard, wood, since they embody such a large sense of vulnerability.

The sense of vulnerability has not diminished. Nor has the sense of gratitude: for the privilege of feeling, the privilege of voluptuousness, the privilege of knowing more rather than less. There is heroism in the vehemence and the lack of irony of Hodgkin's pictures. He labors over them as if painting could still be a vehicle of self-transcendence.

In such matters, with such purposes, the race is to the slow.

[1995]

A Lexicon for *Available Light*

AVAILABLE LIGHT. 1983. Fifty-five-minute work for eleven dancers (five women and six men) commissioned by the Museum of Contemporary Art, Los Angeles: the third of Lucinda Childs's large-scale productions. Music by John Adams, set by Frank Gehry, costumes by Ronaldus Shamask, lighting by Beverly Emmons.

BEAUTY. The visionary authority of Childs's work resides, in part, in its lack of rhetoric. Her strict avoidance of cliché, and of anything that would make the work disjunctive, fragmented. The refusal of humor, self-mockery, flirtation with the audience, cult of personality. The distaste for the exhibitionistic: movement calling attention to itself, isolatable "effects." Beauty as, first of all, an art of refusal.

CHOREOGRAPHY. Childs started by defining herself as a "modern" choreographer; therefore, alienated from "tradition." (Two decades ago, it could still seem plausible to regard modern dance as the antithesis and subversion of classical dance.) When she did start choreographing dances, in 1968, it was with the predilection for keeping the movement vocabulary relatively simple, seeking complexity elsewhere—in the intricate design of spatial forms and of timing. But in the music-based works choreographed since 1979, which propose a much more complex movement vocabulary, Childs has broken radically with the anti-ballet aesthetic of the other ex- or neo-Duchampian choreographers with whom she has been grouped. Of all the adepts of the rigorously modern among contemporary choreographers, she has the subtlest and most fastidious relation to classical dance. If her use of portions of the ballet idiom is less easily recognizable than Merce Cunningham's and Twyla Tharp's, it is because Childs does not feed balletic movements and positions into an eclectic mix but wholly transforms and reinterprets them. In this, as in other matters, she is adamantly anti-collage. Thus the choreography of *Available Light* was not conceived first and then illustrated by the music, the set, and the costumes but solicited, presupposed, and worked out in strict relation to these—to the two-level stage devised by Gehry, the multi-layered music of Adams, the three-color constructivist scheme (black, red, white) of Shamask's costumes.

COMPLEXITY. Cunningham in 1952: "For me, it seems enough that dancing is a spiritual exercise in physical form, and that what is seen is what it is. And I do not believe it is possible to be 'too simple.' " The delicate rhythms and intricate configurations and tempi of Cunningham's work, the way attention is commanded through a simple, unadorned, unexplained, often decentered presence, offered a new standard of the complex.

CUNNINGHAM, MERCE. Childs, who studied with Cunningham between 1959 and 1963, assumes Cunningham's notion that dance should not express something else (an emotion, a story, an interior landscape) but not Cunningham's method, which is to make the elements of dance self-contained, autonomous, even aleatoric in their mix (and sometimes in their look). "I didn't like it," Cunningham once said, "that a movement *meant* something." This liberating stance has been associated with a large element of parody in Cunningham's idiom: post-Graham movements (the Cunningham curved back is an ironic comment on the Graham contraction) and laterally tilted ballet positions. Out of this eclectic aesthetic, much irony. (Cunningham's choreography is an art of disjunction and therefore ultimately comic.) Childs by temperament unifies; her aesthetic refuses the eclectic, the disjunctive—it never quotes. Though playfulness is one of her chief standards of grace, her work is virtually free of irony. Its tone is austere but never cool. Embracing the Cunningham position (the refusal of plot, of "meaning"), Childs has drawn other consequences from it; she has dropped the jokes, the kidding around, the wistful lyricism, and reached for the sublime.

DANCE. 1979. The first of the large-scale productions, a hundred-minute work, for the company of nine. Music by Philip Glass, lighting by Beverly Emmons, and a film by Sol LeWitt of portions of three of the five sections ("Dance #1," "Dance #3," and "Dance #4"). Choreographers as different as Cunningham and Pina Bausch have made works with an accompanying, simultaneous image-record, displayed on a TV monitor placed on the stage; in contrast to this additive, fragmenting use, the projection of LeWitt's film, on a transparent scrim at the front of the stage, is a true setting and literal transfiguration of the dance. The synchronized ongoing of film and dance creates a double space—flat (the scrim/screen) and three-dimensional (the stage)—and provides a double reality, both dance and its shadow (documentation, projection), both intimacy and distance. Recording the dancers from different angles, in long shot and in close-up, LeWitt's film tracks the dancers, sometimes on the same level, sometimes from above—using split-screen and multiple images. Or it immobilizes them, in a freeze-frame (or series of still shots) which the live dancer passes through. Or it waits with the dancer, as in the beginning of "Dance #4," Childs's second solo, when Childs appears both in large mask-like close-up on the scrim and as a small immobile figure in white on the stage. The film is a friendly, intermittent ghost that makes the dancers, seen behind the scrim, seem disembodied, too: each seems the ghost of the other. The spectacle becomes authentically polyvalent, though the film is finally subordinate to the dance. "Dance #2," Childs's first solo, and the concluding "Dance #5" proceed without the film ghost.

DIAGONAL. A signature element in Childs's choreography: a principle of avidity, about space. Dancers often go into low plié arabesque, with the arm continuing the diagonal—the longest line that the body can make. And they often move on the diagonal—the longest distance one can traverse on a stage without changing direction. Childs's adventures with the diagonal have their apotheosis in *Relative Calm*, two of its four sections being choreographed entirely on the diagonal. In the first section, the whole company dances back and forth on parallel paths from upstage right to downstage left for twenty-three increasingly blissful minutes; in the third, solo section, Childs dances for seventeen minutes in phrases of different lengths, punctuated by turns, on the opposite diagonal . . . And moving to the diagonal often means an intensification, as in the finale of "Dance #1" of *Dance*, when suddenly four pairs of dancers dash again and again from upstage left to downstage right. Or in *Available Light*: Childs's arrival upstage right and slow progress downstage left through a corridor formed by eight dancers, four on each side.

DOUBLING. A recurrent structure in Childs's work: splitting the performer into two versions, the action into two levels, which proceed simultaneously. For example, in an early piece, *Street Dance* (1964), Childs's voice, taped, was with the audience assembled in a sixth-floor loft, while she was down on the street, being seen performing the actions that she was heard describing. Doubling in the sense of several dancers performing the same movements on different paths became, starting with *Untitled Trio* (1968), the extended subject of the works she created for small ensembles in the 1970s. *Transverse Exchanges* and *Radial Courses* (both 1976) elaborate, delicately and strenuously, on the counterpoint of dancers who, using the same steps or families of movements, go in and out of sync with each other through changes of gait, direction, and relation to the floor. Having several people doing the same rhythmic thing—side by side, one in front of another, or one above the other—has always been part of choreographing ensembles, military, ceremonial, and balletic. Indeed, doubling is the most basic principle of artifice—of form itself. Childs's work concentrates on the implications of doubling as a formal principle and as the basis of choreographic syntax: the geometrical, or diagrammatic, idealization of movement. Her recent large works, created since 1979, allow for a more complex orchestration of the theme of doubling. The adding of decor is never merely decorative but functions to create richer possibilities of doubling. Thus, the film that LeWitt made as the decor for *Dance* creates a perfectly synchronized double set of dancers. For example, the split screen allows the audience to see the dancers in the film, never less than life-size, on top; the live dancers (behind the scrim) on the bottom. What LeWitt supplied for *Dance* with a film, Frank Gehry supplies for *Available Light* with an architecture. In *Available Light*, the stage itself has become two-level, allowing other variations on the theme of doubling. Instead of traveling ghosts, there are live trackers: one to three dancers are upstairs echoing, playing off, providing counterpoint to what the dancers are unfolding below.

EINSTEIN ON THE BEACH. 1976. The "opera," conceived and directed by Robert Wilson, with music by Philip Glass; Childs was a principal performer and collaborated on the text. The year she spent preparing and touring in *Einstein on the Beach* (Avignon, Venice, Belgrade, Brussels, Paris, Hamburg, Rotterdam, Amsterdam, New York) was a turning point. Her thirty-five-minute solo, constructed on three diagonals, that opens Act I, Scene I was a culmination of the second phase of her work and a bridge to the third. Her longest work so far (both as performer and as choreographer), it was the first time she choreographed to music—and the experience encouraged her to undertake the long work, for which Glass agreed to furnish the score, eventually called *Dance*.

EMOTION. The leading notion of the great modern dance pioneers, from Duncan to Graham and Horton, was to return dance to ritual. Though dance-as-ritual looked more abstract than ballet, actually such dances were heavy with descriptive intentions based, above all, on ideas about the primitive, the authentic, both in movement and in feeling. Thus, Mary Wigman created her "absolute" dances, performed in silence and with a minimum of theatrical support, the better to render extremely emotional "inner states." Childs's turn (in 1968) to dance without props or music or words was an absolute conception of dance, for it did not claim to express anything interior. For Childs, as for Cunningham, all notions of dance as ritual are alien; she was drawn to using game-like forms of ensemble movement, in which the idea of inwardness is irrelevant. The view that dance should not express emotion does not, of course, mean to be against emotion. Valéry defined the poem as a machine made of words whose function is to create a distinctively poetic feeling: it does not "express" emotion, it is a method of creating it.

FORMATIONS. Childs tends to organize choreographic patterns symmetrically, movement contrapuntally. The dancers move in formations—in twos, and their multiples, more than in trios and quintets. Though Childs most often deploys dancers in pairs, this is the smallest formation and has nothing to do with partnering in the traditional sense: neither dancer is the consort of the other, one does not assist or accompany or accommodate another. They are duplicates, and therefore equal. The two dancers are doing the same movements: the existence of a pair doubles the movement image. There are "delicate invasions" (Childs's phrase) of one group by another, each keeping its group contour, as in the traveling diamond formations of the fourth section of *Relative Calm*. Men and women perform the same movements (thus shaving off the gender-specific extremes of movement vocabulary, such as very high jumps), wear the same or virtually identical costumes. All plugged into the same sound, the dancers move on paths, inexorably, to a steady underlying pulse. They rarely take up perilous off-balance positions, such as Cunningham favors. (He also favors asymmetrical formations.) The rule that each element in a Cunningham dance has its own autonomy and can be apprehended in isolation from the other elements of the spectacle also applies to the dancers. In Cunningham's company every dancer is, can be, a star. In Childs's work, as each element of the spectacle is strictly coordinated with every other, so is each dancer: she choreographs for the glorified *corps de ballet*—*they* become the star. Childs's dances are not exercises in polyattentiveness; more generally, they are not examples of art conceived as a tool for perception. Her choreography demands a concentrated all-over attention; it is cumulative; it aims at transporting, not educating the audience.

GEOMETRICAL. *Available Light* is the second act of *Giselle* as revised and corrected by Mondrian.

HEAD. The positioning of the dancer's head in ballet always implies a look—to a partner, or a central (noble) figure, or to the audience. In Childs's choreography, the head is not posed in this sense; there is no such looking elsewhere. One of the basic conventions of Cunningham's technique is a simple, unmannered use of the head and detached, cool expression. Even while taking part in cooperative tasks—a lift, a pull, a support—his dancers usually seem unaware of each other. (Much humor is milked from this incongruity.) In Childs's choreography dancers never engage in cooperative tasks, indeed never touch each other. Hence, their intensely blank performance masks signify another, non-atomized detachment. The effect is never incongruous, or comic; rather, it underscores the feeling of purity, the striving for an elevated state of things that is the register of her work.

IDEAL. *Where* are these dancers dancing? Not in the vernacular space, here and now, of Duchampian performance pieces; nor in the anti-dramatic, democratized space of Cunningham's dances—dance as pure, noncumulative activity with detachable parts and movable borders. (Hence one of Cunningham's characteristic notions: dance as a sequence of open-ended "events.") Instead, Childs's choreography suggests some ideal space, where ideal transactions and transformations take place. (In this, she is close to the ethos of traditional ballet.) Dance as the art of ideal precision; ideal spatial relationships; ideal, undiluted intensity.

ILLUSTRATING. A procedure typical of Childs's early (conceptual or didactic) work, in which she sometimes used words in the form of instructions or descriptions—as in *Street Dance*. This linguistic decor could be live monologues or words on tape that were illustrated by her movements. Some of the early pieces treat movement in the manner of the Surrealist *objet trouvé*: citing already existing positions, "found" through words. In *Model* (1964), Childs gives a mock lecture on modern dance and illustrates a few awkward positions. In *Geranium* (1965), she provides a taped sportscast: as the announcer describes a football player falling, tumbling, Childs illustrates the actions in slow motion. *Museum Piece* (1965) has nineteen dots in three colors cut out of heavy paper, each about ten inches in diameter, which are an enlargement of a tiny portion of Seurat's *Le Cirque*. While delivering a mock lecture on pointillism, Childs sets out the dots like plates in a complex pattern on the floor. Then, gazing into a hand mirror, she walks backward, making a slow, circuitous journey through the dots, without stepping on them, speaking of why she wants "to enter this body of material."

JUDSON DANCE THEATRE. Co-founded in 1962 by Yvonne Rainer (then, like Childs, a student of Cunningham's) and Steve Paxton; disbanded in 1966. Childs was invited to join in 1963, and did a ten-minute piece called *Pastime*—her first work presented publicly—at the Judson Memorial Church, where she went on to present most of the work she did in the next three years, as well as to perform in pieces by Rainer, Paxton, James Waring, and Robert Morris.

KLEIST'S ESSAY ON THE PUPPET THEATRE. Its subject is an ideal state of the spirit; written in 1810, it is also the first great essay on the dance. Kleist exalts as the summit of grace and profundity in art a way of being without inwardness or psychology. Writing when the characteristic modern oppositions of the heart versus the head, the organic versus the mechanical, were invented, Kleist ignores the obloquy already attached to the metaphor of the mechanical, and identifies the mechanical movements of puppets with the sublimity of the impersonal. The Romantic ideal of the absence of affectation is equated not with the free expression of personality but with its transcendence. These Romantic oppositions (and evaluations) continued to dominate sensibility for another century, mutating into what we know as modernism, into "romantic" modernism, which was challenged by "neoclassical" modernism—various ideals of the impersonal as different as those of Duchamp and of Balanchine (who thought ballet should be unconcerned with inner experience). The ideals of the personally expressive and the impersonal or impassive constitute a central contrast in the evolution of contemporary dance. Cunningham is the most important champion of the anti-expressive and anti-subjective, and most of the choreographers who studied with him have extended his emphasis on objectivity and impersonality. Yvonne Rainer's work in the period of the Judson Dance Theatre aimed at "submerging the personality" in impersonal, task-like movements: "So, ideally, one is not even oneself, one is a neutral doer." In Childs's choreography, one is not a neutral but a transpersonal doer. Her emphasis on impersonality is closer to the virtues extolled by Balanchine than by Rainer, for she assumes that dancing is a noble art. The dancers move on paths, imperturbable—their comings and goings seem implacable. Their impassivity is not detachment, the cool ironic tone of Cunningham dancers. It is a positive impassivity that recalls the argument made by Kleist—as if grace and inwardness were opposed.

LIGHTNESS, ART OF. Childs's conception of dance is Apollonian: dance should be lively, playful, joyous. Beauty equals power, delicacy, decorum, unaffected intensity. What is ugly is timidity, anxiety, demagoguery, heaviness. (Other exemplars of the Apollonian style: Seurat, Mallarmé, Morandi, Ozu, Wallace Stevens.)

MEASURABLE. Seurat calculated exactly the place and the disposition of some forty tiny figures in *Le Cirque*—cited by Childs in her early *Museum Piece*. Childs prepares placing of dancers and timing in the same spirit. Seurat believed that the beautiful had an objective, measurable basis; Childs needs to specify the structure of her work in numbers. The early pieces were timed to the second, but not counted. The method of working out choreography by counts started in 1968, with *Untitled Trio*, when Childs began choreographing in the normative sense: to choreograph *means* to give movement a rhythmic, countable time structure. It is through counting that space is connected with time, whether or not time is further articulated by music. All the "silent" works of the 1970s are precisely counted. (An example: a dance from 1976, *Transverse Exchanges*, has 1,449 counts.) In works created since 1979, counts are coordinated to—supplied by—music. For instance, in *Relative Calm*, Childs requested a specific pattern, and numerical phrase base, from the composer Jon Gibson—that the first section be constructed out of fifteen-count phrases and have eleven subsections; that the second section be composed of seventeen-count phrases and have nine subsections, each two to two and a half minutes long; et cetera. The intricate patterning (designed to activate the whole stage space) and subtle variations in timing may seem simple to dance audiences habituated to recognizing only the complexities apparent in movement itself.

MINIMALIST. Unlike some other dumb labels that emerged in visual arts marketing campaigns (Pop Art, Op Art) in the last two decades, this piece of linguistic chewing gum, first applied to some painters and sculptors (Sol LeWitt, Robert Morris, Carl Andre), has spread to architects, choreographers, composers, even to couturiers—imposing, as such label-mongering invariably does, a specious unity among widely different artists. Muybridge, Mondrian, Stein, and Ozu had the good fortune to pursue careers as virtuosi of obsessive repetition and strong patterning without incurring this label. Inevitably succeeded by POST-MINIMALIST.

MOVEMENTS. Childs's movement ideal: clear, clean, deliberate, intense. And directional. The dancers are moving or are absolutely still. When moving, they move continuously, with relatively muted accents and a softer dynamic than in classical choreography, recalling Rainer's prescriptive idea of dance as "movement series"—with "no pauses between phrases and no observable accent . . . the limbs are never in a fixed, still relationship . . . creating the impression that the body is constantly engaged in transitions." Childs has brought the aesthetic of the Judson performers, designed (in Rainer's words) to impart to dance a "factual quality," a deliberately matter-of-fact, more "banal quality of physical being in performance," into confrontation with the high energies and lyrical solemnity of the classical dance ideal. Many of the movements that she recasts are ballet movements. In ballet, positions are reached, then held, allowed to shine. In Childs's choreography, the classical positions (arabesque, attitude, *tendu plié*) are taken, cleanly, but only for a split second. Childs doesn't use in-place movements (like *penché, passé développé, grands battements*) that exhibit positions, that display technique. Reacting against the modern-dance ideal, exemplified by Graham, of dance as a succession of climaxes, Cunningham and, in more radical form, the Judson choreographers proposed a style of movement that has no climaxes, in which nothing is dramatically framed. From that aesthetic Childs has retained the prohibition against devising positions that can be framed; but the taboo on climactic passages is weakening. *Available Light* has several clearly identifiable climaxes. It also has a looser weave—perhaps because, unlike *Dance* and *Relative Calm*, the work is not divided into separate sections. Adams's score is a departure from the music Childs has previously used. Instead of the sharp boundaries of earlier scores, it evolves with soft-edge transitions; it has a more obvious emotional texture and consists, most starkly in the last fifteen minutes, of a succession of climaxes.

NEO-CLASSICAL. It is the hallmark of a neo-classical style, whether in dance or in architecture, to be accused of being merely mathematical. If mathematical means quantifiably precise, insistently formal, majestic, stripped down—as in some Platonic or Palladian kingdom of forms—there is truth in the accusation.

OPENINGS. In *Dance*: an empty stage, and the propulsive joyousness of the music . . . and then the dancers springing in pairs from the wings, spinning, prancing, skimming across the stage. In *Relative Calm*: the drone . . . and the dancers already in place, sitting (in diagonal formation) on their carpets of light. In *Available Light*: the blast of sound that fades into a drone-like hum . . . and the dancers coming on slowly to take their positions.

ORDER. Beauty is identified with order, liveliness, serenity, inevitability.

POLITENESS. The classical tradition of dance is related to courtesy. Ballet gestures are based on a system of deference, of hierarchy, and descend from the gestures of real courts. Childs's dancers comport themselves as members of an imaginary, cosmic court, behaving with egalitarian courtesy. There are no angry or erotic emotions. The dancers are grave, imperturbable. They always leave each other enough space.

POST-MODERN. The aging of modernism was remarked by astute observers when modernism was still in its prime. "The word 'modern' has changed meaning," Cocteau observed in 1932, already situating himself safely beyond the modern (everyone's favorite vantage point) and predicting that "the modern age will be a period between 1912 and 1930." One of modernism's perennial ventures, its demise, has recently been celebrated with the most successful of new labels—the word "post-modern," first applied to architects, now as well to visual artists and to choreographers after Cunningham. Frequently a synonym for eclectic. But sometimes conflated with MINIMALIST.

PRESENCE/ABSENCE. Dance, most present, incarnate of arts, is used by Childs in the service of an aesthetic of absence. This principle was first acknowledged in a Dadaist way, in the notion of the blank, the gap—as in the unpainted painting that is conjured up by discussing its absence, or the drawing that is illustrated by its erasure. Thus, the third section of *Geranium*, a monologue in which Childs announces: "This is supposed to be the third section, but there really is no third section, so it might be best to refer to the third section as a gap"—and goes on to discuss ideas for the third section, one of which is a glass enclosure that would contain a performer. (It was constructed, and could skim about the stage, in the last piece of Childs's first period, *Vehicle*—presented in 1966 in the series "Nine Evenings: Theater and Engineering": the dancer is inside a mobile Plexiglas box.) Many of the early solos are exercises in absence. *Street Dance* begins with Childs disappearing into the elevator after pushing the button of the tape recorder. (She reappears below on the street.) In *Carnation* (1964), Childs does a vanishing act under a white sheet. In her very first piece, *Pastime*, Childs assumes various poses inside a stretchable blue jersey bag. What starts as a Dadaist performance is eventually raised to a positive principle: a mysticism of space. The dancers are disembodied, dematerialized. The Duchampian whimsicality of non- or anti-appearance is replaced by the Mallarméan idea of beauty as a tribute to the ineffable, to absence.

QUARTETS. Favorite formation in Childs's choreography, the first multiple of two. Among the short works choreographed for four dancers are *Calico Mingling* (1973), for four women, and *Radial Courses*, for two women and two men. In *Relative Calm*, the second section is for a quartet formation restocked several times from among eight dancers. Its sequel is the fourth section, which consists of two quartets, one of women and one of men.

RELATIVE CALM. 1981. The second of Childs's evening-length productions. Music by Jon Gibson, decor and lighting by Robert Wilson. Ninety-five minutes, a prologue and four sections, for nine dancers. Though not so labeled, the sections make up one of the traditional four-part sequences, The Times of Day. This is the Symbolic-Romantic version of the subject—Runge rather than Hogarth. Prologue: a star backdrop and the moon swinging pendulum-like in front of the dancers sitting in diagonal formation in carpets of light. The first section, "Rise," is early dawn—the dancers are in identical white jumpsuits; at the end, the stage brightens and the stars blanch out. "Race" is day; the dancers are in beige; it contains an homage to the quotidian, in the form of some inane sentences projected on the cyclorama and the brief appearance of a live dog. "Reach," the solo, is twilight—the stars start to come out—and both stage and cyclorama are cut diagonally, with half of the stage and half of the cyclorama in shadow, and Childs, in black, dancing in a diagonal wedge of light. "Return," with the dancers in royal blue, is starry, electric night. The conceit of the times of day evolved in conversations between Childs and Wilson; Childs invented the titles of the four sections, whose function was both to convey and to obscure a little the literalness of the scenic underpinning supplied by Wilson's set and lighting.

REPETITION. Childs's early notion of repetition, in the sprightly "silent" dances of the 1970s: dancers using the same steps or families of movements, going in and out of sync with each other. The notion becomes more complex in Childs's solo in *Einstein on the Beach*: repetition as an accumulation of effects, as layering. (Versus the repetition-as-reinterpretation of *Patio*.) Strictly speaking, there is of course no repetition in Childs's work, but rather a certain strict use of thematic materials, which are first stated and then gradually modified at a different rate of change (more evenly, not expressionistically) than audiences are accustomed to. In contrast to Wilson's Judson-derived dynamics of slow movement, thin difference, low-contrast change, Childs's work since the late 1970s has a greater density of movement, fast rhythms and few tableaux. (Whereas Wilson's work tends naturally to take long forms, Childs's work is only gradually assuming them.) Though usually presented as cool choice, repetition always suggests perfectionist zeal. Rainer in 1966 defended repetition because it makes movement appear "more objectlike"—more matter-of-fact, neutral, unemphatic. But repetition is also a method for inducing bliss. Repetition is a technique that seems to suggest simplicity, that in principle enhances legibility or intelligibility. (Rainer: "literally making the material easier to see.") A way of ordering material associated with the idea of the minimal, it could more accurately be called the modern maximalism: repetition as exhaustive patterning; the exhausting of possibilities. Far from making material neutral, repetition has a vertiginous effect, as in much of Childs's recent work—duplications, mirrorings, that are the kinetic equivalent of the static *mise-en-abîme*. See DOUBLING.

ROMANTIC. The "classical" tradition in dance is Romantic, so a neoclassical idiom in dance will inevitably be, in a restrained key, neo-Romantic. (But even this restraint is appropriate. Romantic art is, above all, self-conscious and critical.) The play of ghost, shadow, *doppelgänger* in *Dance*. The Pythagorean beauty of *Relative Calm*, with its allegorical underpinning: the Times of Day. (The contact with Wilson's allegorizing sensibility and its innate affinities with a certain German Romanticism helped Childs move away from a dead-end puritanism in her own sensibility.) There are Romantic echoes in all the

work since 1979. In *Dance*, having two solo sections, one in black
("Dance #2") and one in white ("Dance #4"), like *Swan Lake*'s
Odile/Odette. In *Available Light*, the arrival of Childs in the corridor,
like the Queen of the Wilis in *Giselle*. When *Available Light* was first
presented—in July 1983, at the Châteauvallon Dance Festival in an
open-air version, with no set and with the dancers in the company's all-
purpose touring costumes, the white jumpsuits of the first section of
Relative Calm—one saw the choreography in its naked state: without
white tutus but very much a *ballet blanc*.

SOLOS. Childs choreographs for herself differently than she does for
the rest of the company. As a soloist she gives herself a wider range of
dynamic changes, more evolution in the material (rather than in space).
There are two lengthy solos in *Dance*, one in *Relative Calm*. In
Available Light, which is not divided into separate sections, Childs
functions more as a member of the ensemble, less as a soloist. Still, she
is separate—in white, when most of the dancers are in red or black. Although she has no solo section as such where she appears alone onstage, she is the only dancer who comes and goes. The rest of the
company remains onstage for the entire fifty-five minutes (except for
one brief pause when the music downshifts and all ten go off, then return). From her early solos, with their theme of the absent or disappearing performer, to her privileged comings and goings in *Available
Light*, Childs's solo presence—grave, hieratic, not wholly expressive—
invokes both presence and absence.

SPACE. Dancers are travelers, "space eaters" (Childs's words), using
up a given space in a patterned, comprehensive way. (An early didactic
solo, *Particular Reel*, 1973, in which Childs covers the stage in ten rows
from right to left and then in ten rows from left to right, ending at the
point where she started, is a model demonstration of the project of
using up space.) The more space the better. Dancers are pulled along a
line; and their relations are conceived as parallel or perpendicular.
Dancers are always, indefatigably, going somewhere. In a state of
non-imploring urgency, they never stop; though they may go into

movement-absence, they do so in order to repopulate the space. When dancers "drop out," others come in.

TITLES. After the capers of the mid-1960s, titles have been sober: usually two words, adjective and noun; often a structure or pattern word with a movement word, as in *Checkered Drift, Calico Mingling, Reclining Rondo, Transverse Exchanges, Radial Courses.* A favorite title form is a contradiction, an oxymoron—one that, in recent works, suggests the paradoxes of self-control: *Relative Calm, Formal Abandon.* Or a stylish appreciation of the possible: *Available Light.*

UNAVAILABLE. Dance is about the absent or unavailable object of desire.

VOLITION. The more formal dance is shown to be, the weaker the possible attributions of volition. Dancers in formations—all this mirroring, duplicating, and inverting of movement removes the impression of subjectivity. So does the neutral performance mask—the fact that the dancers don't look at each other, or at the audience. (The effect is comparable to the anti-acting style favored by Bresson.) Dancers stop because they are being rearranged or repatterned, not because of any emotion or volition. To substitute rules or patterns—Kleist imagined them as mechanisms—for subjectivity in demeanor and movement is the prerequisite of grace. But the dancers are anything but automata.

WORLD. Dance, since the Romantics, has been about a phantom world. Childs's counts, like the tiny dots of color in the paintings of Seurat, are the building blocks of an art of phantom presences. Things which both are and are not: the moment of plenitude is an evocation of absence; pleasure—as in *La Grande Jatte*—is shown as rigidity, restraint.

YEARNING. The body in diagonal is a pose of outreach, hailing; of longing—for space itself. However large, the stage is never large enough. Childs's choreography projects onto the finite stage an infinitely large space or territory. Her love of space produces movements and structures—among them, the modalities of repetition—that seem choreographic equivalents of Zeno's arguments (called paradoxes) on the subject of motion, according to which, since any line is infinitely divisible, and will be made up of an infinite number of units, each of which has some magnitude, every finite line or space is in fact infinitely great; and, despite appearances, no moving object ever traverses any distance at all.

ZENO'S TERRITORY. Childs's early, provisional title for the work now known as *Available Light*.

[1983]

In Memory of Their Feelings

1. DANCERS ON A PLANE

I don't see them.

There. The dancers are there, invisible—an analogue to racing thoughts.

Framed by the utensils of eating.

A meal to be eaten?

An invisible meal.

Two meals: one light, one dark. One sprightly, one stained with sexual dread.

Dancers on a plate?

No. They need more space than that.

2. EATING AND DANCING

Recombinant arts.

A domain of pleasure. A domain of courtesy.

Rule-bound. Who sets the rules? Behavior with standards.

"In Memory of Their Feelings" was written for the exhibition catalogue of *Dancers on a Plane: Cage, Cunningham, Johns* at the Anthony d'Offay Gallery, London, 1989. The exhibition centered on Jasper Johns's *Dancers on a Plane* series. Framing the sides of the paintings is a sequence of applied knives, forks, and spoons.

An idea of order. First one thing, then another. Then one is full. Then it is finished—the belly sated, the limbs heavy. After a decent interval: then again. All over again. All over, again.

They remind us we live in the body-house.

Living "in" the body. But where else could we live?

Dancing as the realm of freedom, that's less than half the story.

Eating as the realm of necessity. Not necessarily. What about eating idyllically (as in Paris)?

Everyone eats, everyone can dance. Not everyone dances (alas).

I watch dance, with pleasure. I don't watch eating. If I watch someone eating when hungry, I wish it were I eating. A meal watched by a hungry person is always savory. If I watch someone eating when I'm full, I may turn away.

You can dance for me. (You do the dancing in my place, I'll just watch.) You can't eat for me. Not much pleasure there.

You can dance to please: Salome. You can eat to please too: as a child might eat to please its mother or a nurse. (As Suzanne Farrell is said to have said that she danced for God and for Mr. Balanchine.) But except to doting parents eating is a poor spectator sport. Mildly disgusting unless you're doing it as well.

To eat is to put metal in one's mouth. Delicately. It's not supposed to hurt.

The eater fills the hole.

A dancer eats space.

Space eats time.

Sounds eat silence.

3. THE KNIFE

It cuts. Don't be afraid. This is not a weapon. It's just a tool to help you eat. See. Passing it to you—you asked for it—I proffer it by the handle, keeping the blade pointed at myself. The blade is pointing at me.

One should not move the point of the knife toward someone as in an attack.

You can lay it down two ways. Blade in, blade out.

Don't be timorous. It isn't sharp. It's just a plain, ordinary . . . knife. Straight. Two-sided.

In the fairy tale, a mermaid who has fallen in love with a prince begs to be allowed to assume human form so she can leave the water and make her way to the court. Yes. She will have legs, she will walk. But with each step she takes it will feel as if she were walking on knives.

You can dance with a knife. (Between the teeth? Between the shoulder blades?) Hard to imagine dancing with a fork. Or with a spoon.

The knife seems like the master utensil, the one from which all others depend. (Swiss Army Knife.) You could spear food with your knife, eliminating the fork. (As everyone knows, you *can* eat the peas with your knife. You're just not supposed to.) As for the spoon—well, we could do without that, too. Just lift up the bowl dish cup, and drink it.

Only the knife is really necessary. And it is the knife, more than any other eating utensil, whose use is most circumscribed. The evolution of table manners is mainly about what to do with knives. Use the knife more and more unobtrusively, elegantly. With your finger ends. Don't grasp it against your palm like a stick.

"There is a tendency that slowly permeates civilized society, from the top to the bottom, to restrict the use of the knife (within the framework of existing eating techniques) and wherever possible not to use the instrument at all" (Norbert Elias). For instance, to eliminate or at least limit the contact of the knife with round or egg-shaped objects. Not all restrictions are successful. The prohibition on eating fish with a knife was circumvented by the introduction of a special fish knife.

That oxymoron: the butter knife.

To eat is to put metal in one's mouth. But not knives. The mere sight of someone putting her knife in her mouth produces an uneasy feeling.

4. THE SPOON

The spoon seems to belong in the mouth.

The spoon is not quite grownup in the way the knife and fork are. It doesn't menace. It isn't a tamed weapon.

The spoon is the utensil of childhood, the friendliest utensil. The spoon is childlike. Yum-yum. Scoop me up, pour me in. Like a cradle, a shovel, a hand cupped. Doesn't cut or pierce or impale. It accepts. Round, curved. Can't stick you. Don't trust your child with a knife or a fork, but how can a spoon harm? The spoon is itself a child.

The world is full of pleasures. One has only to be where one is. Here. Now.

Give me my spoon, my big spoon, and I'll eat the world. A metal spoon is an afterthought. While a wooden knife is less of a knife, a wooden spoon isn't less of a spoon. It's just fine.

"Spooning": embracing, kissing, petting. Lovers in bed fit together in sleep like spoons.

To bring about a music "that will be part of the noises of the environment, will take them into consideration. I think of it as melodious, softening the noises of the knives and forks, not dominating them, not imposing itself," wrote John Cage, quoting Erik Satie.

What happened to the spoons? Don't spoons make noises, too?

Softer noises.

And music. Music is made with two spoons (not with two forks, two knives).

Spoon music.

5. THE FORK

There's a hesitation about the fork. You hold down the food with the fork in your left hand while you cut it with the knife held in your right. Then—if you're not only right-handed but also American—you put down the knife, then transfer the fork to your right hand and send the speared morsel up to your mouth.

Grownups throw knives. Children throw spoons. Nobody (I think) would throw a fork. It may be four-thirds of a toy trident, but it can't be thrown as one. It wouldn't arrive, spear-like, tines first.

The weight is in the handle.

The fork as emblem—emblem of the real. Jasper Johns, explaining something about "my general development so far," said: "That is to say,

I find it more interesting to use a real fork as a painting than it is to use a painting as a real fork."

What would a fork that isn't real look like?

The fork is the youngest of the three great eating utensils. The Last Supper was set with knives and spoons only. No forks either at the wedding feast in Cana.

It made its appearance when the knife and spoon were well established. Invented in Italy, thought a foppish pretension when it arrived in England in the early seventeenth century: a set of gold "Italian forkes" presented to Elizabeth I by the Venetian ambassador were put on display at Westminster; she never used them.

The introduction of that vital implement, for a long time despised as effete, enabled people to distance themselves from the eating process by avoiding manual contact with the food.

The principle of fastidiousness. New forms of distance, new forms of delicacy.

New rules of finicky behavior at table proliferated. People were expected to manipulate an increasingly complicated battery of utensils.

It seemed hard, setting up and keeping this distance.

Now we take forks for granted.

6. KNIFE, SPOON, FORK

A secular trinity—knife, spoon, fork.

No hierarchy. The list can only be varied, systematically. As in knife, fork, spoon. As in knife, spoon, fork. As in fork, knife, spoon. As in fork, spoon, knife. As in spoon, fork, knife. As in spoon, knife, fork.

Seemingly immutable (after all that history).

They lie there, flat. On a plain (plane) surface. Perpendicular to the edge of the table.

A trialogue.

A stately relationship. Not all on the same side of the plate. Three divides into two and one. Fork on the left side. Knife and spoon on the right.

The knife is scary by itself. But as part of a setting, something else.

Lying beside the spoon, the knife becomes quite domestic. Knife and spoon: the odd couple. They don't go together, you don't use them together. But they *are* together.

The fork is solitary. Always is. Even in an ampler setting, all you could have next to it is another (smaller, larger) fork.

That's how they're arranged at the start of the meal, one step down from the plate. Escorting the plate on either side.

No excuse now to eat with your hands. Civil eating (versus gluttony).

After finishing eating you arrange them neatly on the plate.

Not alphabetically. Not in order of importance, if there were one.

A trinity but quite contingent.

They seem to complement each other.

We have learned to use all three. But they can be used separately, of course.

7. DANCERS ON A PLAIN

On a plane? An airplane?

On a plain. As open (borderless) as feasible.

Low, level. Don't try for any of those old heights. Depths.

What is essential about a surface that makes it different from another surface? How do we register smoothness in a surface, a movement, a sound, an experience?

Smoothness?

Yes. Something continues, plausibly.

Pleasurably. With parts.

What does it mean to be one part of something (a surface, a movement, a sound, an experience)?

The old heights. Mirroring. Look down. These are my genitals.

Be more modest; elegant.

Sometimes light, sometimes heavy—it's all right to be heavy sometimes.

Makes it new. Yes. And make it plain.

8. SYMMETRIES

Dancers on a plane. No center. Always off-side. Any place is the center.

We seem symmetrical. Two eyes, two ears, two arms, two legs; two ovaries—or two hairy testicles. But we're not. Something is always dominating.

A mirror image: a fantasy of symmetry. The right the reverse of the left, or vice versa.

We *seem* symmetrical. But we are not.

They cross-refer (knife, spoon, fork). As in the brain. Right-handedness means the left side of the brain is dominant. Left-handedness means the brain's right side dominates.

How to find out which side of your brain is dominant. Close your eyes, think of a question, then slowly think of an answer to the question. If while you're doing this you turn your head slightly to the right, that means the left side dominates.

And vice versa.

The question-master.

An art that asks questions.

How do we understand how one part of a surface, a movement, a sound, an experience relates to another? Note: you have a choice of questions. But if that's the question you choose to ask, you can be sure the answer will include a bias toward asymmetry.

"The non-relationship of the movement," Cunningham has declared, "is extended into a relationship with music. It is essentially a non-relationship."

The dancer must be light. Food makes you heavy.

You eat with your hands, dance on your legs. Eating can be right-handed or left-handed. Is dancing left-legged or right-legged?

Any place is the center.

A real symmetry: chopsticks.

9. SILENCES

Lots of prattle. That, too, is a kind of silence. (Since there is no silence.) The deaf hear their deafness. The blind see their blindness.

Controlling through silence. Whoever speaks less is the stronger.

Is there a warm silence?

The noise of ideas.

Take it to language.

No, take it to babble. Cut up the words in strips, like raw vegetables. Make meals out of words. A culinary relation to words . . .

Suppose Knife, Spoon, and Fork are three people. And they get together on a plane (plain). What would they have to say to each other?

I know. "Who brought the marshmallows?"

Mushrooms, surely you mean mushrooms.

As I said, marshmallows.

That's not what I had in mind. Then what?

Then they get very particular about how the marshmallows are to be cooked.

All three of them know a lot about food. (About eating. Preceded by gathering, preparing, cooking . . .)

But these are just marshmallows. American junk.

You can be fastidious about anything. And marshmallows can be botched, too; can disappoint. It's a question of (yes, once again) the relation of inside to outside. The inside has to be cooked very well, while not letting the outside catch fire. Ideally the outside will get crusty but not burnt, while the inside melts. Then, right before it falls off the stick, you pluck it off with your fingers and pop it whole into your mouth.

Stick? What happened to the fork? Don't you toast marshmallows with a fork?

All right, the fork. But this is better as a gooey experience than as a refined one.

"Everywhere and at all times," Lévi-Strauss has observed, "the European code of politeness rules out the possibility of eating noisily."

And you don't always have to be polite.

10. IN MEMORY OF THEIR FEELINGS

In the first—buoyant, *allegro vivace*—painting, this is real flatware that has been painted white. In the second painting, the artist has cast the utensils in bronze.

Repeating as a means of varying. Accepting as a way of discriminating. Indifference as a form of emotional vitality.

Use me as you will.

Savoring non-relatedness. Put the emphasis on savoring. "I am more interested in the *facts* of moving rather than in my feelings about them" (Merce Cunningham).

Would you like to play chess? Chess seriously.

We were younger then. Who would have thought then—when we were younger; then—that it would be like this?

We meet. This could be at a dinner party (forks, knives, spoons, et cetera).

We say things like, How lovely to see you. I've been busy. I think so. I don't know. That must have been very interesting. (Everything is interesting. But some things are more interesting than others.) Probably not. I've heard. In Frankfurt, in Illinois, in London. Next year. What a pity. He's gone away. He'll be back soon. They're organizing something. You'll get an invitation.

We smile. We nod. We are indefatigable. I think I'm free next week. We say we wish we saw more of each other.

We eat, we savor.

Meanwhile, each harbors a secret idea of ascending, of descending. We go on. The plane's edge beckons.

[1989]

Dancer and the Dance

L INCOLN KIRSTEIN, the finest historian of dance and one of
its master ideologues, has observed that in the nineteenth century what the prestige of ballet really amounted to was the reputation
of the dancer; and that even when there were great choreographers
(notably Petipa) and great dance scores (from Adam, Delibes, and
Tchaikovsky), dance was still almost entirely identified for the large
theatrical public with the personality and virtuosity of great dancers.
That triumphant mutation in dance taste and in the composition of
dance audiences which occurred just before World War I, in response
to the authoritative intensity and exoticism of the Ballets Russes, did
not challenge the old imbalance of attention—not even with the subsequent invention by Diaghilev of dance as an ambitious collaboration,
in which major innovative artists outside the dance world were brought
in to enhance this theatre of astonishment. The score might be by
Stravinsky, the decor by Picasso, the costumes by Chanel, the libretto
by Cocteau. But the blow of the sublime was delivered by a Nijinsky or
a Karsavina—by the dancer. According to Kirstein, it was only with the
advent of a choreographer so complete in his gifts as to change dance
forever, George Balanchine, that the primacy of the choreographer
over the performer, of dance over the dancer, was finally understood.

Kirstein's account of the more limited perspectives of dance publics
before Balanchine is, of course, not incorrect. But I would point out

that the exaltation of the performer over all else pervaded not only dance in the nineteenth (and early twentieth) century but all the arts that need to be performed. Recalling the effusive identification of dance with the dancer—say, with Marie Taglioni and with Fanny Elssler—one should recall as well other audiences, other raptures. The concert audiences ravished by Liszt and Paganini were also identifying music with the virtuoso performer: the music was, as it were, the occasion. Those who swooned over La Malibran in the new Rossini or Donizetti thought of opera as the vehicle of the singer. (As for the look of opera, whether it was the staging, the decor, or the often incongruous physique of the singer—this hardly seemed worthy of discussion.) And the focus of attention has been modified in these arts, too. Even the most diva-besotted portion of the opera public of recent decades is prepared to segregate the work from the performance and, within the performance, vocal prowess and expressiveness from acting—distinctions fused by the inflatedly partisan rhetoric of extreme reactions (either ecstasy or the rudest condemnation) that surrounded opera performance in the nineteenth century, particularly early performances of a new work. That the work is now routinely seen as transcending the performer, rather than the performer transcending the work, has come to be felt not just in dance, because of the advent of a supremely great choreographer, but in all the performing arts.

And yet, this being said, there seems to be something intrinsic to dance that warrants the kind of reverential attention paid in each generation to a very few dancers—something about what they do that is different from the achievements of surpassingly gifted, magnetic performers in other arts to whom we pay homage.

Dance cannot exist without dance design: choreography. But dance *is* the dancer.

The relation of dancer to choreographer is not just that of executant to *auteur*—which, however creative, however inspired the performer, is still a subservient relation. Though a performer in this sense, too, the dancer is also more. There is a mystery of incarnation in dance that has no analogue in the other performing arts.

A great dancer is not just performing (a role) but being (a dancer). Someone can be the greatest Odette/Odile, the greatest Albrecht one has ever seen—as a singer can be the best (in anyone's memory) Tosca or Boris or Carmen or Sieglinde or Don Giovanni, or an actor can be the finest Nora or Hamlet or Faust or Phaedra or Winnie. But beyond the already grandiose aim of giving the definitive performance of a work, a role, a score, there is a further, even higher standard which applies to dancers. One can be not just the best performer of certain roles but the most complete exhibit of what it is to be a dancer. Example: Mikhail Baryshnikov.

In any performing art which is largely repertory, interest naturally flows to the contribution of the executant. The work already exists. What is new, each time, is what this performer, these performers, bring to it in the way of new energies, changes in emphasis, or interpretation. How they make it different, or better. Or worse. The relation of work to performer is a musical-structural one: theme and variations. A given play or opera or sonata or ballet is the theme: all readings of it will be, to some extent, variations.

But here as well, although the dancer does what all executants of a work do, dance differs from the other performing arts. For the standard against which dancers measure their performances is not simply that of the highest excellence—as with actors and singers and musicians. The standard is perfection.

In my experience, no species of performing artist is as self-critical as a dancer. I have gone backstage many times to congratulate a friend or acquaintance who is an actor or a pianist or a singer on his or her superlative performance; invariably my praise is received without much demurral, with evident pleasure (my purpose, of course, *is* to give pleasure), and sometimes with relief. But each time I've congratulated a friend or acquaintance who is a dancer on a superb performance— and I include Baryshnikov—I've heard first a disconsolate litany of mistakes that were made: a beat was missed, a foot not pointed in the right way, there was a near slippage in some intricate partnering maneuver. Never mind that perhaps not only I but everyone else failed to observe these mistakes. They were made. The dancer knew. Therefore the performance was not *really* good. Not good enough.

In no other art can one find a comparable gap between what the world thinks of a star and what the star thinks about himself or herself, between the adulation that pours in from outside and the relentless dissatisfaction that goads one from within. The degree and severity of dancers' self-criticism is not simply a case of performers' raw nerves (virtually all great performing artists are worriers, skilled at self-criticism), of artistic conscience—a *déformation professionnelle*. It is, rather, integral to the dancer's *formation professionnelle*. Part of being a dancer is this cruelly self-punishing objectivity about one's shortcomings, as viewed from the perspective of an ideal observer, one more exacting than any real spectator could ever be: the god Dance.

Every serious dancer is driven by notions of perfection—perfect expressiveness, perfect technique. What this means in practice is not that anyone is perfect but that performance standards are always being raised.

The notion of progress in the arts has few defenders now. If Balanchine was the greatest choreographer who ever lived (an unverifiable proposition firmly held by many balletomanes, myself among them), it is surely not because he came after Noverre and Petipa and Fokine, because he was the last (or the most recent) of the breed. But there does seem to be something like linear progress in dance performance— unlike the other performing arts largely devoted to repertory, such as opera. (Was Callas greater than Rosa Ponselle or Claudia Muzio? The question does not make sense.) There is no doubt that the general level of dancing in unison in companies like the Kirov and the New York City Ballet (which have probably the two best *corps de ballet* in the world) and the prowess and power and expressiveness of the leading dancers in today's great ballet companies (the two just mentioned, the Paris Opéra Ballet, the Royal Ballet, and the American Ballet Theatre—among others) are far higher than the level of the most admired dancing of the past. All dance writers agree that, a few immortal soloists apart, the dancing in Diaghilev's Ballets Russes was technically quite limited by today's standards.

Raising the level is the function of the champion: a considerable number of people found they could run the four-minute mile once Roger Bannister had done it. As in sport or athletics, the achievement by a virtuoso dancer raises the achievable standard for everybody else. And this is what Baryshnikov, more than any other dancer of our time, has done—not only by what he can do with his body (he has, among other feats, jumped higher than anyone else, and has landed lower), but by what he can show, in the maturity and range of his expressiveness.

Dance demands a degree of service greater than any other performing art, or sport. While the daily life of every dancer is a full-time struggle against fatigue, strain, natural physical limitations and those due to injuries (which are inevitable), dance itself is the enactment of an energy which must seem, in all respects, untrammeled, effortless, at every moment fully mastered. The dancer's performance smile is not so much a smile as a categorical denial of what he or she is actually experiencing—for there is some discomfort, and often pain, in every major stint of performing. This is an important difference between the dancer and the athlete, who have much in common (ordeal, contest, brevity of career). In sport, the signs of effort are not concealed: on the contrary, making effort visible is part of the display. The public expects to see, and is moved by, the spectacle of the athlete visibly pushing himself or herself beyond the limits of endurance. The films of championship tennis matches or of the Tour de France or any comprehensive documentary about athletic competition (a splendid example: Ichikawa's *Tokyo Olympiad*) always reveal the athlete's strain and stress. (Indeed, the extent to which Leni Riefenstahl, in her film on the 1936 Olympic Games, chose *not* to show the athletes in this light is one of the signs that her film is really about politics—the aestheticizing of politics in totally ordered mass spectacle and in imperturbable solo performance—and not about sport as such.) That is why news of an athlete's injuries is a matter of general knowledge and legitimate curiosity on the part of the public, while news of dancers' injuries is not, and tends to be suppressed.

It is often said that dance is the creation of illusion: for example, the illusion of a weightless body. (This might be thought of as the furthest extension of the phantasm of a body without fatigue.) But it would be more accurate to call it the staging of a transfiguration.

Dance enacts both being completely in the body and transcending the body. It seems to be a higher order of attention, where physical and mental attention become the same.

Dancers of unrivaled talents like Baryshnikov (among woman dancers, Suzanne Farrell comes first to mind) project a state of total focus, total concentration, which is not simply—as for an actor or a singer or a musician—the necessary prerequisite of producing a great performance. It *is* the performance, the very center of it.

Merce Cunningham and Lincoln Kirstein have both offered as a definition of dance: a spiritual activity in physical form. No art lends itself so aptly as dance does to metaphors borrowed from the spiritual life. (Grace, elevation . . .) Which means, too, that all discussions of the dance, and of great dancers, including this one, fit dance into some larger rhetoric about human possibility.

One practice is to pair off the greatest dancers as representing two ideal alternatives. The most astute dance writer of the nineteenth century, Théophile Gautier, so contrasted the reigning dancers of his era, Elssler and Taglioni. Elssler was pagan, earthy; Taglioni was spiritual, transcendent. And critics a decade ago, when absorbing the arrival of a second male Kirov refugee of genius in our midst, tended to compare Nureyev and Baryshnikov in the same way. Nureyev was Dionysian, Baryshnikov was Apollonian. Such symmetries are inevitably misleading, and this particular one does an injustice to Nureyev, who was a supremely gifted and expressive dancer and in the early years an ideal partner (with Fonteyn), as well as to Baryshnikov. For although Baryshnikov has perhaps never in his career been an ideal partner, it has to be said—without any disrespect to the grandeur of Nureyev's dancing and to his heroic tenacities—that the younger dancer proved to be a genius of another magnitude.

Of a magnitude without parallel. Guided by his generosity, his intellectual curiosity, and his unprecedented malleability as a dancer, Baryshnikov has given himself to more different kinds of dancing than any other great dancer in history. He has danced Russian ballet, Bournonville, the British recensions (Ashton, Tudor, MacMillan), Balanchine, Roland Petit, and a range of Americana from jazz dancing (a duo with Judith Jamison, choreographed by Alvin Ailey) to Robbins, Tharp, and Karole Armitage. He may, on occasion, have been abused or misused by his choreographers. But even when the role is not right, he is always more than the role. He is, almost literally, a transcendent dancer. Which is what dance strives to make actual.

[1986]

Lincoln Kirstein

B ORN IN 1907, the "107th year of the nineteenth century," as he once dubbed it, Lincoln Kirstein devoted his life to promoting and exemplifying standards that were both confidently old-fashioned and recklessly visionary. His widest claim to fame is that, through his initiative and unflagging attentions, both a great art and the cultural life of a great city were transformed. Lincoln Kirstein made classical ballet an American art by giving America its first ballet school and giving an American home to one of the supreme artists of the twentieth century. And that artist, George Balanchine, made New York the dance capital of the world: the best dances being made anywhere, performed by consummately trained great dancers, created the most knowledgeable audience anywhere, one better prepared than audiences in any other metropolis to welcome and evaluate dance in all its varieties, "modern" as well as ballet.

Kirstein's actual titles were: general director of the New York City Ballet and president of the School of American Ballet. But his association with dance was only one aspect of his genius. Like Diaghilev, who is often (if not too accurately) invoked when assessing Kirstein's role and importance, he started off as someone with interesting, fiercely partisan tastes in all the arts and literature, a connoisseur and proselytizer of indefatigable appetite, charm, social energies—who narrowed his focus to dance. Great tastemakers need a capacious institution to bend to their will, a vehicle. Diaghilev started, precociously, by founding a magazine (*The World of Art*), well before the Ballets Russes was thought of; Kirstein in the late 1920s, while still an undergraduate at Harvard, founded a magazine, a splendid magazine, *Hound & Horn*, to write for and to discover other talents, new and forgotten. He might have had a career not unlike other exceptionally prescient aesthetes of his generation, such as A. Everett ("Chick") Austin and Julien Levy, who used museums and an art gallery to celebrate and sponsor their disparate enthusiasms: a museum or a gallery is an anthology institution, as is a magazine or a publishing house. But Kirstein had the means, the daring, and the tenacity to put all his avidity, all his piety, into an institution exhibiting one genius. One genius only. And unlike a publishing house or a gallery or a museum or a magazine, institutions that are invaluable in the soliciting and disseminating of work but are not indispensable to its creation, a dance company is a living organism that inspires and makes possible the work which it then exhibits to the public. It was Kirstein's vision, his stamina, his fidelity, that brought into being and guaranteed the survival of the greatest dance company of our time, without which most of the dances made by the genius he imported, who turned out to be the greatest choreographer of all time, would not have been made.

These roles, of tastemaker and supreme enabler of another's genius, are service roles, and Kirstein was devoted to the idea of service. The magnificent *Movement & Metaphor* and many other books (and articles) about the history and ideology of dance made him an important author. What made him something larger, an important, thrilling writer, was the quality of his prose. (I exclude the early novel and volume of poems—interesting mainly because he wrote them. The novel, *Flesh Is Heir*, relates how he happened to be present in Venice at Diaghilev's funeral in 1929; *Rhymes of a PFC*, about his military service during World War II, tells how he loved being in the army.) What's more, when his work with the great institution he founded and kept alive for decades was virtually over ("*Après moi, le Board*," as he quotes Balanchine as saying), his work with English sentences was not. There is more than fifty years of writing, going back to *Hound & Horn*, and he got better all the time, more subtle, more sonorous, more intense. I am thinking of the articles that appeared in the 1980s in *The New York Review of Books* and, in particular, of four stupendous pieces of auto-biographical writing—triumphs of elliptical prose and anguished, ecstatic sensibility—published in the literary quarterly *Raritan*. In 1991 a generous sampling of Kirstein's writing on all subjects (including photography, painting, film, and literature as well as dance) was published under the title *By With To & From: A Lincoln Kirstein Reader*, and in 1994 *Mosaic: Memoirs* appeared, which incorporated some but not all of the material in *Raritan*. And there is much, much more, still to be collected or brought back into print.

A votary of systems of ideal order, Kirstein more than once expressed his love of ballet as a commitment to certain spiritual values—to an exalted abnegation of self. But as the attraction to the impersonal is sometimes the good taste of a truly strong personality, so the militant attraction to ideally regimented communities is, usually, the hallmark of a truly eccentric temperament. The collective enterprise to which Kirstein devoted his life does illustrate the ideals he said it did: perfect discipline, service, devotion. His own life, like any individual life when examined closely, yields a double meaning. Kirstein's life and accomplishments supply model lessons about the necessity of eccentricity—about being eccentric (including being "difficult" personally) as a spiritual value and a precondition of real seriousness.

We were fortunate to have had this noble and complicated man among us.

[1997]

Wagner's Fluids

WATER, BLOOD, HEALING BALM, magic potions—fluids play a decisive role in this mythology.

Wagner's stories are often launched from a water-world. An arrival by water and a departure by water frame the plots of *The Flying Dutchman* and *Lohengrin*. The *Ring* saga begins literally in the water, below the Rhine's surface (to end, four operas later, with a cosmic duet of water and fire). Wagner's most delirious exploration of fluidity, *Tristan und Isolde*, begins and ends with journeys over water. Act I takes place on a noble vessel commanded by Tristan that is taking the Irish princess Isolde, who is affianced to Tristan's uncle, King Marke, to Cornwall. Preceding this journey was an earlier sea voyage, when Tristan, grievously wounded, had set off alone in a frail skiff for Ireland, in hopes of being ministered to by Isolde, renowned for her healing arts. Since the foe who wounded him and whom he killed was Isolde's fiancé, he could not say who he was. (Solitary people with mysterious or disguised identities—Lohengrin, the Dutchman, the wounded Tristan at the Irish court—usually arrive by water.) Act III takes place on a rampart overlooking the sea, where Tristan, re-wounded mortally at the end of Act II, waits for a boat to arrive bearing Isolde, who has been summoned not as his lover but as his once successful healer. But as she appears Tristan dies, and she follows him in death. Journeys over water are associated in Wagner's mythology with a redemption that does not happen, as in *Lohengrin*, or happens in terms other than those originally sought, as in *Tristan und Isolde*, which has almost everybody die, either senselessly or beatifically.

Parsifal, like *Tristan und Isolde*, is very much a story of fluids. However, in this last of Wagner's thirteen operas, what is defined as redemption—finding someone who will heal, and succeed, the wounded king Amfortas—does take place, and in the hoped-for terms. A virgin, this time male, a holy fool, appears as foretold. Perhaps this fulfillment of expectations makes it inevitable that the water-world is largely excluded from the opera. A majestic outdoors, the forest, and a vast sanctified indoors, the Grail Hall, are its two positive locations (the negative ones, Klingsor's domain, being a castle tower and a garden of dangerous flowers). To be sure, Act I has water just offstage: a lake to which the wounded king is brought for his hydrotherapy, and a spring where Kundry procures water to revive the fainting Parsifal after brutally announcing to him his mother's death; and in Act III, there is water for a consecration, for a baptism. But the main story of fluids is about blood: the unstanchable hemorrhaging of the wound in Amfortas's side, Christ's blood that should stream in the Grail chalice. Amfortas's essential duty as king of the Grail knights, which is to make Christ's blood appear in the chalice on a regular basis, for the knights' eucharistic meal, has become agony for him to perform—weakened as he is by this wound, inflicted by Klingsor with the very spear that pierced Jesus' side while He hung on the Cross. The plot of *Parsifal* could be summarized as the search, eventually successful, for a replacement for someone who is having trouble making a fluid appear.

SEVERAL KINDS OF FLUID enter the body in Wagner's stories, but in only one form does fluid leave it, blood, and this in male bodies only. Women have bloodless deaths: usually they simply expire abruptly (Elsa, Elisabeth, Isolde, Kundry), or they immolate themselves, in water (Senta) or in fire (Brunnhilde). Only men bleed—bleed to death. (Therefore, it doesn't seem too fanciful to regard semen as subsumed, metaphorically, under blood.) Though Wagner makes the prostrate, punctured, hemorrhaging male body the result of some epic combat, there is usually an erotic wound behind the one inflicted by spear and sword. Love as experienced by men, in both *Tristan und Isolde* and *Parsifal*, is tantamount to a wound. Isolde had healed Tristan, but Tristan had fallen in love with Isolde; Wagner's way of signaling the emotional necessity of a new physical wound is to make it, shockingly, virtually self-inflicted. (Tristan drops his sword at the end of Act II and lets the treacherous Melot run him through.) Amfortas had already been seduced by Kundry; Klingsor's spear just made that wound literal.

In Wagner's misogynistic logic, a woman, who characteristically doubles as healer and seducer, is often the true slayer. This figure, of whom Isolde is a positive version, appears in *Parsifal* with both the negativity and the eroticism made far more explicit. The person who flies in, early in Act I, bearing a vial of precious medicinal balm for the stricken king—it can relieve but not cure him—is the same person who caused the King's wound. Wagner makes Kundry systematically dual: in her service role, a bringer of fluids; in her seducer's alter ego, a taker of them.

Seduction is eloquence; service is mute. After the failure of Kundry's maximal eloquence, her attempt to seduce Parsifal in Act II, she is represented as having nothing left to say. "*Dienen! Dienen!*" (To serve! To serve!) are the only words she is allowed in all of Act III. In contrast, Isolde, who is characterized first as a healing woman, one who successfully administered balm (the background of the opera's story), and then as a focus of desire, becomes more and more eloquent. It is with Isolde's rush of ecstatic words that Wagner concludes the opera.

THE FLUID ADMINISTERED by Isolde in her role as healer is in the past. In the story Wagner has chosen to tell, the fluid she offers Tristan is what they both believe to be a lethal poison. Instead, it is a disinhibitor, which makes them—just as the boat is about to land—confess their love for each other.

A fluid-that-changes-everything is essential to the Celtic legend of Tristan and Isolde that has been circulating through the veins of European culture for more than seven centuries. In the fullest account, from the thirteenth century, Gottfried von Strassburg's novel-length verse epic *Tristan*, it is a love-philter concocted by Isolde's mother (also named Isolde, and the healing woman in the original tale) for her daughter and King Marke to drink on their wedding night which, during the voyage, an ignorant servant offers to Marke's nephew and the bride-to-be as wine. Wagner's version turns accidental calamity into necessity. "*Der Liebestrank*," the draught of love that Brangäne, Isolde's servant, has deliberately substituted for the poison, does not make Tristan and Isolde feel their own feelings—they already feel them, are being martyred by them. It simply makes it impossible for them to go on not acknowledging their love.

The love-potion is treated in a comic register in another opera, Donizetti's *L'elisir d'amore* (1832), which opens with the well-to-do heroine reading to a group of peasants a reduction of the Celtic legend to a tale of conventionally unrequited love with a happy ending. Handsome Tristan procures from a "*saggio incantatore*" (a wise sorcerer) a "*certo elisir d'amor*" (a certain elixir of love); no sooner has the beautiful but indifferent Isolde taken a sip than a matching love is created—instantly. "*Cambiata in un istante / quella beltà crudele / fu di Tristano amante / visse Tristan fedel.*" (Changed in an instant / that unkind beauty / became Tristan's true love / and lived faithful to him.) The drink that makes someone fall in love belongs to the same family of potions, spells, and charms that transforms princes into frogs and mermaids into princesses: it is the instant metamorphosis of fairy tales. Mere fairy tales. Donizetti's *buffa* realism has no place for magic: the fluid sold by an itinerant quack to the opera's hero to woo the woman he thinks (wrongly) doesn't love him is actually Bordeaux. Instead of what is given as wine being really a magic potion, what is fobbed off as a magic potion is just wine—the inevitable, comic deflation of the fantasy.

Its tragic dissolution is Wagner's, a quarter of a century later: a potion that, rather than making something possible, heightens impossibility, loosening the tie to life. The fluid that Brangäne gives the hapless pair does not just reveal (and therefore unleash) a feeling. It undoes a world. Love subtracts them instantly, totally, from civil society, from normal ties and obligations, casting them into a vertiginous solitariness (rather than a romantic solitude *à deux*) that brings on an inexorable darkening of consciousness. Where are we? asks Isolde at the beginning of the opera. Where am I? she asks Tristan at the end of Act I, after they have drunk the potion, as the boat lands in Cornwall. The king is here, someone says. What king? asks Tristan. And Tristan does not know where he is when he awakens in Act III. What herds? what castle? what peasants? he asks, as his loyal retainer Kurwenal explains that he has been brought home to Brittany, his own kingdom, that he is lying on the rampart of his own castle. Love is an anti-gnosis, a de-knowing. Each act begins with a tormented, paralyzing, anguished waiting by one for the other, followed by the longed-for arrival—and concluding with other, unanticipated arrivals, which are not only disruptive but, to the lovers, barely comprehensible. What duty? What shame?

Passion means an exalted passivity. Act I opens with Isolde on a couch, her face buried in the cushions (Wagner's stage direction), and Act III has Tristan in a coma at the beginning and supine throughout. As in *Parsifal*, there is a great deal of lying down and many fervent appeals for the surcease of oblivion. If the opera ended after its first two acts, one could regard this pull of the horizontal in *Tristan und Isolde*, the paeans to night, the dark, the equating of pleasure with oblivion and of death with pleasure, as a most extravagant way of describing the voluptuous loss of consciousness in orgasm. Whatever is being said or being done on the stage, the music of the Act II encounter is a thrillingly unequivocal rendering of an ideal copulation. (Thomas Mann was not wrong when he spoke of the opera's "lascivious desire for bed.") But Act III makes it clear that the eroticism is more means than end, a platform for the propaganda against lucidity; that the deepest subject is the surrender of consciousness as such.

Already the emotional logic of the words of the Act II duet is a sequence of annihilating—and nihilistic—mental operations. The lovers do not simply unite, generically, as in the unsurpassably elegant formula of Gottfried von Strassburg's medieval German *Tristan*:

> A man, a woman; a woman, a man;
> Tristan, Isolde; Isolde, Tristan.

Imbued with the elaborate understanding of solitude and the exploration of extremes of feeling that seem the most original achievements of the Romantic movements in the arts of the last century, Wagner is able to go much further:

> TRISTAN: *Tristan du, ich Isolde, nicht mehr Tristan!*
> ISOLDE: *Du Isolde, Tristan ich, nicht mehr Isolde!*
>
> (TRISTAN: Tristan you, I Isolde, no more Tristan!
> ISOLDE: You Isolde, Tristan I, no more Isolde!)

When the world is thought to be so easily negated by the pressure of extreme feeling (the still regnant mythology of the self we owe to the nineteenth-century writers and composers), the feeling self expands to fill the empty space: "*Selbst dann bin ich die Welt*" (I myself am the world), Tristan and Isolde had already sung in unison. The inevitable next move is the elimination of the self, gender, individuality. "*Ohne Nennen, ohne Trennen*" (no names, no parting), they sing together . . . "*endlos, ewig, einbewusst*" (ever, unendingly, one consciousness). For one self to seek to fuse with another is, in the absence of the world, to seek the annihilation of both.

When lovers unite in opera, what they do, mainly, is utter the same words; they speak together, as one. Their words unite, rhyme, to the same music. Wagner's libretto for *Tristan und Isolde* carries out this formal principle more literally and insistently than any other opera: the lovers return to echo each other's words throughout. Their fullest exchange, in the garden of Act II, has them voluptuously repeating their words back to each other, competing in their expressions of desire to unite, to die, and their denunciations of light and day. Of course their texts are not identical—and neither, for all their desire to merge, even to exchange identities, are the two lovers. Tristan is given a more complex awareness. And having sung with Isolde of the bliss of their death-bound yearning in Act II, Tristan expresses another relation to death in the last act, in the form of a soliloquy in which he separates himself from Isolde, cursing love. It had been Tristan alone in Act II who dwelled ecstatically on the potion that flowed through him, that he drank with endless delight. Now in Act III the fluids he invokes are all bitter: *"Liebestränen"* (lovers' tears) and the accursed potion, which he now proclaims in his delirious unraveling of the story's deepest layer of emotion that he himself brewed.

THE CHARACTERISTIC, plot-generating situation in Wagner's operas is one that has gone on too long, and is infused with the anguished longing to terminate. ("Unending melody"—Wagner's phrase for his distinctive musical line—is one formal equivalent of this essential subject of prolongation, of excruciation.) Blood flows unceasingly from Amfortas's wound, but he can't die. Meanwhile, his father, Titurel, the former Grail king, who already lies in his tomb, is being kept alive by the Grail ceremony. And ageless Kundry, painfully revived in each act, wants nothing more than to go back to sleep. Wagner turns the legend of Tristan and Isolde into an earlier, secular version of the longings expressed in *Parsifal*—with Tristan taking the lead. The Tristan of Act III is a proto-Amfortas: a suffering man who wants to die but can't until, finally, he can. Men are given a more developed death wish than women. (Kundry, whose longing for extinction seems even stronger than Amfortas's, is the exception.) Isolde tries to die only in Act I, when, with Tristan, she drinks the potion she believes to be poison, while Tristan actively provokes his death in all three acts, succeeding at the end by tearing the bandages from his wound when he is told that Isolde is approaching. Isolde even has a moment in Act II of doubt (or common sense), when she evokes *"dies süsse Wörtlein: und"* (this sweet little word: and), as in Tristan *and* Isolde. But won't dying separate them? she asks. No, he answers.

Viewed from the narrowing and even more excruciating perspective of the last act, the opera is (or becomes) mostly Tristan's story. Viewed more inclusively, as the story of both, Wagner's version of the old Celtic legend has an arbitrariness in its dénouement that makes it closer in feeling to the traditional Japanese tragedy of the double suicide—the voluntary death of lovers whose situation is *not* entirely hopeless—than to, say, *Romeo and Juliet*. (And Wagner's depiction of love as tormentingly painful, consciousness-dissolving yearning recalls sentiments in the love poetry of Heian Japan.) His Tristan and Isolde are not, as in Gottfried von Strassburg's poem, star-crossed lovers thwarted by the standard obstacles: that the man has slain a close relative of the woman's; that the woman is betrothed to an older male relative of the man's to whom loyalty is owed. Wagner requires something beyond these objective impediments, whose importance signifies that the lovers are members of a society, a world. The world-transcending obstacle is, then, the very nature of love—an emotion always in excess of its object; insatiable. The eroticism that Wagner exalts is one that *has* to self-destruct.

When Marke arrives at the end, it is not to grasp for the first time the claims of this passion and now to wish, when it's too late, as Capulets and Montagues do, that he had been more understanding. Having learned from Brangäne that the lovers were compelled by a love-philter to betray him, Marke (who functions as Tristan's father, and in some early versions of the story is his father) has decided to release Isolde from her vow and let the lovers marry. But union is not what Tristan and Isolde want, what they ever wanted. They want the lights turned off. Isolde's last words—the last words of the opera—are a description of losing consciousness: "*ertrinken, versinken / unbewusst höchste Lust!*" (drowning, sinking / unconscious supreme bliss!). The music overflows. Consciousness drowns.

TRISTAN UND ISOLDE is about being overcome, destroyed by feeling—and not only *about* extreme experience but intended to *be* one. That Wagner equates being satisfied or inspired with being overwhelmed is a typically Romantic idea of art, art that not only is about excess (Tristan and Isolde overwhelmed by their passion) but employs, in an almost homeopathic spirit, extravagant and outsized means, such as unusual bulk or duration. The element of ordeal for the audience in all this, even of risk, seemed only appropriate. A good performance of

Tristan und Isolde, Wagner had predicted to Mathilde Wesendonk while composing the last act, is "bound to drive people mad." One of Wagner's favorite notions about his work was that only the strong could immerse themselves in it with impunity. When the first Tristan, the tenor Ludwig Schnorr, fell ill after the first performances in Munich in 1865, both he and Wagner worried that it would be said that he had been laid low by the role's unprecedented exertions and intensities; and when Schnorr unexpectedly died a few weeks later, Wagner (and not only Wagner) felt that perhaps the opera had killed him.

Wagner was hardly the first composer to associate the lethal, at least metaphorically, with the lyrical. But previous notions of the lethal lyrical had focused on the singer. To the librettist with whom he was working on *I Puritani*, Bellini wrote, "Grave on your mind in adamantine letters: A musical drama must make people weep, shudder, and die through the singing." The great singers were those who could provoke audiences to an ecstasy bordering on delirium, a standard that was set by Farinelli, Pacchierotti, and other celebrated castrati of the eighteenth and early nineteenth centuries, the first divas in the modern sense, whose voices made people swoon and weep and feel that they were being driven out of their senses, and whose appearance and extravagantly artificial manner were erotically captivating to both sexes. Napoleon declared, in praise of his favorite singer, that he felt he was going mad when he heard Crescentini sing. It is this longing to have one's normal consciousness ravished by the singer's art that is preserved in an irrepressible phenomenon usually dismissed as an oddity or aberration of the opera world: diva worship. The distinctively high-pitched adulation surrounding several sopranos (and a tenor or two) in every generation affirms this much-prized experience as granted by the voice, not merely the charms of celebrity and glamour.

Wagner opens a new chapter in this operatic tradition of creating beauty that is erotically troubling, soul-piercing—the difference being that the intensity has been heightened by becoming, as it were, diffused. Though borne by the singer's voice, lyricism does not climax in the experience of the voice. Rather than being specifically, corporeally, identified with the singer's voice as it floats above the music, it has become a property of the music as a whole, in which the voice is embedded. (This is what is sometimes called the symphonism of Wagner's operas.)

Audiences have relished being excited, disturbed, troubled by the beauty of voices—their sweetness, their velocity. But there was, at least initially, considerable resistance to a *dérèglement du sens* produced by music as such. What the voice did seemed superhuman and as a display of virtuosity was, in itself, admirable. The sound produced by the castrati suggested something disembodied—the words "seraphic" and "heavenly" were often used to describe these voices, though the singers themselves were clearly objects of erotic fantasy as well. Wagner's maddening lyricism had nothing seraphic about it, whatever the spiritual messages and "higher" feelings being urged on us by the words; if anything, it seemed to come from "below," and, like the potion in the opera, to invite repressed feelings to flow forth. Berlioz described the Prelude to *Tristan und Isolde*, where no voices yet sing, as one long "groaning and moaning." Renouncing all the effects (and relief) of velocity, Wagner had chosen to slow down sequences of deep feeling that then either became enthralling or seemed unbearably oppressive. The Viennese music critic and leader of the anti-Wagnerians, Eduard Hanslick, said that the Prelude to *Tristan und Isolde* "reminds me of the Italian painting of a martyr whose intestines are slowly unwound from his body on a reel." *Parsifal*, he said, made him seasick. "There are no longer any real modulations but rather a perpetually undulating process of modulation so that the listener loses all sense of a definite tonality. We feel as though we were on the high seas, with no firm ground under our feet." Yes. We are.

The new emotional, as distinct from lyrical, intensity that Wagner brought into opera owes most to the way he both amplifies and makes excruciatingly intimate (despite the epic settings) the distinctive mix of feelings depicted: lust, tenderness, grief, pity, euphoria, world-weariness. Wagner utterly transforms feelings that are staples in opera's long tradition of representing exalted sentiments, such as the association of love and death. Hearts wounded by love, death that is preferable to separation from the beloved or the loss of love—this is the common coin of lovers' plaints, of lovers' ecstasies—long before Wagner, long before what we call Romanticism. Wagner, in *Tristan und Isolde* and elsewhere, made these old hyperboles of opera, understood to be expressive exaggerations, shatteringly literal. To speak nakedly and with unprecedented insistence about feeling, to be overwhelmingly intimate with audiences—Wagner's sensualism, his emotionalism, were experienced as invasive—was new territory for art in the mid-nineteenth century, and it seems inevitable that such shamelessness (as it was then judged by many) be attached to the permissions given by opera's rich, unabashed commitment to heightened states of feeling. "But for the opera I could never have written *Leaves of Grass*," Whitman told a disciple late in life (though he meant Italian opera, not Wagner). The treatment of time is one of Wagner's principal innovations: the extending of duration as a means of intensifying emotion. But the depth and grandeur of feeling of which Wagner is capable are combined, in his greatest work, with an extraordinary delicacy in the depiction of emotion. It is this delicacy that may finally convince us that we are indeed in the presence of that rarest of achievements in art, the reinvention of sublimity.

Bruno Walter once said to Thomas Mann, as they were walking home after Walter had conducted a performance of *Tristan und Isolde*, "That isn't even music any longer." Meaning, it is more than music. Wagner thought he was offering some kind of transforming experience or idea that transcended mere art. (Of course, he considered his works much more than mere operas.) But such claims seem mainly like an idea of art, a peculiarly modern idea of art, in which there is a great deal of expressed impatience with art. When artists aren't trying to subvert the art-status of what they do (saying, for instance, that it is really life), they often claim to be doing something more than art. (Religion? Therapy?) Wagner is an important part of this modern story of the inflation and coarsening of expectations about art, which has produced so many great works of art, among them *Tristan und Isolde*.

IT WAS OBSERVED from the beginning that listening to Wagner had an effect similar to consuming a psychotropic drug: opium, said Baudelaire; alcohol, said Nietzsche. And, as with all disinhibiting drugs, sometimes there were violent side effects. In the early years of *Tristan und Isolde* occasionally someone had to be evacuated from the theatre, fainting or vomiting, in the course of the performance. It is perhaps as hard now to imagine the impact on early audiences of Wagner, particularly of this opera, and the scandal which became part of that impact (I mean, of course, aesthetic scandal, leaving aside the issue of Wagner's repugnant political views), as it is to imagine the fainting and spasms of tears produced by the voice of Farinelli. But the scandal was immense, as was the passion with which he was defended—and the incalculable influence of his work. No artist of the nineteenth century was to be more influential.

Though Wagner was the first composer people boasted of not just admiring passionately but being addicted to, there have been others since. And the enchantments of addiction in art are now rarely viewed as anything but positive. In the era of rock 'n' roll and of Philip Glass and John Adams, it seems normal and desirable for music to aspire to be a narcotic. We live in the time of the triumph of the "theatrocracy" that Nietzsche deplored, in which we can find many descendants of Wagner's favorite dramatic form, the pseudo-spiritual pageant of redemption. And Wagner's characteristic means (the garrulous, soft-focus libretto; the exacerbated length; the organized repetitiveness) and themes (the praise of mindlessness, the featuring of the pathos of heroes and rulers) are those of some of the most enchanting spectacles of our own day.

Wagner's adaptations of the myths of the European and specifically the Germanic past (both Christian and pagan) do not involve belief. But they do involve ideas. Wagner was highly literate, and reflective in a literary way; he knew his sources. The creators of *Einstein on the Beach* made it clear that they knew nothing about Einstein, and thought they didn't have to. The emblems and bric-a-brac of heroic mythologies of the past that litter the work of the modern Wagnerians only express an even more generic pathos, and a generalized striving for effect. It is firmly thought that neither the creator nor the audience need have any information (knowledge, particularly historical knowledge, is considered to have a baleful effect on creativity and on feeling—the last and most tenacious of the clichés of Romanticism). The

Gesamtkunstwerk becomes a vehicle for moods—such as paranoia, placidity—that have floated free from specific emotional situations, and for non-knowing as such. And the aptness of these anti-literary, emotionally remote modern redemption-pageants may have confirmed a less troubled way of reacting to Wagner's highly literary, fervent ones. The smarmy, redeeming higher values that Wagner thought his work expressed have been definitively discredited (that much we owe the historic connection of Wagnerian ideology to Nazism). Few puzzle anymore, as did generations of Wagner lovers and Wagner fearers, about what Wagner's operas *mean*. Now Wagner is just enjoyed . . . as a drug.

"His pathos topples every taste." Nietzsche's acerbic remark about Wagner seems, a hundred years after it was made, truer than ever. But is there anyone left even to be ambivalent about Wagner now, in the way that Nietzsche and, to a lesser extent, Thomas Mann were? If not, then indeed much has been lost. I should think that feeling ambivalence (the opposite of being indifferent—you have to be seduced) is still the optimal mood for experiencing how authentically sublime a work *Tristan und Isolde* really is, and how strange and troubling.

[1987]

An Ecstasy of Lament

ALL ART, it has been said, aspires to the condition of music. And all arts made with music—but, more than any other, opera—aspire to the experience of ecstasy.

Originally, opera's ecstasies were provided by the singers. Stories—well-known intrigues from classical mythology, ancient history, and Renaissance epic—were dignified pretexts. The music, often glorious, was a platform. Whatever the pleasures afforded by the other elements (music, dance, poetry, scenography), opera was above all a vehicle for a unique reach of the human voice. This was something much more potent than "beautiful singing." What was released by the dramatic and musical occasion of opera was a substance experienced as sublime, virtually trans-human (in part because it was often transgendered), and so erotically affecting as to constitute a species of ravishment. (Think of the swoons and delirium that Farinelli and the other legendary castrati of the eighteenth and early nineteenth centuries provoked among men and women both—echoed, in diminuendo, by the adulation offered the great bel canto singers of our own century.) The model register was soaring, feminine; the gender line was arbitrary (men sang women's parts), and opera aroused emotions, excesses of reaction identified as feminine.

A more civically responsible idea of the ecstasies delivered by opera emerged when the devoted audience expanded from its aristocratic core to a much larger public, and attendance at "opera houses" became a ritual of urban bourgeois life. Opera experienced as preeminently a vehicle for the voice declined in favor of opera as the most inspiring, irresistible form of drama. Singing was a heroic rather than an uncanny enterprise, which furthered the "progressive" idea that the work of the voice and the work of music were at parity. It is about this time that opera began to reflect the nationalist projects of the European nineteenth century. The enthusiasm produced in opera houses fed on something the audience brought to the occasion: tribal self-congratulation. Being construed as an achievement of a national culture resulted inevitably in a certain normalization of opera ecstasies: sexual roles were locked into place; stories chosen (historical or folkloric) were constructed around the contrasts of feminine and masculine traits, vocal and characterological. The model responses of audiences became less outrageously feminine: invigoration, inspiration, exaltation.

It was precisely the composer with the largest ambition for opera, Richard Wagner, who, in addition to bringing this second idea of what opera can be—the apotheosis of a collective spirit—to its greatest, most solemn conclusion, also ushered in the third, or modern, idea of what opera can be: an isolating, ecstatic commotion of feeling aroused not by the sublime feats of a human voice but by exhausting, relentlessly ecstatic music. The voice rides the music; the music, rather than an independent ideal of vocal virtuosity, makes ever more difficult (initially felt to be impossible) demands on the voice. Music, Wagner's music, depicts the very condition of being flooded by feeling that the uncanny voice once provoked in audiences. The consequence was to weaken the authority of sharply contrasting feminine and masculine styles of emotional reaction—both on the opera stage (for all the masculinist pretensions of Wagnerian ideology) and in the minds of the opera public. But how could reinstating the goal of providing an immoderate, ravishing experience not entail a re-feminizing (in terms of the cultural stereotypes) of the most acute pleasure taken in opera?

FOR WAGNER, who created the idea of opera as overwhelming experience—and whose supreme dramatic subject is the progression of consciousness through ecstasy into oblivion—certain strictures about the story still held. Wagner could not have accepted as satisfying any drama left unresolved by an epiphany of acceptance, of understanding. Since Wagner, however, the stories that operas tell are more likely to end with collective dismay, with the defeat of understanding.

To be sure, some of the greatest operas (*L'incoronazione di Poppea, Così fan tutte, Fidelio, Don Carlo, Moses und Aron*) carry real arguments, real debate. But more commonly favored in opera are stories which are, in effect, tragedies of cognition. This is particularly true of what we could properly call modern opera, the transition to which is made by Wagner's last opera, *Parsifal*, whose protagonist enters the story as a child, a holy innocent, a fool. Subsequently, Parsifal does attain enlightenment—offstage. In later versions of this story the naïf remains in a state of unknowing. The central figure of modern opera is often someone in a state of deficient consciousness, of pathological innocence.

Pelléas et Mélisande is one of the masterpieces in this evolution. Onto one of the most traditional opera stories, that of a young man whose love for a woman his own age or younger is thwarted because she is promised or already married to an older relative (*Tristan und Isolde, Don Carlo, Eugene Onegin*, inter alia), is grafted the modern story about not understanding, not knowing, being balked by a mystery; or creating a mystery, by being afflicted by an unexplained injury or suffering.

Debussy's opera (following the Maeterlinck play used almost in its entirety as the libretto) has its special inflections. We are in the world without clear borders and fixed dimensions of Symbolist enigma: where appearances are known by their shadows or reflections, where debility and inexplicable affliction are equated with voluptuousness, and the emblematic object of desire is a languid childlike woman with Art Nouveau long hair.

In this kingdom of stretched, fairy-tale dualities—ancient and juvenile, ill and well, dark and light, wet and dry—is set a neo-Wagnerian tale of yearning and thwarting, of incurable vulnerability. Maeterlinck's drama can be read as an idealization of depression. It can also be seen as a representation, a literalizing, of once widely accepted ideas about physical illness—which attributed many illnesses, tautologically, to an illness-producing atmosphere ("miasma"). The story is set in precisely such a damp, sun-deprived environment, replete with water sources and subterranean spaces. Debussy began at the play's second scene, with Mélisande at a forest spring: "*Une petite fille qui pleure au bord de l'eau.*" (It was surely not for lack of thematic aptness that he cut the first scene of Maeterlinck's play: a chorus of castle servants calling for water.) The omnipresence of water, which generally signifies purity—or emotional volatility—here signifies a generalized unhealthiness.

Most characters are ill (Pelléas's father, Pelléas's friend Marcellus) or wounded (in the course of the story, Golaud) or infirm (the grandfather, Arkel) or physically weak (Golaud's little son, Yniold, who sings of his inability to lift a stone). Mélisande, of course, is the epitome of fragility—and dies of a wound that, the doctor says, would not kill a bird. (In Maeterlinck's play, the doctor adds, "*Elle est née sans raison . . . pour mourir; et elle meurt sans raison.*") Every reference to Mélisande emphasizes her smallness (her hands are always her "*petites mains*"), her untouchability (her first words are "*Ne me touchez pas! Ne me touchez pas!*"). Her benign discoverer, Golaud, who appears to her like a giant—and possibly a rapist—wins Mélisande by promising not to touch her, and by avowing his own vulnerability ("*Je suis perdu aussi*"). But when he brings Mélisande back to his family and begins to treat his child-bride as a woman, he becomes, despite himself, a brute.

The love of Pelléas and Mélisande cannot be consummated not because the young woman is married to an older relative of the young man's, the usual story, but because she is too fragile, sexually immature. Any adult sexuality would constitute an aggression against the heroine. Golaud is the story's one normally mature male character—in contrast to the ancient grandfather, whose request to kiss Mélisande is ostentatiously chaste, and to Golaud's young half brother, still a boy, who, when he wishes to embrace and be embraced by Mélisande, wraps himself in the part of her body that is not solid, not flesh: her hair. Mélisande seems endowed with a body only for others to marvel at its delicacy. It is startling to realize (I have never seen it depicted in any production of the opera) that Mélisande would be nine months pregnant when she and Pelléas finally do confess their love to each other, only immediately to be torn apart by the jealous Golaud. But her altered, swollen body is unmentionable, perhaps unstageable, and, in a certain sense, unthinkable. It is as if Mélisande herself cannot realize she is pregnant (and therefore a woman), for the same reason that, at the story's close, she cannot take in that she now has a daughter and is about to die.

Eventually the lovers do embrace, body to body, but this moment of shared immolation-in-feeling is cut short, to be followed by amnesia (Mélisande) and excruciating mental confusion (Golaud). Mélisande doesn't remember that Pelléas has been slain by Golaud, isn't aware that she has just given birth (*"Je ne sais pas ce que je dis . . . Je ne sais pas ce que je sais . . . Je ne dis plus ce que je veux"*), and is genuinely incapable of giving the frantically bereaved Golaud the relief of knowing that, however much he regrets what he has done, he was not wrong in suspecting that Mélisande and Pelléas were in love.

The well-intentioned Golaud has turned into one of opera's remorseful, inadvertent murderers who kills an innocent woman whom he truly loves. For in this story in which not just a protagonist but everyone feels inadequate, helpless, baffled by what she or he is feeling, Golaud is the only character physically capable of violence. Mental deficiency or frustrated understanding (combined with feelings of helplessness) is indeed a recipe for violence. Like *Wozzeck* and *Lulu*, like *Bluebeard's Castle*, *Pelléas et Mélisande* is a story of blind cruelty, with the difference that the cruelties perpetrated are not transactions between adult men and women but acts of adults against children. Mélisande is a lost child whom Golaud rescues and pledges to protect but cannot help destroying; in the anguish of jealousy he also manhandles his little son. But all this does not make the ogre any less a victim—like Wozzeck, like Peter Grimes, Golaud is innocently guilty—and therefore a proper object of the audience's pity.

Pity for the innocent lovers; pity for Yniold and the infant Mélisande has left; and pity for Golaud—*Pelléas et Mélisande* completes the process begun long ago whereby opera exalts the feelings regarded as feminine. No work that is now part of opera's standard repertory is so devoid of the triumphalist accents by which opera, traditionally, gives such pleasure. A robust art (compared with, say, chamber music), opera has specialized in broad—broadly contrasting, broadly legible—emotions. The emotional stream of Debussy's master-piece is deliberately narrower: he wagers on a more harrowing, more finely calibrated intensity. But the great modern tragedies of deficient consciousness propose their own voluptuous standards as they rise to an ecstasy of lament. Debussy's portrayal of *lacrimae rerum* is unlike any other in opera. It must be the saddest opera ever composed. (The only rival of *Pelléas et Mélisande* in this respect is *Wozzeck*, which also ends on the excruciating presence of a just-orphaned child.) As the heartbroken Arkel sings: "*Mais la tristesse, Golaud, mais la tristesse de toute que l'on voit!*"

[1997]

One Hundred Years
of Italian Photography

*I*TALY: ONE HUNDRED YEARS OF PHOTOGRAPHY announces a
double narrative: a century of Italy as well as a century of photography.

The earliest photograph in the book, taken in 1884, of the large
conservatory of the Italian Horticultural Society, shows us a place fre-
quented by well-off people of a century ago, some of whom probably
owned cameras and practiced photography at a very expert level as a
hobby; a picture like this could have been taken by one of the Society's
members. The most recent photograph, taken in 1984, shows us not a
real place (not an Italian interior, not even something in Italy) but a
portion of the world (Europe) of which Italy is a part; an aerial view,
it's a picture not so much taken as arranged, by professionals, aided by
computers.

There is nothing distinctively Italian about either photograph,
though both photographs bespeak their period. In the first one we see
a lush example of the glass-and-iron shape given to new exhibition
halls, markets, and railway stations all over Europe in the mid- and late
nineteenth century. The aerial photograph is also an example of a subject that could have been photographed elsewhere in the same way;
what dates it, though, is not *what* we see but *that* we can see it. It is an

example of something that can be seen only in the form of a photo-graph, and could only be photographed (thanks to the existence of other, allied technologies) now.

The subjects of both photographs have an obtrusive geometry; nei-ther includes people. But the conservatory is a site that appears to be just temporarily vacated of people, to get this picture of the overbear-ing architecture and the valiant plants. It is very much a human, histor-ically specific world. One easily imagines people reinserted in this place, milling about in it. The world of the aerial photograph is a world of things beyond the human scale from which people are necessarily absent. Here the human, historical fact has no place.

But history—time—is the unifying topic of this seemingly random collection of subjects. How striking, then, that the anthologist, Cesare Colombo, has selected as the most recent photograph one in which his-tory is annihilated in favor of geography; in which the accents of time are made irrelevant by the scale of this uniformly marked distribution of space.

Are we to read this as a history-minded comment on the part of the anthologist: an acknowledgment of the Euro-destiny of Italy, its demise as a distinctive culture and absorption into the homogenizing system of greeds created by multi-national capitalism? Or is it simply a formal device: the anthologist's perhaps overemphatic way of decreeing a clo-sure for the collection? If only the latter, the device is, of necessity, ar-bitrary. For it defies the very nature of photography, and of collections of photographs, which is that they are open-ended; that they cannot conclude. There can be no definitive or summative or terminal photo-graph, or collection of photographs. Only more photographs. More collections . . .

A COLLECTION OF IMAGES of the Italian past published by Alinari—though most of the photographs aren't from the Alinari archives—reminds us that a photograph is rarely a work of individual seeing but almost inevitably a (potential) unit in an archive. The archive can be that of the Alinari enterprise, which appears less as the very successful business it was than as a cultural operation, a vast collective endeavor for documenting Italian society that extended over many decades, in which the names of individual photographers have been suppressed, like those of the artisans who worked on the Gothic cathedrals. More often, the archive is that of single photographers— prolific professionals with studios from the nineteenth and the first half of the twentieth century, and also contemporary photographers whose manipulations of their subjects, in the service of fashion and other kinds of advertising, produce results that are most unlike the innocently scrupulous documentation practiced by older forms of commercial photography. Avowed proponents of bad taste such as Carlo Mollino and celebrants of celebrity such as Elio Luxardo are now museum-worthy, no less than such illustrious proponents of the serious and beautiful in photography as Paul Strand and Henri Cartier-Bresson. The most eccentric, partial view could constitute an archive of invaluable images of (from, about) the past. Even the soft-focus superimpositions of the self-styled Futurist Anton Bragaglia which are located nowhere and the staged *al fresco* fantasies of the erotomane Baron von Gloeden located in turn-of-the-twentieth-century Taormina have their period charm, their status as documents.

(Though the destiny of all photographs is to end up in an archive housed in a museum, they can still lead, singly, a life outside the museum—the extramural life of a document being that of a souvenir; here, too, time effects its droll mutations. In a journal entry of 1952 Jean Cocteau relates the story of a forty-year-old fisherman in Taormina, furious because one of the shops in the main street was exhibiting von Gloeden's photographs of his grandfather completely naked with a crown of roses. Surely it was just a few years later that, in all shops in town catering to tourists, von Gloeden's daintily erotic photographs of naked local youths of yesteryear were to be found as postcards.)

Italian photography is exceptionally rich in superb photographs which have a primary status as documents. One thinks, first of all, of the best images from the Alinari holdings and of the work of Giuseppe Primoli, the most fascinating figure in the history of Italian photography, who was himself something of a one-person Alinari enterprise. (A photograph by Primoli—of someone taking a photograph—begins this book.) If the collective activities of the Alinari firm and the ultra-individual enterprise practiced by the dilettante aristocrat Primoli were both supremely archive-creating ventures, it should be noted that the word "archive," with its implicit claim of disinterested curiosity, conceals much of the complex ideological agenda behind this glorious burst of picture-taking.

Consider the Alinari collection, more than a hundred thousand pictures. It seems like a nineteenth-century updating of the eighteenth-century *Wunderkammer*, or cabinet of curiosities, which was less an instrument of learning than an expression of collecting mania, the appetite for accumulation and classification; wonder, a favorite sentiment of that era, and one unburdened by historical understanding, depends on ignorance as much as on knowledge. But it also seems an example of a distinctively nineteenth-century ideological project, shared by some of the century's greatest novelists, which was to provide an encyclopedic understanding of social reality, from the highest to the lowest levels, as something that unfolds historically. Last, and perhaps most decisively, it seems like a proto-twentieth-century project: a mode of advertising, of creating needs and boosting consumption.

The Alinari photographers started by specializing in the great works of art of their native city, Florence. For a small, wealthy class of travelers on their Grand Tour, Italy had long been the country where one came to look at the art, and the art in Florence more than in any other Italian city. Collectible photographic documentation played an essential role in the democratizing of this construction of Italy by the happy few, which has made the country into the world's single most desired, most prestigious target for the instant appreciations of mass tourism.

The dissemination of art in the form of photographs—a first version of what André Malraux, who lifted the idea from Walter Benjamin, described as the museum without walls—was soon extended to the whole physical environment, which could be collected as pictures. Exhaustive documentation meant, in fact, a preference for the strongly *contrasting*: feats of urban renewal (as that was understood in the last century) juxtaposed with ancient sites and monuments, the vitality of the swarthy poor as well as the glamour and remoteness of the rich and powerful. Photographs disseminated not just art (the art of the past) but all of the past—and the present, inexorably on its way to becoming the past (that is, art). The notion of art is extended to include the past as such: we look at the past, any part of it, aesthetically.

PHOTOGRAPHS ARE NOT windows which supply a transparent view of the world as it is, or more exactly, as it was. Photographs give evidence—often spurious, always incomplete—in support of dominant ideologies and existing social arrangements. They fabricate and confirm these myths and arrangements.

How? By making statements about what is in the world, what we should look at. Photographs tell us how things ought to look, what their subjects should reveal about themselves.

Photographs taken in the nineteenth and early twentieth centuries rarely fail to make visible the markers of status. We associate this with posing. The process itself took time: one couldn't take photographs on the run. With posing, whether in a studio portrait or in pictures of people taken on the sites of work and recreation, there can be a conscious construction of what is seemly, appropriate, attractive. The way most old photographs look expounds the value of uprightness, explicitness, informativeness, orderly spacing; but from the 1930s on, and this cannot only be due to the evolution of camera technology, the look of photographs confirms the value of movement, animation, asymmetry, enigma, informal social relations. Modern taste judges the way workers in the old photographs of building sites and factories were stiffly posed to be a kind of lie—concealing, for instance, the reality of their physical exertion. We prefer to see the sweat, in informal, unposed-looking shots in which people are caught in a movement—that is what looks truthful (if not always beautiful) to us. We feel more comfortable with what features exertion, awkwardness, and conceals the realities of control (self-control, control by others), of power—revelations we now judge, oddly enough, to be "artificial."

Two contrasts, a century apart.

On the front endpaper, a celebrated image. It is the ordered, heavily signifying decor and spaciousness of the bourgeois photography

studio (in fact, the Alinari salon). Deep space: everyone is seen full figure, remotely, discreetly. Someone (seated, weighty) is being photographed. People seem becalmed. Everyone is taking his or her time.

On the endpaper at the back, a familiar kind of image. A pack of
journalists, *paparazzi*, standing, densely crowded together, straining,
shoving, taking their images by force. (Is there any justice in the fact
that the international word for predatory photographers who jump
their celebrity targets is Italian?) Shallow space: everyone is seen partially, close up, indiscreetly. Not enough of the room to identify it, no
decor—this is a placeless space. And everyone is in a big hurry.

THE FUNCTION OF an anthology is to represent a world. This anthology, this token chronicle of a century, represents a world as it sub-
mits to the imperatives of time.

Most of the pictures are records of a highly distinctive society that
is profoundly used (in several senses of the word), the Italy mourned
by Pasolini in *Uccellacci e uccellini*, the Italy that no longer exists, or is
dying, in the throes of being replaced, since the 1950s, by the trans-
Italian Italy of the consumer society. The difference between the two
Italys is enormous, visceral, shocking.

The distinctive Italy was a society in which the photographer's
practice was an incursion: the photographer could be only an observer.
In the new Italy the photograph and photographic activities (TV,
video, monitoring, playback) are central. It seems a new version of the
way that photography has participated in the past not only in the com-
mercialization of reality but in its unification. The Alinari enterprise,
founded in the early 1850s, could be regarded as itself an instrument of
the subsequent political unification of Italy, as the scope of the firm's
activities, which first had only Florence as its subject, broadened to include the countryside and other cities—the whole country. Now, for
several decades, Italian photography—photographic endeavors by
many hands—has participated mightily in the project of unifying Italy
culturally (which also means politically) with Europe, with the Atlantic
world. Photographic images play a large role in making Italy (be? or
only look?) more and more like . . . everywhere else.

All of Europe is in mourning for its past. Bookstores are stocked with albums of photographs offering up the vanished past for our delectation and reflex nostalgia. But the past has deeper roots in Italy than anywhere else in Europe, which makes its destruction more defining. And the elegiac note was sounded earlier and more plangently in Italy, as was the note of rancor—think of the Futurist tantrums about the past: the calls to burn the museums, fill in the Grand Canal and make it a highway, and so on. Comparable anthologies of photographs of, say, premodern France or Germany do not move in quite this way.

The depth possessed by these images of an older Italy is not just the depth of the past. It is the depth of a whole culture, a culture of incomparable dignity and flavor and bulk, that has been thinned out, effaced, confiscated. To be replaced by a culture in which the notion of depth is meaningless. That is not meant to be sauntered through. That becomes an abstraction. To be seen as an image. To be seen from the air . . .

[1987]

On Bellocq

F IRST OF ALL, the pictures are unforgettable—photography's
ultimate standard of value. And it's not hard to see why the
trove of glass negatives by a hitherto unknown photographer working
in New Orleans in the early years of this century became one of the
most admired recoveries in photography's widening, ever incomplete
history. Eighty-nine glass plates in varying states of corrosion, shatter,
and defacement were the treasure that Lee Friedlander came across in
New Orleans in the late 1950s and eventually purchased. When, in
1970, a selection of the ingeniously developed, superb prints Friedlander had made was published by the Museum of Modern Art, the
book became, deservedly, an instant classic. So much about these pictures affirms current taste: the low-life material; the near-mythic prove-
nance (Storyville); the informal, anti-art look, which accords with the
virtual anonymity of the photographer and the real anonymity of his
sitters; their status as *objets trouvés*, and a gift from the past. Add to
this what is decidedly unfashionable about the pictures: the plausibility
and friendliness of their version of the photographer's troubling, highly
conventional subject. And because the subject is so conventional, the
photographer's relaxed way of looking seems that much more distinctive. If there had once been more than eighty-nine glass negatives
and one day a few others turned up, no one would fail to recognize a
Bellocq.

The year is 1912, but we would not be surprised to be told that the pictures were taken in 1901, when Theodore Dreiser began writing *Jennie Gerhardt*, or in 1899, when Kate Chopin published *The Awakening*, or in 1889, the year Dreiser set the start of his first novel, *Sister Carrie*— the ballooning clothes and plump bodies could be dated anywhere from 1880 to the beginning of World War I. The charges of indecency that greeted Chopin's second novel and Dreiser's first were so unrelenting that Chopin retreated from literature and Dreiser faltered. (Anticipating more such attacks, Dreiser, after beginning his great second novel in 1901, put it aside for a decade.) Bellocq's photographs belong to this same world of anti-formulaic, anti-salacious sympathy for "fallen" women, though in his case we can only speculate about the origin of that sympathy. Until recently we knew nothing about the author of these pictures except what some old cronies of Bellocq's told Friedlander: that he had no other interests except photography; that "he always behaved polite" (this from one of his Storyville sitters); that he spoke with a "terrific" French accent; and that he was—shades of Toulouse-Lautrec—hydrocephalic and dwarf-like. It turns out that he was an entirely normal-looking scion of the New Orleans middle class (his grandparents were born in France), who also photographed quite conventional subjects as well as other low-life ones—for example, the opium dens of New Orleans's Chinatown. The Chinatown series, alas, has never been recovered.

The Storyville series includes two pictures of parlor decor. The interest for Bellocq must have been that, above a fireplace in one picture and a rolltop desk in the other, the walls are covered with photographs surrounding a central painting, photographs with the same contrasts as the ones he was taking: all are of women, some dressed to the nines, some erotically naked. The rest of Bellocq's photographs are individual portraits. That is, there is a single subject per picture, except for a shot of two champagne drinkers on the floor absorbed in a card game (there is a similar off-duty moment in Buñuel's unconvincing, notional portrait of a brothel in *Belle de Jour*) and another of a demure girl posing in her Sunday best, long white dress and jacket and hat, beside an iron bed in which someone is sleeping. Typically—an exception is this picture, which shows only the sleeping woman's head and right arm—Bellocq photographs his subjects in full figure, though sometimes a seated figure will be cut off at the knees; in only one picture—a naked woman reclining on some embroidered pillows—does one have the impression that Bellocq has chosen to come in close. Central to the impression the pictures make on us is that there are a large number of them, with the same setting and cast in a variety of poses, from the most natural to the most self-conscious, and degrees of dress/undress. That they are part of a series is what gives the photographs their integrity, their depth, their meaning. Each individual picture is informed by the meaning that attaches to the whole group.

Most obviously, it could not be detected from at least a third of the pictures that the women are inmates of a brothel. Some are fully clothed: in one picture a woman in a large feathered hat, long-sleeved white blouse adorned with brooch and locket, and black skirt sits in the yard in front of a low black backdrop, just beyond which frayed towels are drying on a laundry line. Others are in their underwear or something like it: one poses on a chair, her hands clasped behind her head, wearing a comical-looking body stocking. Many are photographed naked—with unpretentious candor about, mostly, unpretentious bodies. Some just stand there, as if they didn't know what to do once they had taken off their clothes for the camera. Only a few offer a voluptuous pose, like the long-tressed adolescent odalisque on a wicker divan—probably Bellocq's best-known picture. Two photographs show women wearing masks. One is a come-hither picture: an exceptionally pretty woman with a dazzling smile reclines on a chaise longue; apart from her trim Zorro-style mask she is wearing only black stockings. The other picture, the opposite of a pin-up, is of a large-bellied, entirely naked woman whose mask sits as awkwardly on her face as she is awkwardly posed on the edge of a wooden chair; the mask (it appears to be a full mask minus its lower half) seems too big for her face. The first woman seems happy to pose (as, given her charms, well she might); the second seems diminished, even foiled, by her nudity. In some pictures, in which the sitters adopt a genteelly pensive look, the emotion is harder to read. But in others there is little doubt that posing is a game, and fun: the woman in the shawl and vivid striped stockings sitting beside her bottle of "Raleigh Rye," appreciatively eyeing her raised glass; the woman in ample undergarments and black stockings stretched out on her stomach over an ironing board set up in the backyard, beaming at a tiny dog. Clearly, no one was being spied on, everyone was a willing subject. And Bellocq couldn't have dictated to them how they should pose—whether to exhibit themselves as they might for a customer or, absent the customers, as the wholesome-looking country women most of them undoubtedly were.

We are far, in Bellocq's company, from the staged sadomasochistic hijinks of the bound women offering themselves up to the male gaze (or worse) in the disturbingly acclaimed photographs of Nobuyoshi Araki or the cooler, more stylish, unvaryingly intelligent lewdness of the images devised by Helmut Newton. The only pictures that do seem salacious—or convey something of the meanness and abjection of a prostitute's life—are those on which the faces have been scratched out. (In one, the vandal—could it have been Bellocq himself?—missed the face.) These pictures are actually painful to look at, at least for this viewer. But then I am a woman and, unlike many men who look at these photographs, find nothing romantic about prostitution. That part of the subject I do take pleasure in is the beauty and forthright presence of many of the women, photographed in homely circumstances that affirm both sensuality and domestic ease, and the tangibleness of their vanished world. How touching and good-natured the pictures are.

[1996]

Borland's Babies

1

THE TITLE IS *The Babies.* More than one. A group. A fellowship, it appears. More than one such fellowship or band or coterie. A world.

A cunningly sequenced album of pictures inducts us into this world.

It would convey little to have only one photograph. Or two. Or three. To show a world calls for an abundance of photographs, and the photographs have to be arranged. First things first. The last for the last.

The sequence will be a tour of this world. A journey. An initiation.

First we see bits of decor. A small pink satin dress. A teddy bear. A colorful crib sheet printed with cuddly animals. Then, gradually, the presence of the human. A pair of shoes. Bunny slippers. A foot. A knee.

It will be a while before we see faces.

Something doesn't fit. The accoutrements are those of the nursery. But the human presence is too large, ugly—Brobdingnagian.

We expect babies. These seem to be adult men. The skin of babies, real babies, is perfect. This skin is rough, blotchy, hairy (with here and there a tattoo), the bodies mostly flabby or scrawny—and Polly Borland's camera scrutinizes them very closely.

Close is ugly. And adult is ugly, when compared with the perfection of the recently born.

As Gulliver observes after reaching a country whose inhabitants are over eighty feet tall: to see enlarged *is* to be taken aback by imperfections. He recalls that in the country from which he's come, where *he* was a giant, the complexion of the diminutive Lilliputians had appeared to him "the fairest in the world," while his tiny new friends found him ugly beyond imagining. One of them

> said that my face appeared much fairer and smoother when he looked on me from the ground, than it did upon a nearer view when I took him up in my hand and brought him close, which he confessed was at first a very shocking sight. He said he could discover great holes in my skin; that the stumps of my beard were ten times stronger than the bristles of a boar, and my complexion made up of several colors altogether disagreeable: although I must beg leave to say for myself, that I am as fair as most of my sex and country, and very little sunburnt by all my travels.

Stranded among the people of Brobdingnag, Part II of *Gulliver's Travels*, where he's the tiny person, Gulliver finds these mountainous bodies and faces repulsive in exactly the same way that he was, in close-up, to the people of Lilliput. But, even while recoiling from their gross imperfections, Gulliver reminds himself—good cultural relativist that he's become—that the Brobdingnagians are no doubt just as handsome as any other people in the world.

A world, according to Jonathan Swift, and as depicted by Polly Borland, replete with disconcerting oddities.

By the standard of the baby, any adult is ugly, coarse. No beauty of skin can withstand the too intimate scrutiny of the camera.

Beauty, adorableness—and repulsiveness—are mainly a matter of favoring or disfavoring scale, and proximity. And that—scale, proximity—is what photographers deal with all the time.

2

OF COURSE, BEING "CLOSE" is essential to the impact and the meaning of these photographs.

Virtually all of them were taken in some generic, meanly furnished indoors. We may suppose Borland's subjects to be hiding in these drab, wallpapered rooms which we never see most of, but which feel small. They may only be lying about. (Babies need a lot of rest.) As well as coming and going. We also seem to be offered glimpses of the convening of a boisterous clan. A party of tots. A children's sleepover.

The photographer has penetrated a space where a secret identity unfolds. An intimate, private space whose banal activities—yowling, drooling, eating, sleeping, bathing, masturbating—here acquire the character of weird rituals, because they're done by adult men dressed as, and carrying on like, babies.

It has to come as a surprise when, late in the book, there is a photograph of three of the babies in full regalia on a suburban street. (Australia? England?) Surprise that some of Borland's subjects are willing to offer themselves to the gaze of casual passersby.

3

A PROGRESS OF PHOTOGRAPHS. We are introduced to this world in the guise of parts of bodies, oddly framed and cropped. The initial withholding of faces, and the number of pictures taken from a high angle, bolster the relation of superiority that we, the consumers of Borland's images, seem invited to have (at first) to these clandestine shenanigans.

We look at them. They don't look at us. We are rarely shown the babies seeing; when we are, it's a baby-style gaze, wobbly focus and all, or a look of concentrated self-absorption.

Properly, the book ends with a straight-on portrait of one of the babies, looking adult, even handsome, gazing intently at the camera, at us. Staring back. At last.

4

FOR A LONG TIME the camera has been bringing us news about zanies and pariahs, their miseries and their quirks. Showing the banality of the non-normal. Making voyeurs out of us all.

But this is particularly gifted, authoritative work. Borland's pictures seem very knowing, compassionate; and too close, too *familiar*, to suggest common or mere curiosity. There is nothing of the ingenuous stare of a Diane Arbus picture. (I don't doubt that Arbus would have felt invited by these subjects, but surely she would have photographed them very differently.)

Zeal in colonizing new, especially transgressive, subject matter is one of the main traditions of photographic practice.

Here—says this book—is a specimen of behavior that has a legitimate claim on our interest and attention. The pictures register a truth about human nature which seems almost too obvious to spell out—the temptation of regression? the pleasures of regression?—but which has never received so keen, so direct a depiction. They invite our identification ("nothing human is alien to me")—daring us to admit that we, too, can imagine such feelings, even if we are astonished that some people actually go to the trouble, and assume the shame, of acting them out.

5

ARE THESE PICTURES shocking?

Some people apparently find them so. Probably not the same people made indignant by the sex-pictures of Robert Mapplethorpe. Here the shock is produced by scenes from the intimate life of adult men who appear to have all but completely renounced their sexuality.

I, for one, don't find these pictures shocking or even upsetting. (What shocks me is cruelty, not sadness.)

Shock—which then dilates into aggressive disapproval—seems to me a somewhat pointless reaction to adults who have so dramatically embraced the role of being helpless.

In most of the pictures, the subjects are sitting, lying down, crawling. They are often on beds or close to the floor. They are rarely vertical.

They *want* to look small. But of course they're not. So, instead, they look mortified.

There is a presumption, when picture-taking assumes an anthropological or ethnographic function, that the subjects—who happen to look the way they do—don't really see themselves.

What these pictures suggest—what some may find *is* disturbing about them—is that not only do Borland's subjects want to look like this but they relish being seen.

6

MOST OF THE sexual acting-out understood as deviant is theatre. It requires dressing up. It relies on props. And the world created by these adults must be counted as a sexual fantasy, even if, most of them being "baby purists," they don't have sex.

What goes on in these depressing rooms is a kind of theatre. Playtime.

But entirely unfeigned.

And without manipulation by the camera. Nothing is digitalized. Borland's project depends on the photographs being—as of old—a trace or imprint of the real. There is an implicit contract: these are people who really are (part of the time) like this; they aren't putting on a show for the photographer. Indeed, she had to spend long periods of time with them, win their confidence, become friends, in order to take these pictures.

Imagine what we would feel if we learned that the men are actors, and that the pictures were taken in the course of an afternoon in one house rather than (as they were) over years and in several countries.

The force of these pictures depends on our trusting the photographer that nothing was devised *for* the camera.

That something is being revealed.

7

ARE THE BABIES really unattractive—like, say, the folk in Roger Ballen's *Platteland* (1994)?

In Ballen's marvelous album of portraits of degenerate-looking whites in rural South Africa, the unattractiveness of his subjects and the rooms they inhabit delivers a moral, ultimately political, message. Here ugliness seems to attest to an appalling impoverishment of spirit as well as of material circumstances. In Borland's album, the message of her subjects' unattractiveness is harder to read. We might decide it is mainly one of scale: that is, of the mismatch between the enacted fantasy of smallness and feebleness and these hefty grownup bodies. But we might also suppose, perhaps wrongly, that only adults who look as they do would want to do "this" to themselves.

What are the frontiers of attractiveness—and of unattractiveness? Images produced by cameras have more to tell us, in unpacking this question, than any other resource. Maybe we are no longer capable of thinking about the attractiveness of bodies and faces except in the ways we've learned through the camera's presumptuous seeing. Enlarging, miniaturizing—the camera judges, the camera reveals. Looking at the world to which Borland has given us entry, we don't know whether we're in Lilliput or in Brobdingnag. Her brilliant achievement makes us realize that, when we see photographically, we're living in both.

[2001]

Certain Mapplethorpes

ALTHOUGH REASON TELLS ME the camera is not aimed like a gun barrel at my head, each time I pose for a photographic portrait I feel apprehensive. This is not the well-known fear, exhibited in many cultures, of being robbed of one's soul or a layer of one's personality. I do not imagine that the photographer, in order to bring the image-replica into the world, robs me of anything. But I do register that the way I ordinarily experience myself is turned around.

Ordinarily I feel coextensive with my body, in particular with the command station of the head, whose orientation to the world (that is, frontality)—and articulation—is my face, in which are set eyes that look out on, into, the world; and it is my fantasy, and my privilege, perhaps my professional bias, to feel that the world awaits my seeing. When I am photographed, this normally outgoing, fervent relation of consciousness to the world is jammed. I yield to another command station of consciousness, which "faces" me, if I have agreed to cooperate with the photographer (and, customarily, a photographic portrait is one that requires the subject's cooperation). Stowed away, berthed, brought to heel, my consciousness has abdicated its normal function, which is to provide amplitude, to give me mobility. I don't feel threatened. But I do feel disarmed, my consciousness reduced to an embarrassed knot of self-consciousness striving for composure. Immobilized for the camera's scrutiny, I feel the weight of my facial mask, the jut and fleshiness of my lips, the spread of my nostrils, the unruliness of my hair. I experience myself as *behind* my face, looking out through the windows of my eyes, like the prisoner in the iron mask in Dumas's novel.

Being photographed, by which I mean posing for a photograph (at a session usually lasting several hours, in which many photographs are taken), I feel transfixed, trapped. In response to a look of desire I can look back, with desire. The looking can, ideally should, be reciprocal. But to the photographer's look I cannot respond with anything equivalent, unless I were to decide to be photographed with my head behind my own camera. The photographer's look is looking in a pure state; in looking at me, it desires what I am not—my image.

(Of course, the photographer may in fact desire the subject. It is obvious that many of Robert Mapplethorpe's photographs record objects of his desire. Subjects may seem worth photographing because the photographer feels lust, or romantic attachment, or admiration—any of a myriad of positive feelings. But at the moment the picture is taken, the look trained upon the subject is sightless, generic: a look that discerns form. At that moment, it cannot be responded to in kind.)

I become the looked-at. Docilely, eagerly, I follow the photographer's instructions, if she or he is willing to give any, as to how I may "look" more attractive. For as much as I am a professional see-er, I am a hopelessly amateurish see-ee. An eternal photographic virgin, I feel the same perplexity each time I'm photographed. I forget the makeup tricks I've been taught, what color blouse photographs well, which side of my face is the "good" side. My chin is too low. Too high. I don't know what to do with my hands.

Considering that I have been browsing through the history of photography for decades, have been photographed professionally countless times, and spent five years writing six essays about the aesthetic and moral implications of photographic images, this blankness with which I face the camera can hardly be ascribed to inexperience or to lack of reflectiveness. Some deeper stubbornness on my own part is at work: the refusal fully to take in the fact that I not only look but have a look, look good (or bad), look "like" that.

As I've never been photographed without feeling apprehensive, so I have never looked at the result of a photographic session without feeling embarrassment. Is it that I'm too powerfully an observer myself to be comfortable being observed? Is it a puritan anxiety about pretending, posing? Is it my moral narcissism, which has erected a taboo against whatever narcissism of the usual kind to which I might be prone? All of these, perhaps. But what I mainly feel is dismay. While some ninety percent of my consciousness thinks that I am in the world, that I am me, about ten percent thinks I am invisible. That part is always appalled whenever I see a photograph of myself. (Especially a photograph in which I look attractive.)

The photograph comes as a kind of reproof to the grandiosity of consciousness. Oh. So there "I" am.

I see my own photograph differently from the others in Mapplethorpe's *Certain People*. I can't look at my own photograph with longing, I can't have a fantasy about the person in *that* photograph. The eros of photography, which identifies subject and surface, is suspended. What I feel is the difference between me and the image. To me, the expression in the photograph Mapplethorpe has taken of me is not really "my" look. It is a look fabricated for the camera: an unstable compromise between trying to be cooperative with a photographer I intensely admire (who is also a friend) and trying to preserve my own dignity, which is hinged to my anxiety. (When I look at my picture I read stubbornness, balked vanity, panic, vulnerability.) I doubt that I have ever looked exactly the way Mapplethorpe has photographed me—or that I will look exactly this way the next time he takes my picture.

At the same time that I recognize in this portrait another record of how I feel being photographed, Mapplethorpe's photograph looks different to me from any other that has ever been taken of me. I cooperated as best I could, and he saw something that no one had ever seen. Being photographed by Mapplethorpe was different from being photographed by anyone else. He reassures differently, encourages differently, is permissive differently . . .

Taking pictures is an anthologizing impulse, and Mapplethorpe's book offers no exception. This mix of subjects, the non-famous and the celebrated, the solemn and the lascivious, illustrates a characteristic spread of photographic interests. Nothing human is alien to me, the photographer is saying. By including a sexy self-portrait, Mapplethorpe is rejecting the typical photographer's stance, in which, from a godlike distance, the photographer confers reality upon the world but declines to be a subject himself.

Most photography comes with a built-in cognitive claim: that the photograph conveys a truth about the subject, a truth that would not be known were it not captured in a photograph. In short, that photographing is a form of knowledge. Thus, some photographers have said they photograph best someone whom they don't know, others that their best photographs are of subjects they know best. All such claims, however contradictory, are claims of power over the subject.

Mapplethorpe's claims are more modest. He is not looking for the decisive moment. His photographs do not aspire to be revelatory. He is not in a predatory relation to his subjects. He is not voyeuristic. He is not trying to catch anyone off guard. The rules of the game of photography, as Mapplethorpe plays it, are that the subject must cooperate—must be lit. In the eloquence and subtlety of cropping, rendering of textures of clothing and skin, and variations on the color black, his photographs clearly proclaim their relation to an artistic, rather than documentarist, impulse. The photographer himself would probably prefer to say they are a record of his own avidity.

Mapplethorpe wants to photograph everything, that is, everything that can be made to pose. (However broad his subject matter, he could never become a war photographer or a photographer of accidents in the street.) What he looks for, which could be called Form, is the quiddity or *is*ness of something. Not the truth about something, but the strongest version of it.

I once asked Mapplethorpe what he does with himself when he poses for the camera, and he replied that he tries to find that part of himself that is self-confident.

His answer suggests a double meaning in the title he has chosen for his book: there is certain in the sense of some, and not others, and certain in the sense of self-confident, sure, clear. *Certain People* depicts, mostly, people found, coaxed, or arranged into a certainty about themselves. That is what seduces, that is what is disclosed in these bulletins of a great photographer's observations and encounters.

[1985]

A Photograph Is Not an Opinion.
Or Is It?

U NDERTAKE TO DO a book of photographs of people with
nothing more in common than that they are women (and living in America at the end of the twentieth century), all—well, almost
all—fully clothed, therefore not the *other* kind of all-women picture
book . . .

Start with no more than a commanding notion of the sheer interestingness of the subject, especially in view of the unprecedented changes
in the consciousness of many women in these last decades, and a resolve to stay open to whim and opportunity . . .

Sample, explore, revisit, choose, arrange, without claiming to have
brought to the page a representative miscellany . . .

Even so, a large number of pictures of what is, nominally, a single
subject will inevitably be felt to be representative in *some* sense. How
much more so with this subject, with this book, an anthology of destinies and disabilities and new possibilities; a book that invites the sympathetic responses we bring to the depiction of a minority (for that is
what women are, by every criterion except the numerical), featuring

This essay was written to accompany a book of photographs, *Women*, by Annie Leibovitz
(Random House, 1999).

many portraits of those who are a credit to their sex. Such a book has to feel instructive, even if it tells us what we think we already know about the overcoming of perennial impediments and prejudices and cultural handicaps, the conquest of new zones of achievement. Of course, such a book would be misleading if it did not touch on the bad news as well: the continuing authority of demeaning stereotypes, the continuing violence (domestic assault is the leading cause of injuries to American women). Any large-scale picturing of women belongs to the ongoing story of how women are presented, and how they are invited to think of themselves. A book of photographs of women must, whether it intends to or not, raise the question of women—there is no equivalent "question of men." Men, unlike women, are not a work in progress.

Each of these pictures must stand on its own. But the ensemble says, So this is what women are now—as different, as varied, as heroic, as forlorn, as conventional, as unconventional as *this*. Nobody scrutinizing the book will fail to note the confirmation of stereotypes of what women are like and the challenge to those stereotypes. Whether well known or obscure, each of the nearly one hundred and seventy women in this album will be looked at (especially by other women) as models: models of beauty, models of self-esteem, models of strength, models of transgressiveness, models of victimhood, models of false consciousness, models of successful aging.

No book of photographs of men would be interrogated in the same way.

But then a book of photographs of men would not be undertaken in the same spirit. How could there be any interest in asserting that a man can be a stockbroker or a farmer or an astronaut or a miner? A book of photographs of men with sundry occupations, men only (without any additional label), would probably be a book about the beauty of men, men as objects of lustful imaginings to women and to other men.

But when men are viewed as sex objects, that is not their primary identity. The traditions of regarding men as, at least potentially, the creators and curators of their own destinies and women as objects of male emotions and fantasies (lust, tenderness, fear, condescension, scorn, dependence), of regarding an individual man as an instance of humankind and an individual woman as an instance of women, are still largely intact, deeply rooted in language, narrative, group arrangements, and family customs. In no language does the pronoun "she" stand for human beings of both sexes. Women and men are differently weighted, physically and culturally, with different contours of selfhood, all presumptively favoring those born male.

I do this, I endure this, I want this . . . because I am a woman. I do that, endure that, I want that . . . even though I'm a woman. Because of the mandated inferiority of women, their condition as a cultural minority, there continues to be a debate about what women are, can be, should want to be. Freud is famously supposed to have asked, "Lord, what do women want?" Imagine a world in which it seems normal to inquire, "Lord, what do men want?" But who can imagine such a world?

No one thinks the Great Duality is symmetrical—even in America, noted since the nineteenth century by foreign travelers as a paradise for uppity women. Feminine and masculine are a tilted polarity. Equal rights for men has never inspired a march or a hunger strike. In no country are men legal minors, as women were until well into the twentieth century in many European countries, and are still in many Muslim countries, from Morocco to Afghanistan. No country gave women the right to vote before giving it to men. Nobody ever thought of men as the second sex.

AND YET, AND YET: there is something new in the world, starting with the revoking of age-old legal shackles regarding suffrage, divorce, property rights. It seems almost inconceivable now that the enfranchisement of women happened as recently as it did—that, for instance, women in France and Italy had to wait until 1945 and 1946 to be able to vote. There have been tremendous changes in women's consciousness, transforming the inner life of everyone: the sallying forth of women from women's worlds into the world at large, the arrival of women's ambitions. Ambition is what women have been schooled to stifle in themselves, and what is celebrated in a book of photographs that emphasizes the variety of women's lives today.

Such a book, however much it attends to women's activeness, is also about women's attractiveness.

Nobody looks through a book of pictures of women without noticing whether the women are attractive or not.

To be feminine, in one commonly felt definition, *is* to be attractive, or to do one's best to be attractive, to attract. (As being masculine is being strong.) While it is perfectly possible to defy this imperative, it is not possible for any woman to be unaware of it. As it is thought a weakness in a man to care a great deal about how he looks, it is a moral fault in a woman not to care enough. Women are judged by their appearance as men are not, and women punished more by the changes brought about by aging. Ideals of appearance such as youthfulness and slimness are in large part now created and enforced by photographic images. And, of course, a primary interest in having photographs of well-known beauties to look at over the years is seeing just how well or badly they negotiate the shame of aging.

In advanced consumer societies, it is said, these "narcissistic" values are more and more the concern of men as well. But male primping never loosens the male lock on initiative taking. Indeed, glorying in one's appearance is an ancient warrior's pleasure, an expression of power, an instrument of dominance. Anxiety about personal attractiveness could never be thought defining of a man: a man is, first of all, seen. Women are looked at.

We assume a world with a boundless appetite for images, in which people, women and men, are eager to surrender themselves to the camera. But it is worth recalling that there are many parts of the world where being photographed is off-limits to women. In a few countries, where men have been mobilized for a veritable war against women, women scarcely *appear* at all. The imperial rights of the camera—to gaze at, to record, to exhibit anyone, anything—are an exemplary feature of modern life, as is the emancipation of women. And just as the granting of more and more rights and choices to women is a measure of a society's embrace of modernity, so the revolt against modernity initiates a rush to rescind the meager gains toward equal participation in society won by women, mostly urban, educated women, in previous decades. In many countries struggling with failed or discredited attempts to modernize, there are more and more *covered* women.

THE TRADITIONAL UNITY of a book of photographs of women is some ideal of female essence: women gaily displaying their sexual charms, women veiling themselves behind a look of soulfulness or primness.

Portraits of women featured their beauty; portraits of men their "character." Beauty (the province of women) was smooth; character (the province of men) was rugged. Feminine was yielding, placid, or plaintive; masculine was forceful, piercing. Men didn't look wistful. Women, ideally, didn't look forceful.

When in the early 1860s a well-connected, exuberant, middle-aged Englishwoman named Julia Margaret Cameron took up the camera as a vocation, she invariably photographed men differently than she photographed women. The men, who included some of the most eminent poets, sages, and scientists of the Victorian era, were posed for their portraits. The women—somebody's wife, daughter, sister, niece— served mostly as models for "fancy subjects" (Cameron's label). Women were used to personify ideals of womanliness drawn from literature or mythology: the vulnerability and pathos of Ophelia; the tenderness of the Madonna with her Child. Almost all the sitters were relatives and friends—or her parlor maid, who, suitably reclothed, incarnated several exalted icons of femininity. Only Julia Jackson, Cameron's niece (and the future mother of the future Virginia Woolf), was, in homage to her exceptional beauty, never posed as anyone but herself.

What qualified the women as sitters was precisely their beauty, as fame and achievement qualified the men. The beauty of women made them ideal subjects. (Notably, there was no role for picturesque or exotic beauty, so that after Cameron and her husband moved to Ceylon, she took very few pictures.) Indeed, Cameron defined photography as a quest for the beautiful. And quest it was: "Why does not Mrs. Smith come to be photographed?" she wrote to a friend about a lady in London whom she had never met. "I hear she is Beautiful. Bid her come, and she shall be made Immortal."

IMAGINE A BOOK of pictures of women in which none of the women could be identified as beautiful. Wouldn't we feel that the photographer had made some kind of mistake? Was being mean-spirited? Misogynistic? Was depriving us of something that we had a right to see? No one would say the equivalent thing of a book of portraits of men.

THERE WERE ALWAYS several kinds of beauty: imperious beauty, voluptuous beauty, beauty signifying the character traits that fitted a woman for the confines of genteel domesticity—docility, pliancy, serenity. Beauty was not just loveliness of feature and expression, an aesthetic ideal. It also spoke to the eye about the virtues deemed essential in women.

For a woman to be intelligent was not essential, not even particularly appropriate. It was in fact considered disabling, and likely to be inscribed in her appearance. Such is the fate of a principal character in *The Woman in White*, Wilkie Collins's robustly, enthrallingly clever novel, which appeared in 1860, just before Cameron started making her portraits. Here is how this woman is introduced, early in the book, in the voice of its young hero:

> I looked from the table to the window farthest from me, and saw a lady standing at it, with her back turned towards me. The instant my eyes rested on her, I was struck by the rare beauty of her form, and by the unaffected grace of her attitude. Her figure was tall, yet not too tall; comely and well-developed, yet not fat; her head set on her shoulders with an easy, pliant firmness; her waist, perfection in the eyes of a man, for it occupied its natural place, it filled out its natural circle, it was visibly and delightfully undeformed by stays. She had not heard my entrance into the room; and I allowed myself the luxury of admiring her

for a few moments, before I moved one of the chairs near me, as the least embarrassing means of attracting her attention. She turned towards me immediately. The easy elegance of every movement of her limbs and body as soon as she began to advance from the far end of the room set me in a flutter of expectation to see her face clearly. She left the window—and I said to myself, The lady is dark. She moved forward a few steps—and I said to myself, The lady is young. She approached nearer—and I said to myself (with a sense of surprise which words fail me to express), The lady is ugly!

Reveling in the effrontery and delights of the appraising male gaze, the narrator has noted that, seen from behind and in long shot, the lady satisfies all the criteria of female desirability. Hence his acute surprise, when she turns and comes toward him, at her "ugly" face (it is not allowed to be just plain or homely), which, he explains, is a kind of paradox:

Never was the old conventional maxim, that Nature cannot err, more flatly contradicted—never was the fair promise of a lovely figure more strangely and startlingly belied by the face and head that crowned it. The lady's complexion was almost swarthy, and the dark down on her upper lip was almost a moustache. She had a large, firm, masculine mouth and jaw; prominent, piercing, resolute brown eyes; and thick, coal-black hair, growing unusually low down on her forehead. Her expression—bright, frank, and intelligent—appeared, while she was silent, to be altogether wanting in those feminine attractions of gentleness and pliability, without which the beauty of the handsomest woman alive is beauty incomplete.

Marian Halcombe will turn out to be the most admirable character in Collins's novel, awarded every virtue except the capacity to inspire desire. Moved only by generous, noble sentiments, she has a near-angelic, that is, archetypally feminine, temperament—except for the troubling matter of her uncommon intelligence, her frankness, her want of "pliability." Marian Halcombe's body, so ideally feminine that it is judged ripe for appropriation by a presumptively male artist, conveys "modest graces of action." Her head, her face, signifies something more concentrated, exacting—unfeminine. The body gives one message, the face another. And face trumps body—as intelligence, to the detriment of female sexual attractiveness, trumps beauty. The narrator concludes:

> To see such a face as this set on shoulders that a sculptor would have longed to model—to be charmed by the modest graces of action through which the symmetrical limbs betrayed their beauty when they moved, and then to be almost repelled by the masculine form and masculine look of the features in which the perfectly shaped figure ended—was to feel a sensation oddly akin to the helpless discomfort familiar to us all in sleep, when we recognise yet cannot reconcile the anomalies and contradictions of a dream.

Collins's male narrator is touching a gender fault line, which typically arouses anxieties and feelings of discomfort. The contradiction in the order of sexual stereotypes may seem dream-like to a well-adjusted inhabitant of an era in which action, enterprise, artistic creativity, and intellectual innovation are understood to be masculine, fraternal orders. For a long time the beauty of a woman seemed incompatible, or at least oddly matched, with intelligence and assertiveness. (A far greater novelist, Henry James, in the preface to *The Portrait of a Lady*, speaks of the challenge of filling the "frail vessel" of a female protagonist with all the richness of an independent consciousness.) To be sure, no novelist today would find it implausible to award good looks to a woman who is both cerebral and self-assertive. But in real life, it's still common to begrudge a woman who has beauty as well as intellectual brilliance—one would never say there was something odd or intimidating or "unfair" about a man who was so fortunate—as if beauty, the ultimate enabler of feminine charm, should by rights have barred other kinds of excellence.

IN A WOMAN BEAUTY is something total. It is what stands, in a woman, for character. It is also, of course, a performance; something willed, designed, obtained. Looking through an old family photograph album, the Russian-born French writer Andreï Makine recalls a trick used to get the particular glow of beauty he saw in some of the women's faces:

> These women knew that in order to be beautiful, what they must do several seconds before the flash blinded them was to articulate the following mysterious syllables in French, of which few understood the meaning: "*pe-tite-pomme*." As if by magic, the mouth, instead of being extended in counterfeit bliss, or contracting into an anxious grin, would form a gracious round . . . The eyebrows arched slightly, the oval of the cheeks was elongated. You said "*petite pomme*," and the shadow of a distant and dreamy sweetness veiled your gaze, refined your features . . .

A woman being photographed aspired to a standardized look that signified an ideal refinement of "feminine" traits, as conveyed *through* beauty; and beauty was understood to be a distancing from the ordinary. As photographed, it projected something enigmatic, dreamy, inaccessible. Today idiosyncrasy and forthrightness of expression are what make a photographic portrait interesting. And refinement is passé, and seems pretentious or sham.

Beauty—as photographed in the mainstream tradition that prevailed until recently—blurred women's sexuality. And even in photographs that were frankly erotic, the body might be telling one story and the face another: a naked woman lying in a strenuously indecent position, spread-eagled or presenting her rump, with the face turned toward the viewer wearing the vapidly amiable expression of respectable photographic portraiture. Newer ways of photographing women are less concealing of women's sexuality, though the display of once forbidden female flesh or carnal posturing is still fraught as a subject, so inveterate are responses that reassert male condescensions to women in the guise of lecherous appreciation. Women's libidinousness is always being repressed or held against them.

The identification of women with beauty was a way of immobilizing women. While character evolves, reveals, beauty is static, a mask, a magnet for projection. In the legendary final shot of *Queen Christina*, the queen—Greta Garbo—having abdicated the Swedish throne, renouncing the masculinizing prerogatives of a monarch for the modesty of a woman's happiness, and boarded the ship to join her foreign lover and depart with him into exile only to find him mortally wounded by a vengeful rejected suitor from her court, stands at the ship's prow with the wind in her face, a monument of heartbreak. While the lighting for the shot was being prepared, Garbo asked the director, Rouben Mamoulian, what she should be thinking during the take. Nothing, he famously replied. Don't think of anything. Go blank. His instruction produced one of the most emotion-charged images in movie history: as the camera moves in and holds on a long close-up, the spectator has no choice but to read mounting despair on that incomparably beautiful, dry-eyed, vacant face. The face that is a mask on which one can project whatever is desired is the consummate perfection of the looked-at-ness of women.

The identification of beauty as the ideal condition of a woman is, if anything, more powerful than ever, although today's hugely complex fashion-and-photography system sponsors norms of beauty that are far less provincial, more diverse, and favor brazen rather than demure ways of facing the camera. The downcast gaze, a staple of the presentation of women to the camera, should have a touch of sullenness if it is not to seem insipid. Ideas of beauty are less immobilizing now. But beauty itself is an ideal of a stable, unchanging appearance, a commitment to staving off or disguising the marks of time. The norms of sexual attractiveness for women are an index of their vulnerability. A man ages into his powers. A woman ages into being no longer desired.

Forever young, forever good-looking, forever sexy—beauty is still a construction, a transformation, a masquerade. We shouldn't be surprised—though of course we are—that in real life, when she is not decked out as a cliché of desirability, the flamboyant, bespangled, semi-nude Las Vegas showgirl can be a mature woman of unremarkable features and sober presence. The eternal feminine project of self-embellishment has always been able to pull off such triumphs.

SINCE TO BE FEMININE is to have qualities which are the opposite, or negation, of ideal masculine qualities, for a long time it was hard to elaborate the attractiveness of the strong woman in other than mythic or allegorical guise. The heroic woman was an allegorical fantasy in nineteenth-century painting and sculpture: Liberty leading the People. The large-gestured, imperiously draped, convulsively powerful woman danced by Martha Graham in the works she created for her all-women troupe in the 1930s—a turning point in the history of how women's strength, women's anger have been represented—was a mythic archetype (priestess, rebel, mourning daimon, quester) presiding over a community of women, not a real woman compromising and cohabiting with and working alongside men.

Dentist, orchestra conductor, commercial pilot, rabbi, lawyer, astronaut, film director, professional boxer, law-school dean, three-star general . . . no doubt about it, ideas about what women can *do*, and do well, have changed. And what women *mind* has changed. Male behavior, from the caddish to the outright violent, that until recently was accepted without demurral is seen today as outrageous by many women who not so long ago were putting up with it themselves and who would still protest indignantly if someone described them as feminists. To be sure, what has done most to change the stereotypes of frivolity and fecklessness afflicting women are not the labors of the various feminisms, indispensable as these have been. It is the new economic realities that oblige most American women (including most women with small children) to work outside their homes. The measure of how much things have *not* changed is that a woman earns between one-half and three-fourths of what a man earns in the same job. And nearly all occupations are still gender-labeled: with the exception of a few occupations (prostitute, nurse, secretary) where the reverse is true and it needs to be specified if the person is a man, one has to put "woman" in front of most job titles when it's a woman holding them; otherwise the assumption will always be that one is referring to a man.

Any woman of accomplishment becomes more acceptable if she can be seen as pursuing her ambitions, exercising her competence, in a feminine (wily, nonconfrontational) way. "No harsh feminist, Ms. X has attained . . ." begins the reassuring accolade to a woman in a job with executive responsibilities. That women are the equals of men—the new idea—continues to collide with the age-old presumption of female inferiority and serviceability: that it is normal for a woman to be in an essentially dependent or self-sacrificingly supportive relation to at least one man.

So ingrained is the expectation that the man will be taller, older, richer, more successful than the woman with whom he mates that the exceptions, of which there are now many, never fail to seem noteworthy. It seems normal for a journalist to ask the husband of a woman more famous than himself if he feels "threatened" by his wife's eminence. No one would dream of wondering if the non-famous wife of an important industrialist, surgeon, writer, politician, actor, feels threatened by her husband's eminence. And it is still thought that the ultimate act of love for a woman is to efface her own identity—a loving wife in a two-career marriage having every cause for anguish should her success overtake and surpass her husband's. ("Hello, everybody. This is Mrs. Norman Maine.") Accomplished women, except for those in the performing professions, continue to be regarded as an anomaly. It appears to make sense, for many reasons, to have anthologies of women writers or exhibits of women photographers; it would seem very odd to propose an anthology of writers or an exhibit of photographers who had nothing in common except that they were men.

WE WANT PHOTOGRAPHY to be unmythic, full of concrete information. We are more comfortable with photographs that are ironic, unidealizing. Decorum is now understood as concealment. We expect the photographer to be bold, even insolent. We hope that subjects will be candid, or naïvely revealing.

Of course, subjects who are accustomed to posing—women of achievement, women of notoriety—will offer something more guarded, or defiant.

And the way women and men really look (or allow themselves to appear) is not identical with how it is thought appropriate to appear to the camera. What looks right, or attractive, in a photograph is often no

more than what illustrates the felt "naturalness" of the unequal distribution of powers conventionally accorded women and men.

Just as photography has done so much to confirm these stereotypes,
it can engage in complicating and undermining them. In Annie Leibovitz's *Women*, we see women catering to the imperatives of looked-
at-ness. We see women for whom, because of age or because they're
preoccupied with the duties and pleasures of raising children, the rules
of ostentatiously feminine performance are irrelevant. There are many
portraits of women defined by the new kinds of work now open to
them. There are strong women, some of them doing "men's jobs,"
some of them dancers and athletes with the powerful musculature that
only recently began to be visible when such champion female bodies
were photographed.

ONE OF THE TASKS of photography is to disclose, and shape our
sense of, the variety of the world. It is not to present ideals. There is no
agenda except diversity and interestingness. There are no judgments,
which of course is itself a judgment.

And that variety is itself an ideal. We want now to know that for
every *this* there is a *that*. We want to have a plurality of models.

Photography is in the service of the post-judgmental ethos gaining
ascendancy in societies whose norms are drawn from the practices of
consumerism. The camera shows us many worlds, and the point is that
all the images are valid. A woman may be a cop or a beauty queen or an
architect or a housewife or a physicist. Diversity is an end in itself—
much celebrated in today's America. There is the very American, very
modern faith in the possibility of continuous self-transformation. A
life, after all, is commonly referred to as a *lifestyle*. Styles change. This
celebration of variety, of individuality, of individuality as style, saps the
authority of gender stereotypes, and has become an inexorable counterforce to the bigotry that still denies women more than token access
to many occupations and experiences.

That women, in the same measure as men, should be able to fulfill
their individuality is, of course, a radical idea. It is in this form, for

better and for worse, that the traditional feminist call for *justice* for women has come to seem most plausible.

A BOOK OF PHOTOGRAPHS; a book about women; a very American project: generous, ardent, inventive, open-ended. It's for us to decide what to make of these pictures. After all, a photograph is not an opinion. Or is it?

[1999]

THERE AND HERE

Homage to Halliburton

B EFORE THERE WAS travel—in my life, at least—there were
travel books. Books that told you the world was very large but
quite encompassable. Full of destinations.

The first travel books I read, and surely among the most important
books of my life, were by Richard Halliburton. I was seven, and the
year was 1940, when I read his *Book of Marvels*. Halliburton, the handsome, genteel American youth, born in Brownsville, Tennessee, who
had devised for himself a life of being forever young and on the move,
was my first vision of what I thought had to be the most privileged of
lives, that of a writer: a life of endless curiosity and energy and countless enthusiasms. To be a traveler, to be a writer—in my child mind
they started off as the same thing.

To be sure, there was a good deal in that child mind that prepared
me to fall in love with the idea of insatiable travel. My parents had
lived abroad most of my first six years—my father had a fur business in
northern China—while my sister and I remained in the care of relatives
in the States. As far back as I can remember, I was already conducting
a potent dream-life of travel to exotic places. But my parents' unimag-
inable existence on the opposite side of the globe had inspired a too
precise, hopeless set of travel longings. Halliburton's books informed
me that the world contained *many* wonderful things. Not just the
Great Wall of China.

Yes, he had walked on the Great Wall, and he'd also climbed the Matterhorn and Etna and Popocatepetl and Fujiyama and Olympus; he'd visited the Grand Canyon and the Golden Gate Bridge (in 1938, when the book was published, the bridge counted as the newest of the world's marvels); he'd rowed into the Blue Grotto and swum the length of the Panama Canal; he'd made it to Carcassonne and Baalbek and Petra and Lhasa and Chartres and Delphi and the Alhambra and Timbuktu and the Taj Mahal and Pompeii and Victoria Falls and the Bay of Rio and Chichén Itzá and the Blue Mosque in Isfahan and Angkor Wat and, and, and . . . Halliburton called them "marvels," and wasn't this my introduction to the notion of "the masterpiece"? The point was: the faraway world was full of amazing sites and edifices, and I, too, might one day see and learn the stories attached to them. Looking back now, I realize that *Book of Marvels* was a prime awakener of my own ardor and appetite.

The year before I read *Book of Marvels*, Halliburton had ventured a trip under sail in that quintessentially Chinese vessel, a junk, from Hong Kong to San Francisco, and had vanished somewhere mid-Pacific without a trace. He was thirty-nine years old. Did I know he had died when I was reading his book? Probably not. But then, I'd not entirely taken in the death of my own thirty-three-year-old father in Tientsin, which I learned about in 1939, several months after my mother returned from China for good.

And a sad end couldn't taint the lessons of pluck and avidity I drew from reading Halliburton. Those books—from *The Royal Road to Romance*, his first, published in 1925, to *Book of Marvels*, his last; I eventually read them all—described for me an idea of pure happiness. And of successful volition. You have something in mind. You imagine it. You prepare for it. You voyage toward it. Then you see it. And there is no disappointment; indeed, it may be even more captivating than you imagined.

Halliburton's books convey in the most candid and ingenuous—which is to say, unfashionable—way the "romance" of travel. Enthusiasm for travel may not be expressed so giddily today, but I'm sure that the seeking out of what is strange or beautiful, or both, remains just as

pleasurable and addictive. It has certainly proved so for me. And because of the impact of those books read when I was so young, my more
enviable sightings throughout grownup life, mostly by-products of opportunity or obligation rather than pilgrimages undertaken, continue
to bear Halliburton's imprint. When I finally did walk on the Great
Wall, and was rowed into the Blue Grotto, and was shat on by mon-
keys in the Taj Mahal, and wandered in the ruins of Angkor Wat, and
wangled permission to spend a night in a sleeping bag on the rosy
rocks of Petra, and surreptitiously climbed the Great Pyramid at Giza
before daybreak, I thought: I've done it. They were on *his* list. Truth is,
although San Francisco is anything but an unusual destination for me,
I never drive across the Golden Gate Bridge without recalling where it
figures in Halliburton's book. Even a place I've assumed isn't very interesting and haven't visited, Andorra, remains on my interior map because he went there. And when Machu Picchu or Palmyra or Lhasa or
Fujiyama comes to mind, I think, I haven't done that. Yet.

The cult of youth that animates Halliburton's books could hardly
have meant something to a seven-year-old. But it is the association of
travel with youth, beautiful youth, that seems most dated now. As an
undergraduate at Princeton just after World War I, he succumbed to
the spell of *The Picture of Dorian Gray*; and throughout his brief life his
beau idéal remained Rupert Brooke, whose biography he hoped one
day to write. Even more remote than these references is Halliburton's
assumption that he is bringing news to his readers, that what will entice
and seduce are his words—not the photographs in the books, most no
better than snapshots: the author standing in front of the Taj Mahal,
and so forth. Today, when lust for travel is awakened primarily through
images, still and moving, we expect the sights, many of them all too familiar, to speak for themselves. Indeed, we've seen the famous sights
unrolling in color long before we actually travel to see them.

Halliburton's travel narratives are stocked with people: guides, fa-
cilitators, scam artists, and other locals. The busy world that he encounters fills his mind. Today it is possible to travel solo, without
traveling, to vacancy itself. The distraught heroine of Don DeLillo's
The Body Artist logs on to her computer at odd hours to watch a live-

streaming video feed from the edge of a two-lane road outside Kotka, Finland, where a webcam is always trained on asphalt. "It emptied her mind and made her feel the deep silence of other places."

To me, travel is filling the mind. But that means, by launching me beyond the self, it also empties my mind: I find it almost impossible to write when I am traveling. To write I have to stay put. Real travel competes with mental traveling. (What is a writer but a mental traveler?) When I recall now how much Halliburton's books meant to me at the beginning of my reading life, I see how the notion of "traveler" infiltrated, perfumed, abetted my nascent dream of becoming a writer. When I acknowledge to myself that I'm interested in everything, what am I saying but that I want to travel everywhere. Like Richard Halliburton.

[2001]

Singleness

WHO'S YOUR FAVORITE WRITER? an interviewer asked me many years ago. —Just one? —Uh-huh. —Then it's easy. Shakespeare, of course. —Oh, I would never have thought you'd say Shakespeare! —For heaven's sake, why? —Well, you've never written anything about Shakespeare.

Oh.

So I'm supposed to be what I write? No more? No less? But every writer knows this isn't so.

I write what I can: that is, what's given to me and what seems worth writing, by me. I care passionately about many things that don't get into my fiction and essays. They don't because what's in my head seems to me to lack originality (I never thought I had anything compelling to say about Shakespeare), or because I haven't yet found the necessary inner freedom to write about them. My books aren't me—all of me. And in some ways I am less than them. The better ones are more intelligent, more talented, than I am; anyway, different. The "I" who writes is a transformation—a specializing and upgrading, according to certain literary goals and loyalties—of the "I" who lives. It feels true only in a trivial sense to say I make my books. What I really feel is that they are made, through me, by literature; and I'm their (literature's) servant.

The me through whom the books make their way has other yearnings too, other duties. For instance: as me, I believe in right action.

But, for the writer, it's far more complicated. Literature is not about doing the right thing—though it is about expressiveness (language) at a noble level and wisdom (inclusiveness, empathy, truthfulness, moral seriousness). And my books are not a means of discovering or expressing who I am, either; I've never fancied the ideology of writing as therapy or self-expression.

There is a deeper reason why the books are not me. My life has always felt like a becoming, and still does. But the books are finished. They liberate me to do, be, feel, aspire to something else—I'm a fierce learner. I've moved on. Sometimes I feel I'm in flight from the books, and the twaddle they generate. Sometimes the momentum is more pleasurable. I enjoy beginning again. The beginner's mind is best.

It's the beginner's mind I embrace and permit myself now, when I'm very far from being a beginning writer. When I began publishing thirty years ago, I entertained a simpler version of the figment that there were two people around here: I and a writer of the same name. Admiration—no, veneration—for a host of books had brought me to my vocation, on my knees. So, naturally, I was scared that I wasn't talented enough, worthy enough. How then did I find the courage to launch my frail vessel into literature's wide waters? Through a sense of two-ness that expressed, and enforced, my awareness of the gap between my own gifts and the standards I wished to honor in my work.

In fact, I never called what I did "my" work but "the" work. By extension, there was that one, the one who had dared to become a writer. And I, the one with the standards, who happily made sacrifices to keep her going, though I didn't think all that much of what she wrote.

Going on as a writer didn't allay this dissatisfaction, not for a very long time; it only upped the ante. (And I think I was right to be dissatisfied.) In my "Sontag and I" game, the disavowals were for real. Oppressed by as well as reluctantly proud of this lengthening mini-shelf of work signed by Susan Sontag, pained to distinguish myself (I was a seeker) from her (she had merely found), I flinched at everything written about her, the praise as much as the pans. My one perennial form of self-flattery: I know better than anyone what she is about, and nobody is as severe a judge of her work as I am myself.

Every writer—after a certain point, when one's labors have resulted

in a body of work—experiences himself or herself as both Dr. Frank-
enstein and the monster. For while harboring a secret sharer is probably not often the fantasy of a beginning writer, the conceit is bound to
appeal to a writer who has gone on. And on. A persona now: enduring,
and trying to ignore, the nibblings of alienation from the earlier work
which time, and more work, are bound to worsen. It also playfully affirms the dismaying disparity between the inside (the ecstasy and ardu-
ousness of writing) and the outside (that congeries of misunderstandings
and stereotypes that make up one's reputation or fame). I'm not that
image (in the minds of other people), it declares. And, with more
poignancy: don't punish me for being what you call successful. I've got
this onerous charge, this work-obsessed, ambitious writer who bears
the same name as I do. I'm just me, accompanying, administering,
tending to *that* one, so she can get some work done.

Then, more specifically, this doubling of the self puts a winsome
sheen on the abandonment of self required to make literature, which
invariably incurs the stigma of selfishness in "real" life. To write, as
Kafka said, you can never be alone enough. But the people you love
tend not to appreciate your need to be solitary, to turn your back on
them. You have to fend off the others to get your work done. And to
appease them—that issue is especially keen if the writer is a woman.
Don't be mad, or jealous. I can't help it. You see, *she* writes.

Yeats said one must choose between the life and the work. No. And
yes. One result of lavishing a good part of your one and only life on
your books is that you come to feel that, as a person, you are faking it.
I remember my merriment when, many years ago, I first came across
Borges's elegy to himself, the most delicate account ever given of a
writer's unease about the reconciling of life and work. Writers' pathos.
Writers' humility. (I envied him the slyness of his humility.)

Rereading it now, I still grin. But I'm not so prone to make use of
that balm to writers' self-consciousness which Borges's fable so charm-
ingly evokes.

Far from needing the consolation of a certain ironic distance from
myself (the earlier distance wasn't ironic at all), I've slowly evolved in
the opposite direction and at last come to feel that the writer is me: not
my double, or familiar, or shadow playmate, or creation. (It's because I

got to that point—it took almost thirty years—that I was finally able to write a book I really like: *The Volcano Lover.*) Now I think there's no escaping the burden of singleness. There's a difference between me and my books. But there's only one person here. That is scarier. Lonelier. Liberating.

[1995]

Writing As Reading

R EADING NOVELS SEEMS to me such a normal activity, while writing them is such an odd thing to do—at least so I think until I remind myself how firmly the two are related. (No armored generalities here. Just a few remarks.)

First, because to write is to practice, with particular intensity and attentiveness, the art of reading. You write in order to read what you've written, and see if it's OK and, since of course it never is, to rewrite it—once, twice, as many times as it takes to get it to be something you can bear to reread. You are your own first, maybe severest, reader. "To write is to sit in judgment on oneself," Ibsen inscribed on the flyleaf of one of his books. Hard to imagine writing without rereading.

But is what you've written straight off never all right? Yes, sure: sometimes even better than all right. And that only suggests, to this writer at any rate, that with a closer look, or voicing aloud—that is, another reading—it might be better still. I'm not saying that the novelist *has* to fret and sweat to produce something good. "What is written without effort is in general read without pleasure," said Dr. Johnson, and the maxim seems as remote from contemporary taste as its author. Surely, much that is written without effort gives a great deal of pleasure. No, the question is not the judgment of readers—who may well prefer a writer's more spontaneous, less elaborated work—but a sentiment of writers, those professionals of dissatisfaction. You think, If I can get it to this point the first go-around, without too much struggle, couldn't it be better still?

And though this, the rewriting—and the rereading—sounds like effort, it is actually the most pleasurable part of writing. Sometimes the only pleasurable part. Setting out to write, if you have the idea of "literature" in your head, is formidable, intimidating. A plunge in an icy lake. Then comes the warm part, when you already have something to work with, upgrade, edit.

Let's say it's a mess. But you have a chance to fix it. You try to be clearer. Or deeper. Or more eloquent. Or more eccentric. You try to be true to a world. You want the book to be more spacious, more authoritative. You want to winch yourself up from yourself. You want to winch the book out of your balky mind. As the statue is entombed in the block of marble, the novel is inside your head. You try to liberate it. You try to get this wretched stuff on the page closer to what you think your book should be—what you know, in your spasms of elation, it *can* be. You read the sentences over and over. Is this the book I'm writing? Is this all?

Or let's say it's going well, for it does go well, some of the time (if it didn't, you'd go crazy). There you are, and even if you are the slowest of scribes and the worst of touch typists, a trail of words is being laid down, and you want to keep going. Then you reread it. Perhaps you don't dare be satisfied, but at the same time you like what you've written. You find yourself taking pleasure—a reader's pleasure—in what's there on the page.

Writing is, finally, a series of permissions you give yourself to be expressive in certain ways. To invent. To leap. To fly. To fall. To find your own characteristic way of narrating and insisting; that is, to find your own inner freedom. To be strict without being too self-excoriating. Not stopping too often to reread. Allowing yourself, when you dare think it's going well (or not too badly), simply to keep rowing along. No waiting for inspiration's shove.

Of course, blind writers can never reread what they dictate. Perhaps this matters less for poets, who often do most of their writing in their head before setting down anything on paper. (Poets live by the ear much more than prose writers do.) And being unable to see doesn't mean that one can't make revisions. Don't we imagine that Milton's daughters, at the end of each day of the dictation of *Paradise Lost*, read it all back to their father and then took down his corrections? But prose writers—who work in a lumberyard of words—can't hold it all in their heads. They need to see what they've written. Even the most forthcoming, prolific writers must feel this. (Hence, Sartre announced, when he went blind, that his writing days were over.) Think of portly, venerable Henry James pacing up and down in a room in Lamb House composing *The Golden Bowl* aloud to a secretary. Leaving aside the difficulty of imagining how James's late prose could have been dictated at all, much less to the racket made by a Remington typewriter circa 1900, don't we assume that James reread what had been typed, and was lavish with his corrections?

When I became, again, a cancer patient two years ago and had to break off work on the nearly finished *In America*, a friend in Los Angeles, knowing my despair and fear that now I'd never finish it, offered to come to New York and stay with me to take down my dictation of the rest of the novel. True, the first eight chapters were done (that is, rewritten and reread many times) and I'd begun the next-to-last chapter, with the arc of the last two chapters clearly in view. And yet I had to refuse his touching, generous offer. It wasn't just that I was probably too befuddled by drastic chemotherapy and morphine to remember what I was planning to write. I had to be able to see what I wrote, not just hear it. I had to be able to reread.

READING USUALLY PRECEDES writing. And the impulse to write is almost always fired by reading. Reading, the love of reading, is what makes you dream of becoming a writer. And, long after you've become a writer, reading books others write—and rereading the beloved books of the past—constitutes an irresistible distraction from writing. Distraction. Consolation. Torment. And, yes, inspiration.

Not all writers will admit to this. I remember once saying something to V. S. Naipaul about a nineteenth-century English novel I loved, a very well known novel, which I assumed that he, like everyone I knew who cared for literature, admired as I did. But no, he'd not read it, he said, and, seeing the shadow of surprise on my face, added sternly, "Susan, I'm a writer, not a reader."

Many writers who are no longer young claim, for various reasons, to read very little, indeed, to find reading and writing in some sense incompatible. Perhaps, for some writers, they are. If the reason is anxiety about being influenced, then this seems to me a vain, shallow worry. If the reason is lack of time—there are only so many hours in the day, and those spent reading are evidently subtracted from those in which one could be writing—then this is an asceticism to which I don't aspire.

Losing yourself in a book, the old phrase, is not an idle fantasy but an addictive, model reality. Virginia Woolf famously said, in a letter, "Sometimes I think heaven must be one continuous unexhausted reading." Surely the heavenly part is that—again, Woolf's words—"the state of reading consists in the complete elimination of the ego." Unfortunately, we never do lose the ego, any more than we can step over our own feet. But that disembodied rapture, reading, is trance-like enough to make us *feel* egoless.

Like reading, rapturous reading, writing fiction—inhabiting other selves—feels like losing yourself, too.

Most people seem to think now that writing is just a form of self-regard. Also called: self-expression. As we are no longer supposed to be capable of authentically altruistic feelings, we are not supposed to be capable of writing about anyone but ourselves.

But that's not true. William Trevor speaks of the boldness of the *non*-autobiographical imagination. Why wouldn't you write to escape yourself as much as you might write to express yourself? It's far more interesting to write about others.

Needless to say, I lend bits of myself to all my characters. When, in *In America*, my immigrants from Poland reach southern California—they're just outside the village of Anaheim—in 1876, stroll out into the desert, and succumb to a terrifying, transforming vision of emptiness, I was drawing on my own memory of childhood walks into the desert of southern Arizona—outside what was then a small town, Tucson—in the 1940s. In the first draft of that chapter, there were saguaros in the southern California desert. By the third draft I had taken the saguaros out, reluctantly. (Alas, in 1876, there weren't any saguaros west of the Colorado River.)

What I write about is other than me. As what I write is smarter than I am. Because I can rewrite it. My books know what I once knew—fitfully, intermittently. And getting the best words on the page does not seem any easier, even after so many years of writing. On the contrary.

Here is the great difference between reading and writing. Reading is a vocation, a skill at which, with practice, you are bound to become more expert. What you accumulate as a writer is mostly uncertainties and anxieties.

All these feelings of inadequacy on the part of the writer—this writer, anyway—are predicated on the conviction that literature matters. "Matters" is surely too pale a word. That there are books which are necessary, that is, books which, while reading them, you know you'll reread. Maybe more than once. Is there a greater privilege than to have a consciousness expanded by, filled with, pointed to literature?

Book of wisdom, exemplar of mental playfulness, dilator of sympathies, faithful recorder of a real world (not just the commotion inside one head), servant of history, advocate of contrary and defiant emotions—a novel that feels necessary can be, should be, most of these things.

As for whether there will continue to be readers who share this high notion of fiction, well, "There's no future to that question," as Duke Ellington replied when asked why he was to be found playing morning programs at the Apollo. Best just to keep rowing along.

[2000]

Thirty Years Later . . .

T O L O O K B A C K on writings of thirty or more years ago is not a wholesome exercise. My energy as a writer impels me to look forward, to feel still that I am beginning, really beginning, now, which makes it hard to curb my impatience with that beginning writer I once was in the literal sense.

Against Interpretation, my second book, was published in 1966, but some essays in it date from 1961, when I was still writing *The Benefactor*. I had come to New York at the start of the 1960s—eager to put to work the writer I had, since adolescence, pledged myself to become. My idea of a writer: someone interested in "everything." I'd always had interests of many kinds, so it was natural for me to conceive of the vocation of a writer in this way. And reasonable to suppose that such fervency would find more scope in a great metropolis than in any variant of provincial life, including the excellent universities I had attended. The only surprise was that there weren't more people like me.

I'm aware that *Against Interpretation* is regarded as a quintessential text of that now mythic era known as the Sixties. I evoke the label with reluctance, since I'm not keen on the omnipresent convention of packaging one's life, the life of one's time, in decades. And it wasn't the Six-

"Thirty Years Later . . ." was written in the summer of 1995 as the preface to the republication the following year in Madrid of the Spanish translation of *Against Interpretation*.

ties then. For me it was chiefly the time when I wrote my first and second novels, and began to discharge some of the cargo of ideas about art and culture and the proper business of consciousness which had distracted me from writing fiction. I was filled with evangelical zeal.

The radical change I'd made in my own life, a change embedded in my moving to New York, was that I was not going to settle for being an academic: I would pitch my tent outside the seductive, stony safety of the university world. No doubt, there were new permissions in the air, and old hierarchies had become ripe for toppling, but not that I was aware, at least not until after the time (1961 to 1965) these essays were written. The freedoms I espoused, the ardors I was advocating, seemed to me—still seem to me—quite traditional. I saw myself as a newly minted warrior in a very old battle: against philistinism, against ethical and aesthetic shallowness and indifference. And I could never have imagined that both New York, where I had come to live after my long academic apprenticeship (Berkeley, Chicago, Harvard), and Paris, where I had started spending the summers, in daily attendance at the Cinémathèque, were in the early throes of a period that would be judged as exceptionally creative. They were, New York and Paris, exactly as I'd imagined them to be—full of discoveries, inspirations, the sense of possibility. The dedication and daring and absence of venality of the artists whose work mattered to me seemed, well, the way it was supposed to be. I thought it normal that there be new masterpieces every month—above all in the form of movies and dance events, but also in the fringe theatre world, in galleries and improvised art spaces, in the writings of certain poets and other, less easily classifiable writers of prose. Maybe I *was* riding a wave. I thought I was flying, getting an overview, sometimes swooping down to get close.

I had so many admirations: there was so much to admire. I looked around and saw importance to which no one was giving its due. Perhaps I was particularly well fitted to see what I saw, to understand what I understood, by virtue of my bookishness, my Europhilia, and the energy I had at my disposal in the search for aesthetic bliss. Still, it surprised me at first that people found what I said "new" (it wasn't so new to me), that I was thought to be in the vanguard of sensibility and, from the appearance of my very first essays, regarded as a tastemaker. Of course, I was elated to be apparently the first to pay attention to some of the matters I wrote about; sometimes I couldn't believe my good fortune that they had waited for me to describe them. (How odd, I thought, that Auden hadn't written something like my "Notes on Camp.") As I saw it, I was merely extending to some new material the aesthete's point of view I had embraced, as a young student of philosophy and literature, in the writings of Nietzsche, Pater, Wilde, Ortega (the Ortega of "The Dehumanization of Art"), and James Joyce.

I was a pugnacious aesthete and a barely closeted moralist. I didn't set out to write so many manifestos, but my irrepressible taste for aphoristic statement conspired with my staunchly adversarial purposes in ways that sometimes surprised me. In the writings collected in *Against Interpretation* this is what I like best: the tenacity, the succinctness (I suppose I should say here that I still agree with most of the positions I took), and certain psychological and moral judgments in the essays on Simone Weil, Camus, Pavese, and Michel Leiris. What I don't like are those passages in which my pedagogic impulse got in the way of my prose. Those lists, those recommendations! I suppose they are useful, but they annoy me now.

The hierarchies (high/low) and polarities (form/content, intellect/feeling) I was challenging were those that inhibited the proper understanding of the new work I admired. Although I had no programmatic commitment to the "modern," taking up the cause of new work, especially work that had been slighted or ignored or misjudged, seemed more useful than defending old favorites. In writing about what I was discovering, I assumed the preeminence of the canonical treasures of the past. The transgressions I was applauding seemed altogether salutary, given what I took to be the unimpaired strength of the old taboos. The contemporary work I praised (and used as a platform to relaunch my ideas about art-making and consciousness) didn't detract from the glories of what I admired far more. Enjoying the impertinent energy and wit of a species of performance called Happenings did not make me care less about Aristotle and Shakespeare. I was—I am—for a pluralistic, polymorphous culture. No hierarchy, then? Certainly there's hierarchy. If I had to choose between the Doors and Dostoyevsky, then—of course—I'd choose Dostoyevsky. But do I have to choose?

The great revelation for me had been the cinema: I felt particularly marked by the films of Godard and Bresson. I wrote more about cinema than about literature, not because I loved movies more than novels but because I loved more new movies than new novels. It was clear to me that no other art was being so widely practiced at such a high level. One of my happiest achievements in the years when I was doing the writing collected in *Against Interpretation* is that no day passed without my seeing one, sometimes two or three movies. Most of them were "old." My absorption in cinema history only reinforced my gratitude for certain new films, which (along with my favorites from the silent era and the 1930s) I saw again and again, so exalting were their freedom and inventiveness of narrative method, their sensuality and gravity and beauty.

Cinema was the exemplary art activity during the time these essays were written, but there were astonishments in the other arts as well. Artists were insolent again, as they'd been after World War I until the rise of fascism. The modern was still a vibrant idea. (This was before the capitulations embodied in the idea of the "post-modern.") And I have said nothing here about the political struggles which took shape around the time the last of these essays were being written: I mean the nascent movement against the American war on Vietnam, which was to consume a large part of my life from 1965 through the early 1970s (those years were still the Sixties, too, I suppose). How marvelous it all does seem, in retrospect. How one wishes some of its boldness, its optimism, its disdain for commerce had survived. The two poles of distinctively modern sentiment are nostalgia and utopia. Perhaps the most interesting characteristic of the time now labeled the Sixties was that there was so little nostalgia. In that sense, it was indeed a utopian moment.

The world in which these essays were written no longer exists.

Instead of a utopian moment, the time we live in is experienced as the end—more exactly, just past the end—of every ideal. (And therefore of culture: there is no possibility of true culture without altruism.) An illusion of the end, perhaps—and not more illusory than the conviction of thirty years ago of being on the threshold of a great positive transformation of culture and society. No, not an illusion, I think.

It is not simply that the Sixties have been repudiated, and the dissident spirit quashed, and made the object of intense nostalgia. The ever more triumphant values of consumer capitalism promote—indeed, impose—the cultural mixes and insolence and defense of pleasure that I was advocating for quite different reasons. No recommendations exist outside a certain setting. The recommendations and enthusiasms expressed in the essays collected in *Against Interpretation* have become the possession of many people now. Something was operating to make these marginal views more acceptable, something of which I had no inkling—and, had I understood better my time, that time (call it by its decade-name if you want), would have made me more cautious. Something that it would not be an exaggeration to call a sea change in the whole culture, a transvaluation of values—for which there are many names. Barbarism is one name for what was taking over. Let's use Nietzsche's term: we had entered, really entered, the age of nihilism.

So I can't help viewing the writings collected in *Against Interpretation* with a certain irony. I still like most of the essays—a few of them, such as "Notes on Camp" and "On Style," quite a lot. (Indeed, there's only one thing in the collection I don't like at all: two theatre chronicles, the brief result of a commission I had accepted, against my better judgment, from a literary magazine with which I was allied.) Who would not be pleased that a collection of contentious writings from more than three decades ago continues to matter to new generations of readers in English and in many foreign languages. Still, I urge the reader not to lose sight of—it may take some effort of imagination—the larger context of admirations in which these essays were written. To call for an "erotics of art" did not mean to disparage the role of the critical intellect. To laud work condescended to then as "popular" culture did not mean to conspire in the repudiation of high culture and its complexities. When I denounced (for instance, in the essays on science-fiction films and on Lukács) certain kinds of facile moralism, it was in the name of a more alert, less complacent seriousness. What I didn't understand (I was surely not the right person to understand this) was that seriousness itself was in the early stages of losing credibility in the culture at large, and that some of the more transgressive art I was enjoying would reinforce frivolous, merely consumerist transgressions. Thirty years later, the undermining of standards of seriousness is almost complete, with the ascendancy of a culture whose most intelligible, persuasive values are drawn from the entertainment industries. Now the very idea of the serious (and of the honorable) seems quaint, unrealistic, to most people, and when allowed—as an arbitrary decision of temperament—probably unhealthy, too.

I suppose it's not wrong that *Against Interpretation* is read now, or reread, as an influential, pioneering document from a bygone age. But that is not how I read it, or—lurching from nostalgia to utopia—wish it to be read. My hope is that its republication now, and the acquisition of new readers, could contribute to the quixotic task of shoring up the values out of which these essays and reviews were written. The judgments of taste expressed in these essays may have prevailed. The values underlying those judgments did not.

[1996]

Questions of Travel

BOOKS ABOUT TRAVEL to exotic places have always opposed an "us" to a "them"—a relation that yields a limited variety of appraisals. Classical and medieval travel literature is mostly of
the "us good, them bad"—typically, "us good, them horrid"—sort. To
be foreign was to be abnormal, often represented as physical abnormality; and the persistence of those accounts of monstrous peoples, of
"men whose heads / Do grow beneath their shoulders" (Othello's win-
ning tale), of anthropophagi, Cyclopes, and the like illustrates to us the
astonishing gullibility of past ages. But even this gullibility had its limits. A Christian culture could more easily believe in the existence of the
monstrous than of the perfect or near perfect. Thus, while the king-
doms of freaks appear century after century on maps, exemplary races
figure mostly in books of travel to utopia; that is, nowhere.

Not until the eighteenth century are there many examples of a more
daring geography: literature about model societies which describes
purportedly real places. Documentary literature and fiction were, of
course, closely related in the eighteenth century, with nonfiction narratives in the first person an important model for the novel. It is the heyday of travel hoaxes, as well as of fiction in the form of travel books.
And the greatest of the imaginary voyages, *Gulliver's Travels*, mixes the
two main fantasies of the wholly alien. Consisting mostly of visits to a
series of monstrous races, it ends with its burnt-out hero settled among

an ideal race: a high moment in the soon-to-be-flourishing "us bad, them good" tradition.

The travel literature that can be understood as premodern takes for granted the contrast between the traveler's society and those societies defined as anomalous, barbaric, backward, odd. To speak in the persona of the traveler, a professional (or even amateur) observer, was to speak for civilization; no premodern travelers thought of themselves as the barbarians. Modern travel literature starts when civilization becomes a critical as well as a self-evident notion—that is, when it is no longer so clear who is civilized and who is not.

Travel is a didactic fantasy in the discourse of the *philosophes* (the first intellectuals in the modern sense), who often invoke distant non-European societies, described as either more "natural" or more "rational," in order to illuminate the evils of their own. Tales of physical anomaly attested to by voyagers to remote lands still circulate in the late eighteenth century—the nine-foot-tall giants of Patagonia, for example—but the sense of anomaly is increasingly the moral one. And "we" become the moral defectives. There is a large literature of journeys to exotic places whose fanciful virtues are recounted to point an instructive contrast with Europe. The journey was out of civilization— the present—to something better: the past or the future.

America was the beneficiary of many trips, real and fabricated, of this kind. "In the beginning," said John Locke, "all the world was America." Crèvecoeur and Chateaubriand found in the New World something better than, unspoiled by, civilization: health, vigor, moral integrity, a refreshing naïveté and directness. After such fantasies came the inevitable counter-literature, that of acerbic British travelers of the mid-nineteenth century like Fanny Trollope and Dickens, who found us simply not very civilized, in a word, vulgar; Harriet Martineau in the 1830s, sensing abolitionism and feminism on the march, had liked us rather better. Much of modern judgments about exotic places is reactive. Turks were one of the model races in the eighteenth century; in the 1850s the intrepid Martineau actually visited two examples of the "Turkish" harem and described its inmates as the most injured, depressed, and corrupted human beings she had ever seen.

Although these travel judgments—the idealizing of an exotic society, and the report on its barbarity—seem to alternate in cycles of hope and disillusionment, certain countries (following the mysterious laws of stereotyping) have proved more susceptible to idealizing than others. China has been a fantasy kingdom since Marco Polo's visit; and in the eighteenth century it was widely believed that in China, a land of reason, there was no war, debauchery, ignorance, superstition, or widespread illness. America, too, for all its denigrators, keeps recurring as an object of idealization. In contrast, Russia is a land whose customs and energies have been perennially deplored. Since Ivan the Terrible, the first Muscovite monarch to capture the imagination of Europe, reports on the infamy of Russian society have constituted a flourishing branch of travel literature in the West. The only memorable counter-reports—those made by some foreign visitors from the 1930s to the 1950s, precisely the period of the Greatest Terror, about the unprecedented heights of freedom and justice attained in the Soviet Union—have strengthened this tradition.

One cannot imagine anyone being exactly disillusioned by the Marquis de Custine's account of the barbarism and despotism he found when he went to Russia in 1839, as many people were sharply disillusioned by Simon Leys's account, in the mid-1970s, of the barbarism of China's Cultural Revolution. And this centuries-old propensity to think the best of China and the worst of Russian society still has its echo today, when, though by many criteria Chinese communism is infinitely more repressive, more (literally) totalitarian than Soviet communism, the Chinese version still enjoys a far better press than the Soviet one. (Indeed, most self-righteous anti-communists at the highest reaches of the American foreign policy establishment behave as if they are not supposed to notice the tragically Stalinist character of current Chinese political life.) Some countries are perennial objects of fantasy.

THE *PHILOSOPHES* HAD ATTRIBUTED ideal virtues not only to a noble savage—the Hurons of Voltaire and Rousseau, Diderot's wise old Tahitian—but also to existing non-European ("Eastern") peoples such as Turks, Persians, and Chinese. The fantasies of succeeding generations of writers were not so easily disconfirmed. The only "ideal" civilization allowed by the Romantic poets was a thoroughly dead one: the Greek.

Once travel was itself an anomalous activity. The Romantics construe the self as essentially a traveler—a questing, homeless self whose true citizenship is of a place that does not exist at all, or yet, or no longer exists; one consciously understood as an ideal, opposed to something real. It is understood that the journey is unending, and the destination, therefore, negotiable. To travel becomes the very condition of modern consciousness, of a modern view of the world—the acting out of longing or dismay. On this view everyone is, potentially, a traveler.

The generalizing of travel results in a new genre of travel writing: the literature of disappointment, which from now on will rival the literature of idealization. Europeans visited America, prospecting the possibilities of a new, simpler life; cultivated Americans journeyed to Europe to appraise the Old World sources of civilizations—both often profess to be disappointed. From the early nineteenth century on, European letters resound with the sentiment of being *Europamüde*, tired of Europe. Travelers continue, in ever larger numbers, to make trips to exotic, non-Western lands, which seem to answer to some of the old stereotypes: that simpler society, where faith is pure, nature pristine, discontent (and its civilization) unknown. But paradise is always being lost. One of the recurrent themes of modern travel narratives is the depredations of the modern, the loss of the past—the report on a society's decline. The nineteenth-century travelers are noting the inroads in the idyllic life in, say, the South Seas made by the modern money-economy, for travelers who would never dream of living like the natives generally still want the natives to stay wholesome, rustic, sexy, and uncomfortable.

Another characteristic modern incitement to travel, what makes a country worth seeing, and describing, is that a revolution has taken place in it. That most unromantic and profound of travel writers, Alexis de Tocqueville, saw in America the vanguard of a radical process soon to transform Europe as well, irrevocably destroying the past; it was to examine that revolution, democracy, that Tocqueville traveled about the United States. Trips to countries to see how they have been transformed by a revolution, a revolution which claims to be about the enactment of ideals, have been one of the great subjects of modern travel literature. In the twentieth century these are trips to specific revolutions, seeking that ideal homeland, revolution-in-general. Much of the literature of travel from the "West" to communist countries reads as a late variant of the old genre, in which visitors from corrupt, oversophisticated Europe hail the healthy energies of a "new world"—now a self-designated "new man."

In this version of the ideal destination, "revolutionary" has replaced "primitive" but still retains many of the attributes of what was once understood as primitive. "I have seen the future and it works," notoriously declared Lincoln Steffens after his visit to the Soviet Union in the early 1930s—perhaps the high point of identifying communism with modernization. But as the Soviet model was discredited, and revolution became the fate of struggling agrarian societies more or less under siege, it seemed that what the travelers really felt was: I have seen the past and it is . . . moving.

Trips to those grievously poor countries are perceived as journeys backward in time: leaving affluent, doubt-stricken civilization for the simplicities, pieties, and materially spartan life of an earlier age. Writing of her visit to China in 1973, Barbara Wooten avowed: "To anyone coming from a world which threatens to strangle itself in its own complications it is the apparent simplicity of Chinese life which makes an irresistible appeal." This reaction is not just fantasy. Communist revolutions tend not only to occur in peasant societies but, for all the energy devoted to bringing about a certain modernization, to preserve tenaciously much that is premodern in them, such as old-fashioned family life and the central role of a literary culture; and to abort or at least slow down—in part due to the intractable failures of the economy—the onset of the consumer society, with its affluence, its "permissive" values, and its degraded mass culture. Even the unfortunate countries of Central Europe (now paradigmatically relocated in the "East"), though hardly backward societies when they fell under Russian hegemony, are not exceptions to the rule of delayed advance into the modern which communism enforces; and still visibly preserve more of Europe before World War II than do the countries of Western Europe. A good deal of the favorable reaction of foreign visitors has been precisely to this.

In almost all accounts of modern reflective travel, the master subject is alienation itself. The trip may support a skeptical, acutely sensuous, or speculative view of the world. Or the trip is an exercise in overcoming alienation in which travelers celebrate virtues—or liberties—found in a distant society that are lacking in their own. In another trip that has become common with the enlarging possibilities of travel to non-European countries, the affluent traveler, on vacation from bourgeois restraints, explores the "picturesque," takes advantage of unlimited sexual opportunities. One celebrated nineteenth-century example is the trip that Flaubert, in the company of Maxime Du Camp, made to Egypt in 1850–1851. (In the twentieth century, homosexual writers have been specialists in this kind of libertine travel to colonies and ex-colonies.) In the trip to the revolution, another kind of picturesque is in evidence. Part of what is perceived in communist countries as old-fashioned is the sexual decorousness. Untrammeled sexuality is now associated not with the primitive but with decadence. The revolution represents itself as a kingdom of virtue, and visitors have been ready to believe that behavior in a revolutionary society really has been thus transformed. In the early 1970s many Western visitors accepted the solemn assurances of their Chinese hosts that there was no theft, no homosexuality, and no premarital sex in China.

Though travel for debauch is the opposite of the high-minded, edifying trip made to a poor country in the throes of a revolution, the latter trip often inspires similar condescensions and detachments. Sympathetic visitors who cannot even imagine the local hardships often have a high standard of revolutionary consciousness, and when, for example, the ghastly rigors and lethal zealotry of Chinese communism in the time of the Cultural Revolution were somewhat abated, starting in the mid-1970s, first-time visitors were known to commiserate with each other that they had missed the really good period, when the natives were pure, pious, uncorrupted by consumerism.

Many of the earlier travelers to the capitals of the revolution were, as in an old-fashioned literary journey, going to an exotic land in order to return home and write about it. Travelers to these countries were conscious of traversing a formidable barrier. (Beyond the Great Wall. Behind the Iron Curtain.) They came to write about an exotic country; what they actually wrote about was their itinerary, the strenuous program that is laid out for privileged visitors. Indeed, the common form of these books was the record of the trip, as in *China Day by Day*, the notably ingenuous account Simone de Beauvoir wrote of her trip to China in 1955. By the early 1970s, with an increasing volume of travel to China, travelers were reporting not only similar trips but identical ones: the same tea-growing commune near Hangchow, the same bicycle factory in Shanghai, the same "lane committee" in a Peking neighborhood—the sameness of the trip having not deterred a large number of them from coming back and writing virtually the same book.

Isolated, secretive, besieged—all communist countries have elaborate procedures for receiving foreign visitors, pampering them while putting them through some well-chosen paces, then dispatching them back, laden with trinkets and books, to the outside world. Like the most modern tourist venture in any remote land, the experience in which the traveler to the revolution is enrolled eliminates all risk, denies enigma. Mystery, risk and unpleasantness, isolation are traditional ingredients of travel to remote lands. Even the most independent lone observer needs help in deciphering an exotic country. Such an observer may take on a native cicerone, who will be the traveler's principal interlocutor for part of the trip—as in V. S. Naipaul's *Among the Believers*, about his travels in revolution-convulsed Islam. But the lone observer is unlikely to take at face value the attitudes of this native friend. Group travel to a communist revolution is designed to produce a different result. These are trips organized by travel officials to make the country seem intelligible. And many visitors to communist countries have been easily persuaded to consider the aspirations and needs of their inhabitants to be fundamentally different from ours, when they are all too similar, and institutions and practices to be comparable to our own, which are in fact radically different.

The voyage to be made to new worlds used to be arduous, hazardous—so arduous that travelers often skipped it. Many authors of travel books were fireside travelers, plagiarizing earlier travel accounts. That eventually travel to exotic places became altogether common, and more and more organized, has made the old kind of travel hoax virtually obsolete: people do take the trips they write about. In the modern period there are probably many fewer travel books that consciously intend to deceive, many more in which the author *is* deceived. The chances of being caught out, of course, have also mounted. No Natchez squaw arrived in Paris at the end of the eighteenth century to explain what Chateaubriand hadn't seen or had misinterpreted in the course of his enthusiastic (and, in part, faked) travels to America in 1791. But someone—her name is Eleanor Lipper—who served eleven years in the Gulag and was a prisoner in that slave labor camp in Siberia that both Henry Wallace and Owen Lattimore visited in the early 1940s and pronounced a model workplace (a cross between the Hudson Bay Company and the Tennessee Valley Authority) did turn up a few years later, and wrote about the rage and contempt the prisoners felt for their visitors.

THE ACCOUNTS OF TRAVEL to exotic countries in the nineteenth century suppressed the servants, often a whole retinue, who accompanied the venturesome traveler. The modern traveler touring the revolution tended to suppress the group with which such a trip was accomplished. The sort of person who writes a book about travel to a communist country is, more often than not, the sort who gets invited. And this usually means being a member of a tour—an educational (that is, propaganda) tour sponsored and often paid for by the country being visited. As in all tours, one may not know some or even any of the other people with whom one is packaged. The group may be as small as three (as on my first trip to North Vietnam, in April 1968) or five (as when I went to Poland, in April 1980) or eight (the size of the group I joined to go to China in 1979). Groups of forty in general mean students; the eminent rarely travel in groups of more than five or six; those considered top-drawer celebrities will be invited to travel with a spouse or companion. And, if it is a first trip to a communist country, one will be surprised to learn that this group—however small, however ad hoc—is called a "delegation." You may protest that your group represents nobody back home, that each member speaks only for herself or himself, but your smiling hosts will keep on referring to "your delegation."

The custom is for all those taking part in the trip to rendezvous in a hotel mid-journey on the way "in," the day before entering the country, to be instructed in the ground rules of delegation travel, and to elect a "chairman" (sometimes a vice chairman as well) for the trip, whose duty it will be to respond to official speeches and to sit at the head table at banquets and lead off the toasts. (Some delegations choose to rotate the chairmanship for different segments of the trip, to share the pompousness and the fun.) Wherever you go—at railway stations, where they meet your train; in factories; in schools; at the Writers' Union—your delegation is meeting the representatives of their organization.

No invitation without an inviting—host—organization; no travel without a program. Led from museums to model kindergartens to the birthplace of the country's most famous composer or poet, welcomed and given tea and phony statistics by dignitaries in factories and communes, shepherded from oversized meal to oversized meal, with time off for shopping sprees in stores reserved for foreigners, the travelers will complete the tightly scheduled trip having talked with hardly anyone except each other and the only natives they spend time with, upon whom they will base many a generalization: the inveterately amiable guides assigned to the delegation. These official companions—apart from a few head hacks, they are often young, warmhearted, eager (they have worked hard to get the coveted, thrilling job that puts them in contact with foreigners), and scared (they know the price of a misstep, an indiscretion)—hover and fuss, at the constant disposal of their charges. One is always busy, accompanied by them. They are even busier. During an after-lunch break, they have to arrange tickets and accommodations; up late at night, they will be writing reports on the day's activities and the visitors' reactions, planning activities to come. The tourist's role is, characteristically, a greedy one. But a delegation tour of a communist country tenders an explicit invitation to be selfish, greedy. The visitor has only to express a wish for some unscheduled excursion or entertainment, and more phone calls are made to the people working behind the scenes to conjure up the necessary tickets, a guide on the spot, another limousine.

Educational travel is by definition privileged travel—travel on a round-trip ticket. One model of travel to foreign countries for the sake of education was the eighteenth-century Grand Tour, in which a young gentleman, accompanied by his often ill-born and usually underpaid tutor, was exposed to a variety of customs, places, treasures adjacent to his own. Although these leisurely travels through the Continent were often no more than a rake's progress, their educational point could not be altogether nullified. The graduate of the Grand Tour did return home contaminated in some sense by the foreign. At the least he had experienced that there are many models for being civilized—which is one beginning of true civilization, and civility.

In the Grand Tour offered to visitors to communist countries, travel is designed to make sure the visitor does not encounter anything contaminating. The precondition of such tours or field trips, the visitor's intellectual and cultural distance, is reinforced by the mandatory luxuriousness of delegation travel. The Disneyland of revolution which the traveler will see has for its theme the country's progress, the revolution's benefits, as illustrated by an array of elementary performances, economic and cultural, to which visitors are taken in order to admire. But few visitors from very rich countries, including many who identify with the left, are able to evaluate these performances. If on their first trip to a communist country, it is probably the first time most of them will have been in a truck factory, on a breeding ranch, in a paper mill. Most visitors will know nothing about communism, about the country they are visiting (often they have not even taken the time to study a map and seem unaware of the most salient facts of its history), about peasant life and major industrial procedures.

So-called fellow travelers, whether informed or ignorant, are not the best participants in a delegation trip. Indeed, travel officials in communist countries have learned to distrust Western leftists and— this is clearest in Richard Nixon's favorite foreign vacation spot, Ronald Reagan's "so-called communist China"—prefer to entertain travelers untouched by radical sentiments: better a chairman of the board than a leftist assistant professor of history. Such travelers tend to depart with a much more favorable impression of the country than they had before their trip, partly on the basis of their discovery that it contains many friendly, attractive people, that the exotic streets swarm with human beings "just like us."

What had they imagined before they came?

[1984]

The Idea of Europe
(One More Elegy)

EUROPE? What Europe means to me?

What it doesn't mean: the Europe of Euro-business, Euro-dollars—the so-called, would-be European "community" that is supposed to help the individual countries of capitalist Western Europe "to stand up to the bracing economic challenges of the late 20th century" (I quote from today's *Herald Tribune*, America's world newspaper); the Euro-kitsch acclaimed as art and literature in these countries; Euro-festivals and Euro-exhibitions and Euro-journalism and Euro-television. But *that* Europe is inexorably reshaping the Europe I love, the polyphonic culture within whose traditions, some of them, I create and feel and think and grow restless, and to whose best, humbling standards I align my own.

America is not, of course, totally disjunct from Europe, though it is far more unlike Europe (more "barbaric") than many Europeans like to think. And although, like the majority of my compatriots, if a smaller majority than before, I am of European descent—specifically of European-Jewish descent (my great-grandparents immigrated to the northeastern part of the United States a century ago from what are now Poland and Lithuania)—I don't often think of what Europe means to me as an American. I think of what it means to me as a writer, as a citizen of literature—which is an international citizenship.

If I must describe what Europe means to me as an American, I would start with liberation. Liberation from what passes in America for a culture. The diversity, seriousness, fastidiousness, density of European culture constitute an Archimedean point from which I can, mentally, move the world. I cannot do that from America, from what American culture gives me, as a collection of standards, as a legacy. Hence Europe is essential to me, more essential than America, although all my sojourns in Europe do not make me an expatriate.

To be sure, Europe means a good deal more than that ideal diversity, that stupendous nourishment . . . those pleasures, those standards. Both an old reality, since at least the Latin Middle Ages, and a perennial, often hypocritical, aspiration, "Europe" as a modern rallying cry for political unification has invariably promoted the suppression and erasure of cultural differences, and the concentration and augmentation of state power. It is chastening to recall that not only Napoleon but also Hitler proclaimed a pan-European ideal. Much of Nazi propaganda in France during the Occupation was devoted to portraying Hitler as Europe's savior from Bolshevism, from the Russian or "Asiatic" hordes. The idea of Europe has often been associated with the defense of "civilization" against alien populations. Usually, to defend civilization meant to extend the military power and business interests of a single European country which was competing for power and wealth with other European countries. Besides meaning something that could indeed be called civilization (for this must not be denied, either), "Europe" meant an idea of the moral rightness of the hegemony of certain European countries over large parts of what is not Europe. Seeking to convince non-Jews of the desirability of a Jewish state in Palestine, Theodor Herzl declared that "we shall form part of Europe's fortified wall against Asia, and fulfill the role of cultural vanguard facing the barbarians." I cite this sentence from Herzl's *Judenstaat* not to inveigh (along with everyone else these days) against Israel in particular but to underline the fact that virtually every act of colonization in the nineteenth and the early twentieth centuries by a European people was justified as an extension of the moral boundaries of "civilization"—

considered identical with European civilization—and a rolling back of the tides of barbarism.

For a long time the very idea of "universal" values, of world institutions, was itself Eurocentric. There is a sense in which the world *was*, once, Eurocentric. That Europe is "the world of yesterday," which is the title that Stefan Zweig gave to his lament for Europe in the form of a memoir, his last book, written almost half a century ago after this preeminent good European was forced to flee Europe, to flee a triumphant barbarism that was (need it be said?) entirely generated from within, in the heart of Europe. One might think that the notion of Europe would have been thoroughly discredited, first by imperialism and racism, and then by the imperatives of multi-national capitalism. In fact, it has not. (Nor is the idea of civilization unusable—no matter how many colonialist atrocities are committed in its name.)

The place where the idea of Europe has the greatest cultural vivacity is in the central and eastern parts of the continent, where citizens of countries in the other empire struggle for some autonomy. I refer, of course, to the debate over Central Europe opened by Milan Kundera's influential essay of some years ago, and continued with essays and manifestos by Adam Zagajewski, Václav Havel, Georgy Konrád, and Danilo Kiš. For a Pole, a Czech, a Hungarian, a Yugoslav (even, for other reasons, for an Austrian or a German), the idea of Europe has an obvious, subversive authority. The ultimate value of the cultural, and eventually political, counter-hypothesis of the existence of Central Europe—and, by extension, of Europe—is to urge a European peace settlement, a settlement that would erode the rivalry of the superpowers that holds all our lives hostage. To have the edges of the two empires, as they meet in Europe, be porous would be in everyone's interest. And I mean everyone, which I shall define arbitrarily as all those who think that their great-grandchildren should be allowed to have great-grandchildren. "As long as it is impossible to go over to Vienna from Budapest for an evening at the opera without special permission," Konrád has observed, "we cannot be said to live in a state of peace."

Do we have anything comparable to the Central Europeans' romantic project of a Europe of small nations, able to communicate freely with one another and pool their experience, their immense civic maturity and cultural depth, which have been acquired at the cost of so much suffering and privation? For us, who can hop from continent to continent without securing permission from anyone for a night at the opera, could Europe mean anything of that value? Or is the ideal Europe rendered obsolete by our prosperity, our liberty, our selfishness? And the idea itself, for us, spoiled beyond repair?

In one respect, our two experiences seem comparable, perhaps due to the very real loss of European power on both sides of the divide of empire. The new idea of Europe is not of extension but of retrenchment: the Europeanization not of the rest of the world but of Europe. Among Poles and Hungarians and Czechs, "Europe" is a not-so-subtle slogan for limiting the power and cultural hegemony of the cloddish, stifling Russian occupiers. Make Europe . . . European. In rich Europe, where we cannot complain of being cut off from one another, there is another anguish. Not about making Europe European but about keeping it European. Clearly, a losing battle. While the highly educated populations of central Europe are suffering from preposterous isolation and rationing of cultural contacts, those of western Europe are afflicted with incessant and isolating admixtures of cultural practice. There are Sikh taxi drivers in Frankfurt and mosques in Marseille. Italian doctors in hospitals in Naples, Rome, and Turin are performing clitoridectomies on the pubescent daughters of African immigrants, at the request of their parents. The only relatively homogeneous countries in Europe are going to be the poor ones, like Portugal and Greece, plus the Central European countries that have been impoverished by forty years of Moscow-directed economic planning. The unremitting influxes of foreigners into the rich European countries have the possibility of turning the slogan "Europe" nasty once more.

Europe, an exercise in nostalgia? Loyalty to Europe like continuing to write by hand when everyone is using a typewriter? (More aptly: like continuing to write on a typewriter when everyone is using a word processor?) It seems worth noting that the countries where an idea of Europe one can take seriously does flourish are those whose inflexible, fearful, militarized systems of governance and dismal economies make them considerably less modern, less prosperous, and more ethnically homogeneous than the western part of the continent. A modern Europe—often mistakenly called an "Americanized" Europe—is certainly a good deal less European. Some experience of Japan over the last decade has shown me that the "modern" is not equivalent to American. (Equating modernization with Americanization and vice versa may be the ultimate Eurocentric prejudice.) The modern has its own logic, liberating and immensely destructive, by which the United States, no less than Japan and the rich European countries, is being transformed. Meanwhile, the center has shifted. (But the center is always being destroyed or modified by the periphery.) Los Angeles has become the eastern capital of Asia, and a Japanese industrialist, when recently describing his plans to put up a factory in the United States in the "northeast," meant not Massachusetts but Oregon. There is a new cultural and political geography, and it will be syncretistic, and increasingly destructive of the past. The future of mainstream Europe is Euroland, nation-sized theme parks, Europe as instant playback, which natives will consume as avidly as tourists (in Europe the distinction has long been obsolete—everyone is a tourist). What remains of the Europe of high art and ethical seriousness, of the values of privacy and inwardness and an unamplified, non-machine-made discourse: the Europe that makes possible the films of Krzysztof Zanussi and the prose of Thomas Bernhard and the poetry of Seamus Heaney and the music of Arvo Pärt? That Europe still exists, will continue to exist for some time. But it will occupy less territory. And increasing numbers of its citizens and adherents will understand themselves as émigrés, exiles, and foreigners.

What then will happen to one's European roots, the real ones and the spiritual ones? I can think of no more consoling response to that question than one given by an American expatriate writer who was once asked if, having spent forty years living in France, she was not worried about losing her American roots. Said Gertrude Stein, her answer perhaps even more Jewish than American: "But what good are roots if you can't take them with you?"

[1988]

The Very Comical Lament
of Pyramus and Thisbe

(AN INTERLUDE)

WALL: Thus have I, Wall, my part discharged so;
    And being done, thus Wall away doth go.
        —*A Midsummer Night's Dream*, Act V, Scene I

THISBE: It's not here anymore.
PYRAMUS: It separated us. We yearned for each other. We grew apart.
THISBE: I was always thinking about it.
PYRAMUS: I thought you were thinking about me.
THISBE: Ninny! (*Gives him a kiss.*) How often have I reassured you. But I'm talking about what I didn't say. With every sentence I uttered, there was another, unspoken half sentence, "And the wall . . ." Example: I'm going to the Paris Bar.
PYRAMUS: "And the wall . . ."
THISBE: Example: What's playing at the Arsenal tonight?
PYRAMUS: "And the wall . . ."
THISBE: Example: It's terrible for the Turks in Kreuzberg.
PYRAMUS: "And the wall . . ."
THISBE: Exactly.

290

PYRAMUS: It was a tragedy. Will it be a comedy now?

THISBE: We won't become normal, will we?

PYRAMUS: Does this mean we can do whatever we want?

THISBE: I'm starting to feel a little nostalgic. Oh, the human heart is a fickle thing.

PYRAMUS: Thisbe!

THISBE: Not about you, beloved! You know I'll always be yours. I mean; you'll be mine. But of course that's the same, isn't it? No, I'm thinking about . . . you know. I miss it a little.

PYRAMUS: Thisbe!

THISBE: Just a little. (*Sees* PYRAMUS *frowning.*) Smile, darling. Oh, you people are so serious!

PYRAMUS: I've suffered.

THISBE: So have I, in my way. Not like you, of course. But it wasn't always easy here, either.

PYRAMUS: Let's not quarrel.

THISBE: *We* quarrel? Never! (*Sound of wall-peckers*) Listen! What an amazing sound!

PYRAMUS: I wish I'd brought my tape recorder. It's a Sony.

THISBE: I'm glad you can buy whatever you want now. I didn't realize you were *so* poor.

PYRAMUS: It was awful. But, you know, it was good for my character.

THISBE: You see? Even you can feel regret. An American artist warned me last year, You'll miss this wall. (*She spies some wall-peckers spraying their hoard of pieces of the wall with paint.*) They're improving it.

PYRAMUS: Let's not be nostalgic.

THISBE: But you agree there's something to be said for it. It made us different.

PYRAMUS: We'll still be different.

THISBE: I don't know. So many cars. So much trash. The beggars. Pedestrians don't wait at corners for the green light. Cars parked on the sidewalk.

Enter the SPIRIT OF NEW YORK.

SPIRIT: O city, I recognize you. Your leather bars, your festivals of independent films, your teeming dark-skinned foreigners, your real-estate predators, your Art Deco shops, your racism, your Mediterranean restaurants, your littered streets, your rude mechanicals—

THISBE: No! Begone! This is the Berkeley of Central Europe.

SPIRIT: Central Europe: a dream. Your Berkeley: an interlude. This will be the New York of Europe—it was ever meant to be so. Only postponed for a mere sixty years.

SPIRIT OF NEW YORK *vanishes.*

THISBE: Well, I suppose it won't be too bad. Since New York isn't America, this city still won't be—

PYRAMUS: Sure, sure, provided it stays shabby as well as full of unwelcome foreigners. (*Sighs.*) Let's not be too hopeful.

THISBE: Oh, let's be hopeful. We'll be rich. It's only money.

PYRAMUS: And power. I'm going to like that.

THISBE: We're not getting anything we don't deserve. We're together. We're free.

PYRAMUS: Everything is going too fast. And costing too much.

THISBE: No one can make us do what we don't want as long as we're together.

PYRAMUS: I'm having a hard time thinking of those less fortunate than we are. But sometimes we'll remember, won't we.

THISBE: I want to forget these old stories.

PYRAMUS: History is homesickness.

THISBE: Cheer up, darling. The world is divided into Old and New. And we'll always be on the good side. From now on.

PYRAMUS: Goethe said—

THISBE: Oh, not Goethe.

PYRAMUS: You're right.

THISBE: In Walter Benjamin's last—

PYRAMUS: Not Benjamin, either!

THISBE: Right. (*They fall silent for a while.*) Let's stroll.

They see a procession of vendors, including some Russian soldiers, coming across an empty field.

PYRAMUS: And to think *that* was no-man's-land.

THISBE: What are they selling?

PYRAMUS: Everything. Everything is for sale.

THISBE: Do say it's better. Please!

PYRAMUS: Of course it's better. We don't have to die.

THISBE: Then let's go on celebrating. Have some champagne. Have a
River Cola.

They drink.

PYRAMUS: Freedom at last.

THISBE: But don't toss your can on the ground.

PYRAMUS: What do you take me for?

THISBE: Sorry. It's just that—I'm sorry. Yes, freedom.

Curtain.

[1991]

Answers to a Questionnaire

I N MAY 1997 the French literary magazine *La Règle du
Jeu*, edited by Philippe Sollers, conducted "an international
survey about intellectuals and their role." I was the sole American
on the list of respondents to whom they sent the following six questions:

1. What does the word intellectual mean to you today? Do you
see yourself as an intellectual or do you reject this term?

2. Who are the intellectual figures who have inspired you in a
profound way and still have influence over your thoughts?

3. What is the role of intellectuals at the end of the XXth century? Is their mission completed or do you think that they still have
an important task in the world?

4. Much has been said about the mistakes of intellectuals, their
blindness and their irresponsibility. What do you think about these
accusations? Do you agree or would you challenge the criticism?

5. What, in your view, are the major obstacles for intellectuals
in your country—the indifference of the media, the chaos of opinions, political repression, or what?

6. What do you consider the most urgent tasks, the most dangerous prejudices, the most important causes, the biggest perils, and the greatest intellectual joys of today?

This provoked nine answers to some of the questions asked and (I thought) implied.

1

WHAT THE WORD intellectual means to me today is, first of all, conferences and roundtable discussions and symposia in magazines about the role of intellectuals in which well-known intellectuals have agreed to pronounce on the inadequacy, credulity, disgrace, treason, irrelevance, obsolescence, and imminent or already perfected disappearance of the caste to which, as their participation in these events testifies, they belong.

2

WHETHER I SEE myself as one (I try to do as little seeing of myself as possible) is beside the point. I answer if so called.

3

BEING A CITIZEN of a country whose political and ethical culture promotes and reinforces distrust, fear, and contempt for intellectuals (reread Tocqueville), the country which has the most developed anti-intellectual tradition on the planet, I incline to a less jaded view of the role of intellectuals than my colleagues in Europe. No, their "mission" (as your question has it) is not completed.

Of course, it's speaking much too well of intellectuals to expect the majority to have a taste for protesting against injustice, defending victims, challenging the reigning authoritarian pieties. Most intellectuals are as conformist—as willing, say, to support the prosecution of unjust wars—as most other people exercising educated professions. The number of people who have given intellectuals a good name, as trouble-makers, voices of conscience, has always been small. Intellectuals responsibly taking sides, and putting themselves on the line for what they believe in (as opposed to signing petitions), are a good deal less common than intellectuals taking public positions either in conscious bad faith or in shameless ignorance of what they are pronouncing on: for every André Gide or George Orwell or Norberto Bobbio or Andrei Sakharov or Adam Michnik, ten of Romain Rolland or Ilya Ehrenburg or Jean Baudrillard or Peter Handke, et cetera, et cetera.

But could it be otherwise?

4

ALTHOUGH INTELLECTUALS COME in all flavors, including the nationalist and the religious, I confess to being partial to the secular, cosmopolitan, anti-tribal variety. The "deracinated intellectual" seems to me an exemplary formula.

By intellectual I mean the "free" intellectual, someone who, beyond his or her professional or technical or artistic expertise, is committed to exercising (and thereby, implicitly, defending) the life of the mind as such.

A specialist may also be an intellectual. But an intellectual is never just a specialist. One is an intellectual because one has (or should have) certain standards of probity and responsibility in discourse. That is the one indispensable contribution of intellectuals: the notion of discourse that is not merely instrumental, conformist.

5

HOW MANY TIMES has one heard in the last decades that intellectuals are obsolete, or that so-and-so is "the last intellectual"?

6

THERE ARE TWO TASKS for intellectuals, today as yesterday. One task, educational, is to promote dialogue, support the right of a multiplicity of voices to be heard, strengthen skepticism about received opinion. This means standing up to those whose idea of education and culture is the imprinting of ideas ("ideals") such as the love of the nation or tribe.

The other task is adversarial. There has been a daunting shift of moral attitudes in the last two decades in advanced capitalist countries. Its hallmark is the discrediting of all idealisms, of altruism itself; of high standards of all kinds, cultural as well as moral. The ideology of Thatcherism is gaining everywhere, and the mass media, whose function is to promote consumption, disseminate the narratives and ideas of value and disvalue by which people everywhere understand themselves. Intellectuals have the Sisyphean task of continuing to embody (and defend) a standard of mental life, and of discourse, other than the nihilistic one promoted by the mass media. By nihilism I mean not only the relativism, the privatization of interest, which is ascendant among the educated classes everywhere, but also the more recent, and more pernicious, nihilism embodied in the ideology of so-called cultural democracy; the hatred of excellence, achievement as "elitist," exclusionary.

7

THE MORAL DUTY of the intellectual will always be complex because there is more than one "highest" value, and there are concrete circumstances in which not all that is unconditionally good can be honored—in which, indeed, two of these values may prove incompatible.

For instance, understanding the truth does not always facilitate the struggle for justice. And in order to bring about justice, it may seem right to suppress the truth.

One hopes not to have to choose. But when a choice (between truth and justice) is necessary—as, alas, it sometimes is—it seems to me that an intellectual ought to decide for the truth.

This is not, by and large, what intellectuals, the best-intentioned intellectuals, have done. Invariably, when intellectuals subscribe to causes, it is the truth, in all its complexity, which gets short shrift.

8

A GOOD RULE BEFORE one goes marching or signing anything:
Whatever your tug of sympathy, you have no right to a public opinion unless you've been there, experienced firsthand and on the ground
and for some considerable time the country, war, injustice, whatever,
you are talking about.

In the absence of such firsthand knowledge and experience: silence.

9

ON THE SUBJECT of the presumption—it's worse than naïveté—
of so many intellectuals who take public positions and endorse collective actions that concern countries they know virtually nothing about,
nobody said it better than one of the most compromised intellectuals
of the twentieth century, Bertolt Brecht (who surely knew whereof he
spoke):

> When it comes to marching many do not know
> That their enemy is marching at their head.
> The voice which gives them their orders
> Is the enemy's voice and
> The man who speaks of the enemy
> Is the enemy himself.

[1997]

Waiting for Godot
in Sarajevo

Nothing to be done. / *Ništa ne može da se uradi.*
      —opening line of *Waiting for Godot*

1

I **WENT TO** Sarajevo in mid-July 1993 to stage a production of *Waiting for Godot* not so much because I'd always wanted to direct Beckett's play (although I had) as because it gave me a practical reason to return to Sarajevo and stay for a month or more. I had spent two weeks there in April, and had come to care intensely about the battered city and what it stands for; some of its citizens had become friends. But I couldn't again be just a witness: that is, meet and visit, tremble with fear, feel brave, feel depressed, have heartbreaking conversations, grow ever more indignant, lose weight. If I went back, it would be to pitch in and do something.

No longer can a writer consider that the imperative task is to bring the news to the outside world. The news is out. Many excellent foreign journalists (most of them in favor of intervention, as I am) have been reporting the lies and the slaughter since the beginning of the siege, while the decision of the western European powers and the United States not to intervene remains firm, thereby giving the victory to Serb fascism. I was not under the illusion that going to Sarajevo to direct a play would make me useful in the way I could be if I were a doctor or a water systems engineer. It would be a small contribution. But it was the only one of the three things I do—write, make films, and direct in the theatre—which yields something that would exist only in Sarajevo, that would be made and consumed there.

In April I'd met a young Sarajevo-born theatre director, Haris Pašović, who had left the city after he finished school and made his considerable reputation working mainly in Serbia. When the Serbs started the war in April 1992, Pašović went abroad, but in the fall, while working on a spectacle called *Sarajevo* in Antwerp, he decided that he could no longer remain in safe exile, and at the end of the year managed to crawl back past UN patrols and under Serb gunfire into the freezing, besieged city. Pašović invited me to see his *Grad* (City), a collage, with music, of declamations, partly drawn from texts by Constantine Cavafy, Zbigniew Herbert, and Sylvia Plath, using a dozen actors; he'd put it together in eight days. Now he was preparing a far more ambitious production, Euripides' *Alcestis*, after which one of his students (Pašović teaches at the still-functioning Academy of Drama) would be directing Sophocles' *Ajax*. One day Pašović asked me if I was interested in coming back in a few months to direct a play.

More than interested, I told him.

Before I could add, "But let me think for a while about what I might want to do," he went on, "What play?" And bravado suggested to me in an instant what I might not have seen had I taken longer to reflect: there was one obvious play for me to direct. Beckett's play, written over forty years ago, seems written for, and about, Sarajevo.

HAVING OFTEN BEEN ASKED since my return from Sarajevo if I worked with professional actors, I've come to understand that many people find it surprising that theatre goes on at all in the besieged city. In fact, of the five theatres in Sarajevo before the war, two are still, sporadically, in use: Chamber Theatre 55 (Kamerni Teater 55), where in April I'd seen a charmless production of *Hair* as well as Pašović's *Grad*, and the Youth Theatre (Pozorište Mladih), where I decided to stage *Godot*. These are both small houses. The large house, closed

since the beginning of the war, is the National Theatre, which presented opera and the Sarajevo Ballet as well as plays. In front of the
handsome ochre building (only lightly damaged by shelling), there is
still a poster from early April 1992 announcing a new production of
Rigoletto, which never opened. Most of the singers and musicians and
ballet dancers left the city soon after the Serbs attacked, it being easier
for them to find work abroad, while many of the actors stayed, and
want nothing more than to work.

Another question I'm often asked is: who goes to see a production
of *Waiting for Godot*? Who indeed if not the same people who would
go to see *Waiting for Godot* if there were not a siege on? Images of
today's shattered city must make it hard to grasp that Sarajevo was
once an extremely lively and attractive provincial capital, with a cultural life comparable to that of other middle-sized old European cities;
that includes an audience for theatre. As elsewhere in Central Europe,
theatre in Sarajevo was largely repertory: masterpieces from the past
and the most admired twentieth-century plays. Just as talented actors
still live in Sarajevo, so do members of this cultivated audience. The
difference is that actors and spectators alike can be murdered or
maimed by a sniper's bullet or a mortar shell on their way to and from
the theatre; but then, that can happen to people in Sarajevo in their living rooms, while they sleep in their bedrooms, when they fetch something from their kitchens, as they go out their front doors.

BUT ISN'T THIS PLAY rather pessimistic? I've been asked. Meaning, wasn't it depressing for an audience in Sarajevo; meaning, wasn't it
pretentious or insensitive to stage *Godot* there?—as if the representation of despair were redundant when people really are in despair; as if
what people want to see in such a situation would be, say, *The Odd
Couple*. The condescending, philistine question makes me realize that
those who ask it don't understand at all what it's like in Sarajevo now,
any more than they really care about literature and theatre. It's not true
that what everyone wants is entertainment that offers them an escape
from their own reality. In Sarajevo, as anywhere else, there are more
than a few people who feel strengthened and consoled by having their

sense of reality affirmed and transfigured by art. This is not to say that people in Sarajevo don't miss being entertained. The dramaturge of the National Theatre, who began sitting in on the rehearsals of *Godot* after the first week, and who had studied at Columbia University, asked me before I left to bring a few copies of *Vogue* and *Vanity Fair* when I return later this month: she longed to be reminded of all the things that had gone out of her life. Certainly there are more Sarajevans who would rather see a Harrison Ford movie or attend a Guns N Roses concert than watch *Waiting for Godot*. That was true before the war, too. It is, if anything, a little less true now.

And if one considers what plays were produced in Sarajevo before the siege began—as opposed to the movies shown, almost entirely the big Hollywood successes (the small cinematheque was on the verge of closing just before the war for lack of an audience, I was told)—there was nothing odd or gloomy for the public in the choice of *Waiting for Godot*. The other productions currently in rehearsal or performance are *Alcestis* (about the inevitability of death and the meaning of sacrifice), *Ajax* (about a warrior's madness and suicide), and *In Agony*, a play by the Croatian Miroslav Krleža, who is, with the Bosnian Ivo Andrić, one of the two internationally celebrated writers of the first half of the century from the former Yugoslavia (the play's title speaks for itself). Compared with these, *Waiting for Godot* may have been the "lightest" entertainment of all.

INDEED, THE QUESTION IS not why there is any cultural activity in Sarajevo now after seventeen months of siege, but why there isn't more. Outside a boarded-up movie theatre next to the Chamber Theatre is a sun-bleached poster for *The Silence of the Lambs* with a diagonal strip across it that says DANAS (today), which was April 6, 1992, the day moviegoing stopped. Since the war began, all of the movie theatres in Sarajevo have remained shut, even if not all have been severely damaged by shelling. A building in which people gather so predictably would be too tempting a target for the Serb guns; anyway, there is no electricity to run a projector. There are no concerts, except for those given by a lone string quartet that rehearses every morning and performs occasionally in a small room that also doubles as an art gallery, seating forty. (It's in the same building on Marshal Tito Street that houses the Chamber Theatre.) There is only one active space for painting and photography, the Obala Gallery, whose exhibits sometimes stay up only one day and never more than a week.

No one I talked with in Sarajevo disputes the sparseness of cultural life in this city where, after all, between 300,000 and 400,000 inhabitants still live. The majority of the city's intellectuals and creative people, including most of the faculty of the University of Sarajevo, fled at the beginning of the war, before the city was completely encircled. Besides, many Sarajevans are reluctant to leave their apartments except when it is absolutely necessary, to collect water and the rations distributed by the United Nations High Commissioner for Refugees (UNHCR); though no one is safe anywhere, they have more to fear when they are in the street. And beyond fear, there is depression—most Sarajevans are very depressed—which produces lethargy, exhaustion, apathy.

Moreover, Belgrade was the cultural capital of the former Yugoslavia, and I have the impression that in Sarajevo the visual arts were derivative; that ballet, opera, and musical life were routine. Only film and theatre were distinguished, so it is not surprising that these continue under siege. A film production company, SAGA, makes both documentary and fiction films, and there are the two functioning theatres.

IN FACT, THE AUDIENCE for theatre expects to see a play like *Waiting for Godot*. What my production of *Godot* signifies to them, apart from the fact that an eccentric American writer and part-time director volunteered to work in the theatre as an expression of solidarity with the city (a fact inflated by the local press and radio as evidence that the rest of the world "does care," when I knew, to my indignation and shame, that I represented nobody but myself), is that this is a great European play and that they are members of European culture. For all their attachment to American popular culture, as intense here as anywhere else, it is the high culture of Europe that represents for them their ideal, their passport to a European identity. People had told me again and again on my earlier visit in April: We are part of Europe. We are the people in the former Yugoslavia who stand for European values—secularism, religious tolerance, and multi-ethnicity. How can the rest of Europe let this happen to us? When I replied that Europe is and always has been as much a place of barbarism as a place of civilization, they didn't want to hear. Now no one would dispute such a statement.

CULTURE, SERIOUS CULTURE, is an expression of human dignity—which is what people in Sarajevo feel they have lost, even when they know themselves to be brave, or stoical, or angry. For they also know themselves to be terminally weak: waiting, hoping, not wanting to hope, knowing that they aren't going to be saved. They are humiliated by their disappointment, by their fear, and by the indignities of daily life—for instance, by having to spend a good part of each day seeing to it that their toilets flush, so that their bathrooms don't become cesspools. That is how they use most of the water they queue for in public spaces, at great risk to their lives. Their sense of humiliation may be even greater than their fear.

Putting on a play means so much to the local theatre professionals in Sarajevo because it allows them to be normal, that is, to do what they did before the war; to be not just haulers of water or passive recipients of humanitarian aid. Indeed, the lucky people in Sarajevo are those who can carry on with their professional work. It is not a question of money, since Sarajevo has only a black-market economy, whose currency is German marks, and many people are living on their savings, which were always in deutsche marks, or on remittances from abroad. (To get an idea of the city's economy, consider that a skilled professional—say, a surgeon at the city's main hospital or a television journalist—earns three deutsche marks a month, while cigarettes, a local version of Marlboros, cost ten deutsche marks a pack.) The actors and I, of course, were not on salary. Other theatre people would sit in on rehearsals not just because they wanted to watch our work but because they were glad to have, once again, a theatre to go to every day.

Far from it being frivolous to put on a play—this play or any other—it is a welcome expression of normality. "Isn't putting on a play like fiddling while Rome burns?" a journalist asked one of the actors. "Just asking a provocative question," the journalist explained to me when I reproached her, worried that the actor might have been offended. He was not. He didn't know what she was talking about.

2

I STARTED AUDITIONING actors the day after I arrived, one role already cast in my head. At a meeting with theatre people in April, I couldn't have failed to notice a stout older woman wearing a large broad-brimmed black hat who sat silently, imperiously, in a corner of the room. A few days later when I saw her in Pašović's *Grad*, I learned that she was the senior actor of the pre-siege Sarajevo theatre, and when I decided to direct *Godot* I immediately thought of her as Pozzo. Pašović concluded that I would cast only women (he told me that an all-woman *Godot* had been done in Belgrade some years ago). But that wasn't my intention. I wanted the casting to be gender-blind, confident that this is one of the few plays where it makes sense, since the characters are representative, even allegorical figures. If Everyman (like the pronoun "he") really does stand for everybody—as women are always being told—then Everyman doesn't have to be played by a man. I was not making the statement that a woman can also be a tyrant—which Pašović then decided I meant by casting Ines Fančović in the role—but rather that a woman can play the role of a tyrant. In contrast, Admir ("Atko") Glamočak, the actor I cast as Lucky, a gaunt, lithe man of thirty whom I'd admired as Death in *Alcestis*, fit perfectly the traditional conception of Pozzo's slave.

Three other roles were left: Vladimir and Estragon, the pair of forlorn tramps, and Godot's messenger, a small boy. It was troubling that there were more good actors available than parts, since I knew how much it meant to the actors I auditioned to be in the play. Three seemed particularly gifted: Velibor Topić, who was playing Death in *Alcestis*; Izudin ("Izo") Bajrović, who was *Alcestis*'s Hercules; and Nada Djurevska, who had the lead in the Krleža play.

Then it occurred to me I could have three pairs of Vladimir and Estragon and put them all on the stage at once. Velibor and Izo seemed likely to make the most powerful, fluent couple; there was no reason *not* to use what Beckett envisaged, two men, at the center; but they would be flanked on the left side of the stage by two women and on the right by a woman and a man—three variations on the theme of the couple.

Since child actors were not available and I dreaded using a nonprofessional, I decided to make the messenger an adult: the boyish-looking Mirza Halilović, a talented actor who happened to speak the best English of anyone in the cast. Of the other eight actors, three knew no English at all. It was a great help to have Mirza as interpreter, so I could communicate with everybody at the same time.

BY THE SECOND DAY of rehearsal, I had begun to divide up and apportion the text, like a musical score, among the three pairs of Vladimir and Estragon. I had once before worked in a foreign language, when I directed Pirandello's *As You Desire Me* at the Teatro Stabile in Turin. But I knew some Italian, while my Serbo-Croatian (or "the mother tongue," as people in Sarajevo call it, the words "Serbo-Croatian" being hard to utter now) was limited when I arrived to "Please," "Hello," "Thank you," and "Not now." I had brought with me an English–Serbo-Croatian phrase book, paperback copies of the play in English and French, and an enlarged photocopy of the text into which I copied in pencil the "Bosnian" translation, line by line, as soon as I received it. I also copied the English and French line by line into the Bosnian script. In about ten days I had managed to learn by heart the words of Beckett's play in the language in which my actors were speaking it.

DID I HAVE a multi-ethnic cast? many people have asked me. And if so, was there conflict or tension among the actors, or did they, as someone here in New York put it to me, "get along with each other"?

But of course I did—the population of Sarajevo is so mixed, and intermarriage is so common, that it would be hard to assemble any kind of group in which all three ethnic identities were not represented. Eventually I learned that Velibor Topić (Estragon I) has a Muslim mother and a Croat father, though he has a Serb first name, while Ines Fančović (Pozzo) had to be Croatian, since Ines is a Croat name and she was born and grew up in the coastal town of Split and came to Sarajevo thirty years ago. Both parents of Milijana Zirojević (Estragon II) are Serb, while Irena Mulamuhić (Estragon III) must have had at least a Muslim father. I never learned the ethnic origins of all the actors. They knew them and took them for granted because they are colleagues—they've acted in many plays together—and friends.

Yes, of course they got along.

WHAT SUCH QUESTIONS show is that the questioner has bought into the propaganda of the aggressors: that this war is caused by age-old hatreds; that it is a civil war or a war of secession, with Milosević trying to save the union; that in crushing the Bosnians, whom Serb propaganda often refers to as the Turks, the Serbs are saving Europe from Muslim fundamentalism. Perhaps I should not have been surprised to be asked if I saw many women in Sarajevo who are veiled, or who wear the chador; one can't underestimate the extent to which the prevailing stereotypes about Muslims have shaped "Western" reactions to the Serb aggression in Bosnia.

To invoke these stereotypes is also to explain—this is another question I'm often asked—why other foreign artists and writers who regard themselves as politically engaged haven't volunteered to do something for Sarajevo. The danger can't be the only reason, though that's what most people *say* is their reason for not considering a visit; surely it was as dangerous to go to Barcelona in 1937 as it is to go to Sarajevo in 1993. I suspect that the ultimate reason is a failure of identification—enforced by the buzzword "Muslim." Even quite well informed people in the United States and in Europe seem genuinely surprised when I mention that, until the siege began, a middle-class Sarajevan was far more likely to go to Vienna to the opera than to go down the street to a mosque. I make this point not to suggest that the lives of non-religious urban Europeans are intrinsically more valuable than the lives of the devout of Tehran or Baghdad or Damascus—every human life has an absolute value—but because I wish it were better understood that it is precisely because Sarajevo represents the secular, anti-tribal ideal that it has been targeted for destruction.

In fact, the proportion of religiously observant people in Sarajevo is about the same as it is among the native-born in London or Paris or Berlin or Venice. In the prewar city, it was no odder for a secular Muslim to marry a Serb or a Croat than for someone from New York to marry someone from Massachusetts or California. In the year before the Serb attack, sixty percent of the marriages in Sarajevo took place between people from different religious backgrounds—the surest index of secularism.

Zdravko Grebo, Haris Pašović, Mirsad Purivatra, Izeta Gradević, Amela Simić, Hasan Gluhić, Ademir Kenović, Zehra Kreho, Ferida Duraković, and other friends of mine there of Muslim origin are as much Muslim as I am Jewish—which is to say, hardly at all. Indeed, it would be correct to say that I'm more Jewish than they are Muslim. My family has been entirely secular for three generations, but I am, as far as I can know, the descendant of an unbroken line of people under the same religious discipline for at least two millennia, and have a complexion and cast of features which identify me as the descendant of a branch of European (probably originally Sephardic) Jewry, while the Sarajevans of Muslim origin come from families that have been Muslim for at most five centuries (when Bosnia became a province of the Ottoman Empire), and are physiologically identical with their southern Slav neighbors, spouses, and compatriots, since they are in fact the descendants of Christian southern Slavs.

What Muslim adherence had existed throughout this century was already a diluted version of the moderate, Sunni faith brought by the Turks, with nothing of what is now called fundamentalism. When I asked friends who in their families are or were religiously observant, they invariably said: my grandparents. If they were under thirty-five, they usually said: my great-grandparents. Of the nine actors in *Godot*, the only one with religious leanings was Nada, who is the disciple of an Indian guru; as her farewell present she gave me a copy of the Penguin edition of *The Teachings of Shiva*.

3

POZZO: There is no denying it is still day.
(*They all look up at the sky.*)
Good.
(*They stop looking at the sky.*)

OF COURSE there were obstacles. Not ethnic ones. Real ones.

To start with, we rehearsed in the dark. The bare proscenium stage was lit usually by only three or four candles, supplemented by the four flashlights I'd brought with me. When I asked for additional candles, I was told there weren't any. Later I was told that they were being saved for our performances. In fact, I never learned who doled out the candles; they were simply in place on the floor when I arrived each morning at the theatre, having walked through alleys and courtyards to reach the stage door, the only usable entrance, at the rear of the freestanding modern building. The theatre's façade, lobby, cloakroom, and bar had been wrecked by shelling more than a year earlier and the debris still had not been cleared away.

Actors in Sarajevo, Pašović had explained to me with comradely regret, expect to work only four hours a day. "We have many bad habits here left over from the old socialist days." But that was not my experience. After a bumpy start—during the first week everyone seemed preoccupied with other performances and rehearsals, or obligations at home—I could not have asked for actors more zealous, more eager. The main obstacle, apart from the siege lighting, was the fatigue of the malnourished actors, many of whom, before they arrived for rehearsal at ten, had for several hours been queuing for water and then lugging heavy plastic containers up eight or ten flights of stairs. Some of them had to walk two hours to get to the theatre, and, of course, would have to follow the same dangerous route at the end of the day.

The only actor who seemed to have normal stamina was the oldest member of the cast, Ines Fančović, who is sixty-eight. Still large, she had lost more than sixty pounds since the beginning of the siege, which may have accounted for her remarkable energy. The other actors were visibly underweight and tired easily. Beckett's Lucky must stand motionless through most of his long scene without ever setting down the heavy bag he carries. Atko, who now weighs no more than one hundred pounds, asked me to excuse him if he occasionally rested his empty suitcase on the floor. Whenever I halted the run-through for a few minutes to change a movement or a line reading, all the actors, with the exception of Ines, would instantly lie down on the stage.

Another symptom of fatigue: they were slower to memorize their lines than any actors I have ever worked with. Ten days before the opening they still needed to consult their scripts, and were not word-perfect until the day before the dress rehearsal. This might have been less of a problem had it not been too dark for them to read the scripts they held in their hands. An actor crossing the stage while saying a line, who then forgot the next line, was obliged to make a detour to the nearest candle and peer at his or her script. (A script was loose pages, since binders and paper clips are virtually unobtainable in Sarajevo. The play had been typed in Pašović's office on a little manual typewriter whose ribbon had been in use since the beginning of the siege. I was given the original and the actors carbon copies, most of which would have been hard to read in any light.)

Not only could they not read their scripts; unless standing face-to-face, they could barely see one another. Lacking the normal peripheral vision that anybody has in daylight or when there is electric light, they could not do something as simple as put on or take off their bowler hats in unison. And they appeared to me for a long time, to my despair, mostly as silhouettes. At the moment early in Act I when Vladimir "smiles suddenly from ear to ear, keeps smiling, ceases as suddenly"— in my version, three Vladimirs—I couldn't see a single one of those false smiles from my stool some ten feet in front of them, my flashlight lying across my scripts. Gradually, my night vision improved.

OF COURSE, it was not just fatigue that made the actors slower to learn their lines and their movements and to be often inattentive and forgetful. It was distraction, and fear. Each time we heard the noise of a shell exploding, there was relief that the theatre had not been hit, but the actors had to be wondering where it had landed. Only the youngest in my cast, Velibor, and the oldest, Ines, lived alone. The others left wives and husbands, parents and children at home when they came to the theatre each day, and several of them lived very close to the front lines, near Grbavica, a part of the city taken by the Serbs last year, or in Alipašino Polje, near the Serb-held airport.

On July 30, at two o'clock in the afternoon, Nada, who was often late during the first two weeks of rehearsal, arrived with the news that at eleven that morning Zlajko Sparavolo, a well-known older actor who specialized in Shakespearean roles, had been killed, along with two neighbors, when a shell landed outside his front door. The actors left the stage and went silently to an adjacent room. I followed them, and the first to speak told me that this news was particularly upsetting to everyone because, up till then, no actor had been killed. (I had heard earlier about two actors who had each lost a leg in the shelling; and I knew Nermin Tulić, the actor who lost both legs at the hip in the first months of the siege and was now the administrative director of the Youth Theatre.) When I asked the actors if they felt up to continuing the rehearsal, all but one, Izo, said yes. But after working for another hour, some of the actors found they couldn't continue. That was the only day that rehearsals stopped early.

THE SET I had designed—as minimally furnished, I thought, as Beckett himself could have desired—had two levels. Pozzo and Lucky entered, acted on, and exited from a rickety platform eight feet deep and four feet high, running the whole length of upstage, with the tree toward the left; the front of the platform was covered with the translucent polyurethane sheeting that UNHCR brought in last winter to seal the shattered windows of Sarajevo. The three couples stayed mostly on the stage floor, though sometimes one or more of the Vladimirs and Estragons went to the upper stage. It took several weeks of rehearsal to arrive at three distinct identities for them. The central Vladimir and Estragon (Izo and Velibor) were the classic buddy pair. After several false starts, the two women (Nada and Milijana) turned into another kind of couple in which affection and dependence are mixed with exasperation and resentment: mother in her early forties and grown daughter. And Sejo and Irena, who were also the oldest couple, played a quarrelsome, cranky husband and wife, modeled on homeless people I'd seen in downtown Manhattan. But when Lucky and Pozzo were onstage, the Vladimirs and Estragons could stand together, becoming something of a Greek chorus as well as an audience to the show put on by the terrifying master and slave.

Tripling the parts of Vladimir and Estragon, which entailed new stage business, more intricate silences, had the result of making the play a good deal longer than it usually is. I soon realized that Act I would run at least ninety minutes. Act II would be shorter, for my idea was to use only Izo and Velibor as Vladimir and Estragon. But even with a stripped-down and speeded-up Act II, the play would be two and a half hours long. And I could not envisage asking people to watch the play from the Youth Theatre's auditorium, whose nine small chandeliers could come crashing down if the building suffered a direct hit from a shell, or even if an adjacent building were hit. Further, there was no way three hundred people in the auditorium could see what was taking place on a deep proscenium stage lit only by a few candles. But as many as a hundred people could be seated close to the actors, at the front of the stage, on a tier of six rows of seats made from wood planks. They would be hot, since it was high summer, and they would be squeezed together; I knew that many more people would be lining up outside the stage door for each performance than could be seated (tickets are free). How could I ask the audience, which would have no lobby, bathroom, or water, to sit so uncomfortably, without moving, for two and a half hours?

I concluded that I could not do all of *Waiting for Godot*. But the very choices I had made about the staging which made Act I as long as it was also meant that the staging could represent the whole of *Waiting for Godot*, while using only the words of Act I. For this may be the only work in dramatic literature in which Act I is itself a complete play. The place and time of Act I are: "A country road. A tree. Evening." (For Act II: "Next day. Same time. Same place.") Although the time is "Evening," both acts show a complete day, the day beginning with Vladimir and Estragon meeting again (though in every sense except the sexual one a couple, they separate each evening), and with Vladimir (the dominant one, the reasoner and information-gatherer, who is better at fending off despair) inquiring where Estragon has spent the night. They talk about waiting for Godot (whoever he may be), straining to pass the time. Pozzo and Lucky arrive, stay for a while and perform their "routines," for which Vladimir and Estragon are the audience, then depart. After this there is a time of deflation and relief: they are waiting again. Then the messenger arrives to tell them that they have waited once more in vain.

Of course, there is a difference between Act I and the replay of Act I which is Act II. Not only has one more day gone by. Everything is worse. Lucky no longer can speak, Pozzo is now pathetic and blind, Vladimir has given in to despair. Perhaps I felt that the despair of Act I was enough for the Sarajevo audience, and I wanted to spare them a second time when Godot does not arrive. Maybe I wanted to propose, subliminally, that Act II might be different. For, precisely as *Waiting for Godot* was so apt an illustration of the feelings of Sarajevans now—bereft, hungry, dejected, waiting for an arbitrary, alien power to save them or take them under its protection—it seemed apt, too, to be staging *Waiting for Godot, Act I.*

4

Alas, alas . . . / *Avaj, avaj . . .*
—from Lucky's monologue

PEOPLE IN SARAJEVO live harrowing lives; this was a harrowing *Godot*. Ines was flamboyantly theatrical as Pozzo, and Atko was the most heartrending Lucky I have ever seen. Atko, who had ballet training and was a movement teacher at the Academy, quickly mastered the postures and gestures of decrepitude, and responded inventively to my suggestions for Lucky's dance of freedom. It took longer to work out Lucky's monologue, which in every production of *Godot* I'd seen (including the one Beckett himself directed in 1975 at the Schiller Theatre in Berlin) was, to my taste, delivered too fast, as nonsense. I divided this speech into five parts, and we discussed it line by line, as an argument, as a series of images and sounds, as a lament, as a cry. I wanted Atko to deliver Beckett's aria about divine apathy and indifference, about a heartless, petrifying world, as if it made perfect sense. Which it does, especially in Sarajevo.

It has always seemed to me that *Waiting for Godot* is a supremely realistic play, though it is generally acted in something like a minimalist or vaudeville style. The *Godot* that the Sarajevo actors were by inclination, temperament, previous theatre experience, and present (atrocious) circumstances most able to perform, and the one I chose to direct, was full of anguish, of immense sadness and, toward the end, violence. That the messenger was a strapping adult meant that when he announces the bad news, Vladimir and Estragon could express not only disappointment but rage: manhandling him as they could never have done had the role been played by a small child. (And there are six, not two, of them, and only one of him.) After he escapes, they subside into a long, terrible silence. It was a Chekhovian moment of absolute pathos, as at the end of *The Cherry Orchard*, when the ancient butler Firs wakes up to find that he's been left behind in the abandoned house.

IT FELT, during the mounting of *Godot* and this second stay in Sarajevo, as if I were going through the replay of a familiar cycle: some of the severest shelling of the city's center since the beginning of the siege (on one day Sarajevo was hit by nearly four thousand shells); the raising once more of the hopes of American intervention; the outwitting of Clinton (if outwitting is not too strong a term to describe so weak a resolve) by the pro-Serb United Nations Protection Force (UNPROFOR) command, which claimed that intervention would endanger UN troops; the steady increase in despair and disbelief of the Sarajevans; a mock cease-fire (that means just a little shelling and sniping, but since more people ventured out in the street, almost as many were murdered and maimed each day); et cetera, et cetera.

The cast and I tried to avoid jokes about "waiting for Clinton," but that was very much what we were doing in late July, when the Serbs took, or seemed to take, Mount Igman, just above the airport. The capture of Mount Igman would allow them to fire shells horizontally into the city, and hope rose again that there would be American air strikes against the Serb gun positions, or at least a lifting of the arms embargo. Although people were afraid to hope, for fear of being disappointed, at the same time no one could believe that Clinton would again speak of intervention and again do nothing. I myself had succumbed to hope again when a journalist friend showed me a dim satellite fax transmission of Senator Biden's eloquent speech in favor of intervention, twelve single-spaced pages, which he had delivered on the floor of the Senate on July 29. The Holiday Inn, the only still functioning hotel, which is on the western side of the city's center, four blocks from the nearest Serb snipers, was crowded with journalists waiting for the fall of Sarajevo or the intervention; one of the hotel staff said the place hadn't been this full since the 1984 Winter Olympics.

SOMETIMES I THOUGHT we were not waiting for Godot, or Clinton. We were waiting for our props. There seemed no way to find Lucky's suitcase and picnic basket, Pozzo's cigarette holder (to substitute for the pipe) and whip. As for the carrot that Estragon munches slowly, rapturously: until two days before we opened, we had to rehearse with three of the dry rolls I scavenged each morning from the Holiday Inn dining room (rolls were the breakfast offered) to feed the actors and assistants and the all-too-rare stagehand. We could not find any rope for Pozzo until a week after we started on the stage, and Ines got understandably cranky when, after three weeks of rehearsal, she still did not have the right length of rope, a proper whip, a cigarette holder, an atomizer. The bowler hats and the boots for the Estragons materialized only in the last days of rehearsal. And the costumes—whose designs I had suggested and the sketches of which I had approved in the first week—did not come until the day before we opened.

Some of this was owing to the scarcity of everything in Sarajevo. Some of it, I had to conclude, was typically "southern" (or Balkan)

mañana-ism. ("You'll definitely have the cigarette holder tomorrow," I
was told every morning for three weeks.) But some of the shortages
were the result of rivalry between theatres. There had to be props at
the closed National Theatre. Why were they not available to us? I discovered, shortly before the opening, that I was not just a visiting member of the Sarajevo "theatre world," but that there were several theatre
clans in Sarajevo and that, being allied with Haris Pašović's, I could not
count on the goodwill of the others. (It would work the other way
around, too. On one occasion, when precious help was offered me by
another producer, who on my last visit had become a friend, I was told
by Pašović, who was otherwise reasonable and helpful: "I don't want
you to take anything from that person.")

Of course this would be normal behavior anywhere else. Why not
in besieged Sarajevo? Theatre in prewar Sarajevo must have had the
same feuds, pettiness, and jealousy as in any other European city. I
think my assistants, as well as Ognjenka Finci, the set and costume de-
signer, and Pašović himself, were anxious to shield me from the knowledge that not everybody in Sarajevo was to be trusted. When I began
to catch on that some of our difficulties reflected a degree of hostility
or even sabotage, one of my assistants said to me sadly: "Now that you
know us, you won't want to come back anymore."

SARAJEVO IS NOT only a city that represents an ideal of pluralism;
it was regarded by many of its citizens as an ideal place: though not important (not big enough, not rich enough), it was still the best place to
be, even if, being ambitious, you had to leave it to make a real career, as
people from San Francisco eventually take the plunge and go to Los
Angeles or New York. "You can't imagine what it used to be like here,"
Pašović said to me. "It was paradise." That kind of idealization produces a very acute disillusionment, so that now almost all the people I
know in Sarajevo cannot stop lamenting the city's moral deterioration:
the increasing number of muggings and thefts, the gangsterism, the
predatory black marketeers, the banditry of some army units, the absence of civic cooperation. One would think that they could forgive

themselves, and their city. For seventeen months it has been a shooting gallery. There is virtually no municipal government; hence, debris from shelling doesn't get picked up, schooling isn't organized for small children, et cetera, et cetera. A city under siege must, sooner or later, become a city of rackets.

But most Sarajevans are pitiless in their condemnation of conditions now, and of many "elements," as they would call them with pained vagueness, in the city. "Anything good that happens here is a miracle," one of my friends said to me. And another: "This is a city of bad people." When an English photojournalist made us the invaluable gift of nine candles, three were immediately stolen. One day Mirza's lunch—a chunk of home-baked bread and a pear—was taken from his knapsack while he was on the stage. It could not have been one of the other actors. But it could have been anyone else, say, one of the stagehands or any of the students from the Academy of Drama who wandered in and out of the rehearsals. The discovery of this theft was very depressing to us all.

Although many people want to leave, and will leave when they can, a surprising number say that their lives are not unbearable. "We can live this life forever," said one of my friends from my April visit, Hrvoje Batinić, a local journalist. "I can live this life a hundred years," a new friend, Zehra Kreho—the dramaturge of the National Theatre—said to me one evening. (Both are in their late thirties.) Sometimes I felt the same way.

Of course, it was different for me. "I haven't taken a bath in sixteen months," a middle-aged matron said to me. "Do you know how that feels?" I don't; I only know what it's like not to take a bath for six weeks. I was elated, full of energy, because of the challenge of the work I was doing, because of the valor and enthusiasm of everyone I worked with—but I could not ever forget how hard it has been for each of them, and how hopeless the future looks for their city. What made my lesser hardships and the danger relatively easy to bear, apart from the fact that I could leave and they couldn't, was that I was totally concentrated on them and on Beckett's play.

5

UNTIL A WEEK before it opened, I did not think the play would be very good. I feared that the choreography and emotional design I had constructed for the two-level stage and the nine actors in five roles were too complicated for them to master in so short a time; or simply that I had not been as demanding as I should have been. Two of my assistants, as well as Pašović, told me that I was being too amicable, too "maternal," and that I should throw a tantrum now and then and, in particular, threaten to replace the actors who had not yet learned all their lines. But I went on, hoping that it would be not too bad; then suddenly, in the last week, they turned a corner, it all came together, and at our dress rehearsal it seemed to me the production was, after all, affecting, continually interesting, well made, and that this was an effort which did honor to Beckett's play.

I was also surprised by the amount of attention from the international press that *Godot* was getting. I had told few people that I was going back to Saravejo to direct *Waiting for Godot*, intending perhaps to write something about it later. I forgot that I would be living in a journalists' dormitory. The day after I arrived I was fielding requests in the Holiday Inn lobby and in the dining room for interviews; and the next day; and the next. I said there was nothing to tell, that I was still auditioning; then that the actors were simply reading the play aloud at a table; then that we'd just begun on the stage, there was hardly any light, there was nothing to see.

But when I mentioned to Pašović the journalists' requests and my desire to keep the actors free from such distractions, I learned that he had scheduled a press conference for me and that he wanted me to admit journalists to rehearsals, give interviews, and get the maximum amount of publicity not just for the play but for an enterprise of which I had not altogether taken in that I was a part: the Sarajevo International Festival of Theatre and Film, directed by Haris Pašović, whose second production, following his *Alcestis*, was my *Godot*. When I apologized to the actors for the interruptions to come, I found that they, too, wanted the journalists to be there. All the friends I consulted in the city told me that the story of the production would be "good for Sarajevo."

And so I obediently changed my policy of no interviews to giving access to anybody who wanted it. This was easy, not only because it was what the actors and Pašović wanted, but because I never saw anything that was printed or televised (even the journalists at the Holiday Inn never saw their stories until they left Sarajevo). I regretted, though, that the rush of interviews in the first two weeks meant that most of the stories were done before the actors had learned their lines, and my conception of the play began to work.

The point is, of course, that any cultural activity in Sarajevo is a sideshow for correspondents and journalists who have come to cover a war. To protest the sincerity of one's motives reinforces suspicion, if there is suspicion to begin with. The best thing is not to speak at all, which was my original intention. To speak at all of what one is doing seems—perhaps, whatever one's intentions, becomes—a form of self-promotion. But this is just what the contemporary media culture expects. My political opinions—I would go on about what I regard as the infamous role now being played by UNPROFOR, railing against "the Serb-UN siege of Sarajevo"—were invariably cut out. You want it to be about *them*, and it turns out—in media land—to be about you.

If it were only a matter of my own discomfort about some of the foreign coverage of my work in Sarajevo, none of this would be worth mentioning. But it illustrates something of the way such long-running stories as the one in Bosnia are transmitted and being reacted to.

Television, print, and radio-journalism are an important part of this war. When, in April, I heard the French intellectual André Glucksmann, on his twenty-four-hour trip to Sarajevo, explain to the local journalists who attended his press conference that "war is now a media event," and "wars are won or lost on TV," I thought to myself, Try telling that to all the people here who have lost their arms and legs. But there is a sense in which Glucksmann's indecent statement was on the mark. It's not that war has completely changed its nature, and is only or principally a media event, but that the media's coverage is a principal object of attention, and the very fact of media attention sometimes becomes the main story.

An example. My best friend among the journalists at the Holiday Inn, the BBC's admirable Alan Little, visited one of the city's hospitals and was shown a semi-conscious five-year-old girl with severe head injuries from a mortar shell that had killed her mother. The doctor said she would die if she was not airlifted to a hospital where she could be given a brain scan and sophisticated treatment. Moved by the child's plight, Alan began to talk about her in his reports. For days nothing happened. Then other journalists picked up the story, and the case of "Little Irma" became the front-page story day after day in the British tabloids and virtually the only Bosnia story on the TV news. John Major, eager to be seen as doing something, sent a plane to take the girl to London.

Then came the backlash. Alan, unaware at first that the story had become so big, then delighted because it meant that the pressure would help to bring the child out, was dismayed by the attacks on a "media circus" that was exploiting a child's suffering. It was morally obscene, the critics said, to concentrate on one child when thousands of children and adults, including many amputees and paraplegics, languish in the understaffed, undersupplied hospitals of Sarajevo and are not allowed to be transported out, thanks to the UN (but that is another story). That it *was* a good thing to do—that to try to save the life of one child is better than doing nothing at all—should have been obvious, and in fact others were brought out as a result. But a story that needed to be told about the wretched hospitals of Sarajevo degenerated into a controversy over what the press did.

THIS IS THE FIRST European genocide in our century to be tracked by the world press and documented nightly on TV. There were no reporters in 1915 sending daily stories to the world press from Armenia, and no foreign camera crews in Dachau and Auschwitz. Until the Bosnian genocide, one might have thought—this was indeed the conviction of many of the best reporters there, like Roy Guttman of *Newsday* and John Burns of *The New York Times*—that if the story could be gotten out, the world would do something. The coverage of the genocide in Bosnia has ended that illusion.

Newspaper and radio reporting and, above all, TV coverage have shown the war in Bosnia in extraordinary detail, but in the absence of a will to intervene by those few people in the world who make political and military decisions, the war becomes another remote disaster; the people suffering and being murdered there become disaster "victims." Suffering is visibly present, and can be seen in close-up; and no doubt many people feel sympathy for the victims. What cannot be recorded is an absence—the absence of any political will to end this suffering: more exactly, the decision not to intervene in Bosnia, primarily Europe's responsibility, which has its origins in the traditional pro-Serb slant of the Quai d'Orsay and the British Foreign Office. It is being implemented by the UN occupation of Sarajevo, which is largely a French operation.

I do not believe the standard argument made by critics of television that watching terrible events on the small screen distances them as much as it makes them real. It is the continuing coverage of the war in the absence of action to stop it that makes us mere spectators. Not television but our politicians have made history come to seem like re-runs. We get tired of watching the same show. If it seems unreal, it is because it's both so appalling and apparently so unstoppable.

Even people in Sarajevo sometimes say it seems to them unreal. They are in a state of shock, which does not diminish, which takes the form of a rhetorical incredulity ("How could this happen? I still can't believe this is happening"). They are genuinely astonished by the Serb atrocities, and by the starkness and sheer unfamiliarity of the lives they are now obliged to lead. "We're living in the Middle Ages," someone said to me. "This is science fiction," another friend said.

People ask me if Sarajevo ever seemed to me unreal while I was there. The truth is, since I've started going to Sarajevo—this winter I hope to direct *The Cherry Orchard* with Nada as Madame Ranevsky and Velibor as Lopakhin—it seems the most real place in the world.

WAITING FOR GODOT OPENED, with twelve candles on the stage, on August 17. There were two performances that day, a Tuesday, one at 2:00 p.m. and the other at 4:00 p.m. In Sarajevo there are only matinees; hardly anybody goes out after dark. Many people were turned away. During the first performances I was tense with anxiety. By the third performance, I started to be able to see the play as a spectator. It was time to stop worrying that Ines would let the rope linking her and Atko sag while she devoured her papier-mâché chicken; that Sejo, the third Vladimir, would forget to keep shifting from foot to foot just before he suddenly rushes off to pee. The play now belonged to the actors, and I knew it was in good hands. And at the end of the 2:00 p.m. performance on August 19, during the long tragic silence of the Vladimirs and Estragons which follows the messenger's announcement that Mr. Godot isn't coming today, but will surely come tomorrow, my eyes began to sting with tears. Velibor was crying, too. No one in the audience made a sound. The only sounds were those coming from outside the theatre: a UN armored personnel carrier thundering down the street and the crack of sniper fire.

[1993]

"There" and "Here"

I WENT TO Sarajevo for the first time in April 1993, one year after the start of the Serb-Croat campaign to carve up the newly independent multi-ethnic Bosnian state. Leaving Sarajevo after that first stay, I flew out as I had come in, on one of the Russian UNPROFOR cargo planes making a regular run between Sarajevo and Zagreb. The heart-stopping drive into the besieged city by the switchback trail over Mount Igman lay far in the future, on my seventh and eighth stays; and by that time, the winter and summer of 1995, my standards of peril were higher, and I was a veteran of dread and shock. Nothing ever equaled the first shock. The shock of Sarajevo itself, the misery of daily life in the shattered city under constant mortar and sniper fire. And the aftershock of re-entry into the outside world.

To leave Sarajevo and be, an hour later, in a "normal" city (Zagreb). To get into a taxi (a taxi!) at the airport . . . to ride in traffic regulated by traffic signals, along streets lined with buildings that have intact roofs, unshelled walls, glass in the windows . . . to flip on the light switch in your hotel room . . . to use a toilet and flush it afterward . . . to run the bath (you haven't had a bath in several weeks) and have water, hot water, come out of the tap . . . to take a stroll and see shops, and people walking, like you, at a normal pace . . . to buy something in a small grocery store with fully stocked shelves . . . to enter a restaurant and be given a menu . . . All this seems so bizarre and upsetting that, for at least forty-eight hours, you feel quite disoriented. And very angry. To speak with people who don't want to know what you know, don't want you to talk about the sufferings, bewilderment, terror, and humiliation of the inhabitants of the city you've just left. And even worse, when you return to your own "normal" city (New York) and your friends say, "Oh, you're back; I was worried about you"—to realize that they don't want to know, either. To understand that you can never really explain to them—neither how terrible it is "there" nor how bad you feel being back, "here." That the world will be forever divided into "there" and "here."

People don't want to hear the bad news. Perhaps they never do. But in the case of Bosnia the indifference, the lack of effort to try to imagine, was more acute than I ever anticipated. You find that the only people you feel comfortable with are those who have been to Bosnia, too. Or to some other slaughter—El Salvador, Cambodia, Rwanda, Chechnya. Or who at least know, firsthand, what a war is.

A few weeks ago—I'm writing in late November 1995—I returned from my ninth stay in Sarajevo. Although once again I came in by the only land route, this was no longer my sole option (UN planes were again landing on a corner of the destroyed Sarajevo airport) and the rutted dirt trail over Mount Igman was no longer the most dangerous route in the world. It had been widened and graded by UN engineers into a narrow dirt road. In the city there was electricity for the first time since the beginning of the siege. The shells were not exploding, snipers' bullets were not whizzing past everyone's heads. There would be gas for the winter. There was the promise of running water. Since my return, an agreement has been signed in Ohio that promises an end to the war. Whether peace, an unjust peace, has actually come to Bosnia I am reluctant to say. If Slobodan Milosević, who started the war, wants the war to end and can impose this decision on his proxies in Pale, then the successful campaign to destroy Bosnia by killing or relocating or driving into exile most of its population is, in most senses, finished. Finished, too, is what the Bosnians had held out for: their internationally recognized unitary state.

So Bosnia (an utterly transformed Bosnia) is to be partitioned. So might, instead of right, has triumphed. Nothing new in that—see Thucydides, Book V, "The Melian Dialogue." It's as if the eastern advance of the Wehrmacht had been halted in late 1939 or early 1940 and the League of Nations called a conference among "the warring parties," at which Germany was awarded half of Poland (the western part), the invading Russians got twenty percent of the east, and while the thirty percent of their country in the middle that the Poles were allowed to keep did include their capital, most of the territory surrounding it went to the Germans. Of course, no one would have claimed that this was very fair by "moral" criteria—quickly adding, Since when have moral standards prevailed in international politics? Because the Poles had no chance of successfully defending their country against the superior forces of Hitler's Germany and Stalin's Russia, they would have to be content with what they got. At least, the diplomats would have said, they still have *some* of their country; they had been on the verge of losing it all. And of course the Poles would have figured as the most difficult at the negotiations, since they didn't see themselves as simply one of three "warring parties." They thought they had been invaded. They thought they were the victims. The diplomats brokering the settlement would have found them quite unreasonable. Divided among themselves. Bitter. Untrustworthy. Ungrateful to the mediators trying to stop the slaughter.

Before, people didn't want to know—you often heard that the war in Bosnia is so complicated, it is hard to know which is the "right" side—but now more people do understand what happened. They also understand that the war—that is, the Serb and Croat aggression— could have been stopped at any moment in the past three years in exactly the same way and by the same minimum application of force by NATO (entirely sparing soldiers on the ground as well as civilians) as finally took place this past August and September. But the Europeans didn't want to stop the conflict (both the British Foreign Office and the Quai d'Orsay are traditionally pro-Serb), and the Americans, the only major power to acknowledge that justice was on the Bosnian side, were reluctant to get involved. Now that the war has, or seems to have been, stopped, it suddenly looks less complicated. The mood is retrospective.

ONE QUESTION I'M OFTEN ASKED after returning from a stay in Sarajevo is why other well-known writers besides myself haven't spent time there. Behind this lies the more general question of the widespread indifference in nearby rich European countries (most notably Italy and Germany) to an appalling historical crime, nothing less than genocide—the fourth genocide of a European minority to take place in this century. But unlike the genocide of the Armenians during World War I and of the Jews and the Gypsies in the late 1930s and early 1940s, the genocide of the Bosniak people has taken place in the glare of worldwide press and TV coverage. No one can plead ignorance of the atrocities that have taken place in Bosnia since the war started in April 1992. Sanski Most, Stupni Do, Omarska, and other concentration camps with their killing houses (for hands-on, artisanal butchery, in contrast to the industrialized mass murder of the Nazi camps), the martyrdom of East Mostar and Sarajevo and Gorazde, the rape by military order of tens of thousands of women throughout Serb-captured Bosnia, the slaughter of at least eight thousand men and boys after the surrender of Srebrenica—this is only a portion of the catalogue of infamy. And no one can be unaware that the Bosnian cause is that of Europe: democracy, and a society composed of citizens, not of the members of a tribe. Why haven't these atrocities, these values, aroused a more potent response? Why have hardly any intellectuals of stature and visibility rallied to denounce the Bosnian genocide and defend the Bosnian cause?

The Bosnian war is hardly the only horror show that has been unfolding in the past four or five years. But there are events—model events—that do seem to sum up the principal opposing forces of one's time. One such event was the Spanish Civil War. Like the war in Bosnia, that struggle was an emblematic one. But intellectuals—the writers, theatre people, artists, professors, scientists who have a record of speaking up on important public events and issues of conscience—have been as conspicuous by their absence from the Bosnian conflict as they were by their presence in Spain in the 1930s. Of course, it's speaking rather too well of intellectuals to think that they constitute something like a perennial class, part of whose vocation is to take up the best causes—as it's unlikely that only every thirty years or so is there a war somewhere else in the world that should inspire even would-be pacifists to take sides. Still, the standard of dissent and activism associated with intellectuals is a reality. Why so little response to what happened in Bosnia?

There are probably many reasons. Heartless historical clichés certainly figure in the paltriness of the response. There is the traditional bad reputation of the Balkans as a place of eternal conflict, of implacable ancient rivalries. Haven't those folks always been slaughtering one another? (This is comparable to having said when confronted with the reality of Auschwitz: Well, what can one expect? You know, anti-Semitism is an ancient story in Europe.) Not to be underestimated, too, is the pervasiveness of anti-Muslim prejudice, a reflex reaction to a people the majority of whom are as secular, and as imbued with contemporary consumer-society culture, as their southern European neighbors. To bolster the fiction that this is at its deepest source a religious war, the label Muslim is invariably used to describe the victims, their army, and their government—though no one would think of describing the invaders as the Orthodox and the Catholics. Do many secular "Western" intellectuals who might be expected to have raised their voices to defend Bosnia share these prejudices? Of course they do.

And this is not the 1930s. Nor the 1960s. Actually, we are already living in the twenty-first century, in which such twentieth-century certainties as the identification of fascism, or imperialism, or Bolshevik-style dictators as the principal "enemy" no longer offer a framework (often a facile one) for thought and action. What made it obvious that one should side with the government of the Spanish Republic, whatever its flaws, was the struggle against fascism. Opposing the American aggression in Vietnam (which took over the unsuccessful French effort to hold on to Indochina) made sense as part of the worldwide struggle against Euro-American colonialism.

If the intellectuals of the 1930s and the 1960s often showed themselves too gullible, too prone to appeals to idealism to take in what was really happening in certain beleaguered, newly radicalized societies that they may or may not have visited (briefly), the morosely depoliticized intellectuals of today, with their cynicism always at the ready, their addiction to entertainment, their reluctance to inconvenience themselves for any cause, their devotion to personal safety, seem at least equally deplorable. (I can't count how many times I've been asked, each time I return to New York from Sarajevo, how I can go to a place that's so dangerous.) By and large, that handful of intellectuals who consider themselves people of conscience can be mobilized now solely for limited actions—against, say, racism or censorship—within their own countries. Only domestic political commitments seem plausible now. Among once internationally minded intellectuals, nationalist complacencies have renewed prestige. (I should note that this seems true more of writers than of doctors, scientists, and actors.) There has been an implacable decay of the very notion of international solidarity.

Not only has the global bilateralism (a "them" versus "us") characteristic of political thinking throughout our short twentieth century, from 1914 to 1989—fascism versus democracy; the American empire versus the Soviet empire—collapsed. What has followed in the wake of 1989 and the suicide of the Soviet empire is the final victory of capitalism, and of the ideology of consumerism, which entails the discrediting of "the political" as such. All that makes sense is private life. Individualism, and the cultivation of the self and private well-being—featuring, above all, the ideal of "health"—are the values to which intellectuals are most likely to subscribe. ("How can you spend so much time in a place where people smoke all the time?" someone here in New York asked my son, the writer David Rieff, of his frequent trips to Bosnia.) It's too much to expect that the triumph of consumer capitalism would have left the intellectual class unmarked. In the era of shopping, it has to be harder for intellectuals, who are anything but marginal and impoverished, to identify with less fortunate others. George Orwell and Simone Weil did not exactly leave comfortable upper-bourgeois apartments and weekend country houses when they volunteered to go to Spain and fight for the Republic, and both of them almost got themselves killed. Perhaps the stretch for intellectuals between "there" and "here" is too great now.

For several decades it has been a journalistic and academic commonplace to say that intellectuals, as a class, are obsolete—an example of an analysis willing itself to be an imperative. Now there are voices proclaiming that Europe is dead, too. It may be more true to say that Europe has yet to be born: a Europe that takes responsibility for its defenseless minorities and for upholding the values it has no choice but to incarnate (Europe will be multicultural, or it won't be at all). And Bosnia is its self-induced abortion. In the words of Emile Durkheim, "Society is above all the idea it forms of itself." The idea that the prosperous, peaceful society of Europe and North America has formed of itself—through the actions and statements of all those who could be called intellectuals—is one of confusion, irresponsibility, selfishness, cowardice . . . and the pursuit of happiness.

Ours, not theirs. Here, not there.

[1995]

Joseph Brodsky

FOR AS LONG AS we *are*, we're always somewhere. Feet are always somewhere, whether planted or running. Minds, notoriously, can be elsewhere. Minds, whether from lack of vitality or from the deepest strengths, can be in the past and the present, or the present and the future. Or simply here and there. For reasons not hard to understand, the making of art at the highest plane of accomplishment during the last century or so has required, more often than not, an exceptional development of the talent for being, mentally, in two places at once. Elated by the landscapes he has been painting and drawing in the south of France, van Gogh writes his brother Theo that he is "really" in Japan. The young, as yet unpublished poet from Leningrad fulfilling a sentence of compulsory labor on a collective farm in a village in the Far North, near the White Sea, receives the news—it is January 1965—that T. S. Eliot has died in London, sits at a table in his icy shack, and within the next twenty-four hours composes a long elegy to Eliot, which is also an homage to the very alive W. H. Auden (the tone and swing of whose elegy on the death of Yeats he adopts).

He was elegant enough always to claim that he had not really suffered during that year and a half of internal exile; that he rather liked farmwork, especially shoveling manure, which he regarded as one of the more honest and rewarding jobs he'd had so far, everyone in Russia being mired in shit, and had got quite a few poems written there.

Then, back in his native Leningrad, a few years later Joseph Brodsky, as he put it succinctly, "switched empires." This happened suddenly, from one day to the next, and entirely against his will: among
other losses, it separated this beloved only son from his elderly parents,
who, in further punishment of the renegade poet, were thereafter repeatedly denied exit permits by the Soviet government to meet for a
brief reunion in, say, nearby Helsinki, and died without his ever embracing them again. Intractable grief, borne with great indignation,
great sobriety.

He even managed to make of his KGB-enjoined departure something self-propelled—

And as for where in space and time one's toe end touches, well, earth is
hard all over; try the States

—landing among us like a missile hurled from the other empire, a benign missile whose payload was not only his genius but his native literature's exalted, exacting sense of the poet's authority. (To be found as
well among its prose writers: think of how Gogol and Dostoyevsky
conceived of the novelist's moral and spiritual task.) Many aptitudes
eased his rapid insertion in America: immense industriousness and self-
confidence, ready irony, insouciance, cunning. But for all the dash and
ingenuity of his connections with his adopted country, one had only to
watch Joseph Brodsky among other Russian exiles and émigrés to realize how viscerally, expressively Russian he had stayed. And how generous his adaptation to us, along with the eagerness to impose himself on
us, actually was.

Such adaptability, such gallantry, may go by the name of cosmopolitanism. But true cosmopolitanism is less a matter of one's relation to
place than to time, specifically to the past (which is simply so much
bigger than the present). This has nothing in common with that sentimental relation to the past called nostalgia. It is a relation, unsparing to
oneself, which acknowledges the past as the source of standards,
higher standards than the present affords. One should write to please
not one's contemporaries but one's predecessors, Brodsky often declared. Surely he did please them—his compatriots agree that he was

his era's unique successor to Mandelstam, Tsvetaeva, and Akhmatova. Raising the "plane of regard" (as he called it) was relentlessly identified with the effortfulness and ambitions and appropriate fidelities of poets.

I think of Joseph Brodsky as a world poet—partly because I cannot read him in Russian; mainly because that's the range he commanded in his poems, with their extraordinary velocity and density of material notation, of cultural reference, of attitude. He insisted that poetry's "job" (a much-used word) was to explore the capacity of language to travel farther, faster. Poetry, he said, is accelerated thinking. It was his best argument, and he made many, on behalf of the superiority of poetry to prose, for he considered rhyme essential to this process. An ideal of mental acceleration is the key to his great achievement (and its limits), in prose as well as in poetry, and to his indelible presence. Conversation with him, as felicitously recalled by his friend Seamus Heaney, "attained immediate vertical takeoff and no deceleration was possible."

Much of his work could be subsumed under the early title of one of his poems, "Advice to a Traveller." Real travel nourished the mental journeying, with its characteristic premium on speedy assimilation of what there was to know and feel, determination never to be duped, mordant avowals of vulnerability. Of course, there were favorite elsewheres, four countries (and the poetry produced within their borders) in particular: Russia, England, the United States, and Italy. Which is to say, empires never ceased to incite his powers of fast-forward association and generalization; hence, his passion for the Latin poets and the sites of ancient Rome, inscribed in several essays and the play *Marbles* as well as in poems. The first, in the end perhaps the only, tenable form of cosmopolitanism is to be a citizen of an empire. Brodsky's temperament was imperial in many senses.

Home was Russian. No longer Russia. Perhaps no decision he made in the later part of his life was as startling (to many), as emblematic of who he was, as his refusal, after the dismantling of the Soviet empire and in the face of countless worshipful solicitations, to go back even for the briefest visit.

And so he lived most of his adult life elsewhere: here. And Russia, the source of everything that was most subtle and audacious and fertile and doctrinaire about his mind and gifts, became the great elsewhere to which he could not, would not, out of pride, out of anger, out of anxiety, ever return.

Now he has rushed away from us, for so it feels, to reside in the largest, most powerful empire of all, the final elsewhere: a transfer whose anticipation (while enduring a serious cardiac ailment for many years) he explored in so many defiant, poignant poems.

The work, the example, the standards—and our grief—remain.

[1998]

On Being Translated

I'LL START WITH a story.

It's the summer of 1993, and I was back in Sarajevo (I'd first gone there three months earlier), this time at the invitation of a local theatre producer to stage a play in one of the besieged city's battered theatres. We'd met at the end of my April stay, he'd asked me if I was interested in coming back to work as a director, I'd said yes, yes, gladly, and my choice of a play to do—Beckett's *Waiting for Godot*—was agreed to with enthusiasm by him and by other theatre people I met. It ought to go without saying that the play would be performed in Serbo-Croatian: it never occurred to me that the actors I chose might or should do otherwise. True, most of them knew some English, as did a portion of the educated Sarajevans who would come to see our production. But an actor's talent is inextricably bound up with the rhythms and sounds of the language in which he or she has developed that talent; and Serbo-Croatian is the only language one could count on everybody in the audience knowing. To those who may think it smacks of presumption to dare to direct in a language one doesn't know, I can only say that repertory theatre now operates with almost as much international circuitry as the opera repertory has always had. Arthur Miller, when he accepted an invitation to direct a production of *Death of a Salesman* in Shanghai a few years ago, knew no more Chinese than I knew Serbo-Croatian. Anyway (trust me), it's not as hard to do as it sounds. You need, besides your theatre skills, a musical ear and a good interpreter.

In besieged Sarajevo, you also needed a lot of stamina.

In July, I flew into Sarajevo on a UN troop plane, my backpack bulging with pocket flashlights and a sack of double-A batteries, and, in a pocket of my flak jacket, copies of the Beckett play in English and French. The day after my arrival I began auditioning a passel of talented, undernourished actors (most of whom I'd met during my first stay), making drawings of how I envisaged the set, and trying to understand how things worked generally in the theatre in Sarajevo—such as that was possible under the privations of siege and the terror of nonstop bombardment. Once chosen, the actors and I huddled in the theatre's basement—no reason to start working upstairs, on the more vulnerable area of the stage, until after the first week—doing improvisations and figuring out rehearsal schedules (everyone had complex family responsibilities, not least of which was several hours' worth of fetching water), and learning to trust each other. The noise from outside the building was incessant. War is noise. Beckett seemed even more appropriate than I'd imagined.

I didn't have to explain Beckett to Sarajevans. And some of my actors were already familiar with the play. But we did not yet have a text in common. Before leaving Sarajevo in April, I'd checked with the producer that I could count on his having enough copies of a translation of the Beckett play on hand for the actors and everyone else involved in working on the production when I returned in July. Not to worry, he said. But when, the day of my return, I asked for copies of the play to distribute at the auditions, he announced that, in honor of the importance of my coming to work in Sarajevo, Beckett's play was being re-translated. In fact, the translation was being worked on right now.

Uh-oh.

"The translation isn't . . . finished?"

"Well, it may be finished," he said.

Hmmm.

So I had another problem besides the Serbs' shells, grenades, and constant gunfire from snipers on rooftops in the center of the city, the absence of electricity and running water, the shattered theatre, the nervousness of the malnourished actors, my own anxiety and fear, the . . .

The problem, as my producer explained, was the typewriter: an old typewriter, but the only one available to the translator, one whose ribbon was very faint (having been in use steadily for a year; this was sixteen months since the beginning of the siege). But, he assured me, this translation would be a real asset to the production—if only I would be patient. I said I would try to be patient.

I knew that in the former Yugoslavia there had been many productions of Beckett's plays—the most frequently performed being none other than *Waiting for Godot*. (Indeed, I'd chosen *Godot* over the other play I'd thought of doing, *Ubu Roi*, partly because the Beckett play was known.) There had to be a translation dating back to the 1950s. Maybe more than one. Perhaps we didn't really need this new translation.

"Is the existing translation not very good?" I asked the producer, who, a director himself, had staged a production of the play in Belgrade a few years earlier.

"No, it's not bad at all," he said. "It's just that this is Bosnia now. We want to translate the play into Bosnian."

"But isn't what you speak Serbo-Croatian?"

"Not really," he said.

"Then why," I said, "did you lend me your Serbo-Croatian–English dictionary the day I arrived?"

"Well, for you it would be good enough to learn Serbo-Croatian."

"But does that mean"—I persisted—"that if I learned Serbo-Croatian there are words or phrases in use here that I wouldn't understand?"

"No, you'd understand everything. The way educated people speak in Sarajevo is the same as educated speech in Belgrade or Zagreb."

"Then what's the difference?"

"I can't explain," he said. "It would be hard for you to understand. But there's a difference."

"A difference for Beckett?"

"Yes, it's a new translation."

"If someone did a new translation in Belgrade, would that be different, too?"

"Maybe," he said.

"And that new translation would be different in a different way from this new translation?"

"Maybe not."

Keep calm, I told myself. "Then what's going to be specifically Bosnian about this translation?"

"Because it's done here in Sarajevo, while the city is under siege."

"But will some of the words be different?"

"That depends on the translator."

"You haven't read any of it?"

"No, because I can't read her handwriting."

"She hasn't started to type it yet?"

"She has, but with that typewriter ribbon it's impossible to read."

"Then how are the actors going to study the play and learn their lines?"

"Maybe we'll have to find someone with good handwriting to make the scripts."

Wow, it really is the Dark Ages, I thought.

AFTER MORE HALLUCINATORY EXCHANGES of this sort, and rising anxiety on my part about when the actors and I would be able really to begin, another typewriter was found and the translation re-typed, using some ancient, scarred carbon paper to provide fifteen double-spaced scripts (for the actors, the set designer, the costume de-signer, my two assistants and interpreter, and me). Between the lines of my script I copied out in ink both the English and the French text, so that I could learn the Bosnian, the sound of it, by heart, and always know what the actors were saying.

(An extra symmetry in this story is that, as Beckett wrote his play in *two* languages—the English *Waiting for Godot* is not merely a transla-tion of the French—the play has two original languages, in both of which I am at home; and now it had two translations, in a language that was completely opaque to me.)

What happened then? After we had gone up on the stage and been working for about a week, and I had blocked a good part of the first act, my assistant and two of the actors—the two who spoke the most English—took me aside.

Problem? Yes. What they felt they had to tell me was that the new translation really wasn't very good, and could we please, please use the translation published in Belgrade in the 1950s.

"Is there a difference?" I asked.

"Yes, the old translation is better."

"Better in what sense?"

"It sounds better. It's more natural. Easier to say."

"There isn't a linguistic difference? Something Serbian about that translation? Or something not Bosnian?"

"Not that anyone would notice."

"So there aren't any words you would have to change to make the translation more Bosnian?"

"Not really. But we could, if you want us to."

"It's not what *I* want," I said, gritting my teeth. "I'm just here to serve. Beckett. You. Sarajevo. Whatever."

"Well," my Vladimir said thoughtfully, "here's what we could do. Let's go back to the old translation, and while we're rehearsing, if we see a word we think should be changed to something more Bosnian, we'll change it."

"Don't forget to tell me," I said.

"*Nema problema,*" said my Estragon.

Which of course means . . . but you know perfectly well what it means. It's a phrase that seems to translate into every language in the world.

THE END OF THE STORY is that—as you may not be surprised to learn—the actors never changed anything. Further, when *Waiting for Godot* opened in mid-August, no member of the theatre public complained that the translation didn't sound Bosnian, or Bosnian enough. (Perhaps they had other, more pressing things on their minds—such as waiting for Clinton.)

Much can be spun from this story, including some consideration of the potent fantasy that people have about language as a carrier of national identity—which can make a translation, or the refusal to make one, the equivalent of an act of treason. What is pathetic about this instance taking place on the territory of the former Yugoslavia is that it concerns newly, lethally self-defined nations that happen to share the *same* spoken language and are therefore deprived of, if I may call it thus, "the right of translation."

It seems appropriate that the story I've just told you happened in a place that—as I realize whenever I try to describe what it's been like to spend so much time in Sarajevo in the past two and a half years (I've just returned, two weeks ago, from my ninth stay there)—seems to most people I talk with like the other side of the moon. It's not just that people can't imagine a war or a siege, or the danger or the fear or the humiliation. More: they simply can't imagine that degree of differentness from their own lives and comforts, from their understandable sense—understandable, for it's based on their own experience—that the world isn't *such* a really terrible place.

They can't imagine that. It must be translated for them.

TRANSLATION IS ABOUT differentness. A way of coping with, and ameliorating, and, yes, denying difference—even if, as my story illustrates, it is also a way of asserting differentness.

Originally (at least in English) translation was about the biggest difference of all: that between being alive and being dead. To translate is, etymologically, to transfer, to remove, to displace. To what end? In order to be rescued, from death or extinction.

Listen to Wycliffe's Englishing of the Hebrew Bible's Book of Enoch:

> Bi feith Enok is translatid, that he shulde not see deeth, and
> he was not founden, for the Lord translatide him.

Eventually "to be translated" did come to mean "to die." Death is translation—one is translated from earth to heaven—and so is resurrection, which is (again in Wycliffe's English) to be "translatid from deeth to lyfe."

In English, the oldest meanings of the verb have nothing to do with language—with a mental act and its transcription. To translate is, mainly, an intransitive verb, and a physical act. It signifies a change of condition or site—usually so far as these, condition and site, imply each other. The "trans" is a physical "across" or crossing, and proposes a geography of action, action in space. The formula is, roughly: where X was, it is no longer; instead it is (or is at) Y.

Consider the following meanings, now obsolete:

In medicine, to translate once meant to transfer a disease from one *person* to another, or from one *part* of the body to another (something like the modern concept of metastasis). In law, it meant to transfer property (such as a legacy). In the words of Thomas Hobbes: "All Contract is mutual translation, or change of Right." Perhaps the latest of these meanings which involve an idea of physical transfer dates from the late nineteenth century. In long-distance telegraphy, to translate is to retransmit a message automatically, by means of a relay.

We retain only the sense of translation as the transfer or handing over or delivery from one language to another. Yet the older meanings expressed in the *tra-* and *trans-* words (welded to *-dere*, *-ducere*) remain as an underpinning. The fruitful affinities of etymology express a real, if subliminal, connection. To translate is still to lead something across a gap, to make something go where it was not. Like tradition, something which is handed "over" or "down" (originally, something material) to others, translation is the conveying or transmitting of something from one person, site, or condition to another. For all that its meaning has been "spiritualized"—what is being passed or transferred is from one language to another—the sense of physical or geographical separateness is still implicit, and potent. Languages are like separate (often antagonistic) communities, each with its own customs. The translator is the one who finds (identifies, formulates) the comparable customs in another language.

I'LL MENTION BRIEFLY three variants of the modern idea of translation.

First, translation as *explanation*. Motivating the translator's effort is the project of replacing ignorance, obscurity ("I don't understand.

Would you please translate that for me?") by knowledge, transparency. The translator's mission is clarification, enlightenment.

Second, translation as *adaptation*. Not simply a freer use of language, which purports to express, in another language, the spirit if not the letter of the original text (a wily distinction), but the conscious creation of another "version" (from *vertere*, to turn, to change direction): "versionist" is the old English word for translator. Indeed, some translators (usually poets) who don't want to be held to the criterion of "mere" accuracy entirely eschew the word "translation" in favor of "adaptation" or "version." Rewriting would be a more accurate description, and if the poet is, say, Robert Lowell, the version stands as a valuable new (if not wholly original) poem—by him.*

Third, translation as *improvement*. The hubristic extension of the translation as adaptation. Of translations which could be considered improvements on the original, Baudelaire's translation of poems of Edgar Allan Poe is one, not too controversial, example. (More controversial, to say the least, is the judgment of several generations of cultivated Germans—Americans old enough to have known German-Jewish Hitler refugees in the academic world or in other professions may remember hearing the fervently held view—that the Shakespeare of the Schlegel-Tieck translation was better than Shakespeare in English.) Translation as improvement has its own sub-variant: translation as *obfuscation* (as in "It sounds better in translation"), a dressing up or paring down of the text, which may or may not entail actively tampering with it.

THE ACCURACY OF a translation is not merely a technical question. It is as well an ideological one. And it has a moral component,

---

*There is a metaphoric use of translation-as-adaptation, which evokes the older, physical sense of translation: translating (transposing) from one *medium* to another. Here there are no guidelines about what may be produced by following the original more, rather than less, literally; or (as is often recommended) choosing an inferior work to strut one's stuff. When *Berlin Alexanderplatz* was "translated to the screen" by Rainer Werner Fassbinder, the filmmaker preserved a large part of the spirit of Döblin's masterpiece, and also made a film that is a masterpiece. What might seem a counterexample, with equally exemplary results: Henry Bernstein's *Mélo* is far from a great play, but Alain Resnais's *Mélo*, which scrupulously follows the text of Bernstein's boulevard melodrama of 1928, is a great film. Resnais did not have to improve Bernstein's play. He only had to add to it his own genius.

which becomes visible when for the notion of accuracy we substitute the notion of fidelity.

In the ethics of translation, what is projected is an ideal servant—one who would be always willing to take more pains, linger longer, revise again. Good, better, best, ideal . . . however good the translation is, it can always be improved, bettered. Can one translation be the best? Of course. But the perfect (or ideal) translation is an ever receding chimera. Anyway, ideal by what standard?

(You will have already noted that I am assuming that there *is* such a thing as an "original" text. Perhaps only now, when ideas utterly devoid of common sense or respect for the practice of writing have great currency in the academy, would this seem to need saying. And not only am I making that assumption, but I am also proposing that the notion of translation not be too broadly extended or metaphorized, which is what allows one to claim, among other follies, that the original should be regarded as itself a translation—the "original translation," so to speak, of something in the author's consciousness.)

The notion of ideal translation is likely to be submitted to two perennially opposed standards of translation. Minimum adaptation is one. It means that the translation will feel like one: it will preserve, even flaunt, the rhythm, syntax, tone, lexical idiosyncrasies of the text in its original language. (The most contentious modern proponent of this literalist idea of translation is Vladimir Nabokov.) Full naturalization is the other. It means that the translator must bring the original text wholly "into" the new language, so that, ideally, one does not ever feel one is reading a translation at all. Inevitably, this work of dispelling all traces of the original lurking behind the translation requires taking liberties with the text: these adjustments or inventions are not only justified but necessary.

Pedestrian trot versus impertinent rewrite—these are, of course, extremes, well within which lies the actual practice of most dedicated translators. Nevertheless, there are two notions of translation in circulation, and behind the difference lies a larger disagreement about what responsibility one has to the "original" text. Everyone agrees that the translator must serve—the image is a powerful one—the text. But for what end? A translator may feel that the text (or "original") is best served by taking certain liberties, perhaps in the interest of making it more accessible or gaining for it new members of the potential audience.

Is it the work to which one is faithful? The writer? Literature? The language? The audience? One might suppose (maybe I mean that *I* might suppose) it to be self-evident that one be faithful to the work, to the words of the book. But this is not a simple matter, either historically or normatively. Take Saint Jerome himself, father of the Latin Bible, who is called the patron saint of translators. Jerome couldn't have received this illustrious title because he was the first to advance a *theory* of translation, for that honor belongs, as we might expect, to Plato. Perhaps it's because Jerome was the first on record to *complain* about translations, about their quality: to rail against ignorant, careless copyists and brazen confectioners of interpolated passages; and to campaign for greater exactitude. And yet it was this same Jerome, in his epistle "The Principles of Good Translation," who said that, except in the case of Scripture, a translator should not feel bound to produce a word-by-word rendering; that it was sufficient to translate the sense.

That a translation from one language to another ought to be reasonably faithful (whatever that may mean) is now received wisdom. Standards of fidelity to the original are certainly higher now than they were a generation, not to mention a century, ago. For some time now, translating, at least into English (though not, say, into French), has been measured by more literalist—I should say more scrupulous—standards, whatever the actual insufficiencies of most translations. This is partly because translation has itself become a subject for academic reflection, and translations (at least of important books) are likely to come under scholarly scrutiny. As part of what may seem like the co-opting by academic standards of the translator's task, it is more and more likely that any literary work of importance which is not contemporary will be accompanied by the translator's "notes," either at the bottom of the page or at the end of the book, explaining references in the text presumed to be obscure. Indeed, less and less do translations presuppose that the reader possesses the most elementary information about history or literature, or any language skills. The recent, much heralded re-translation of *The Magic Mountain* puts the delirious conversation in the pivotal "Walpurgis Nacht" chapter between Hans Castorp and Clavdia Chauchat, which transpires, crucially to the story, in French (and is in French in the old H. T. Lowe-Porter translation of 1927), into English. English in italics, so the Anglo-American reader (whose ignorance of French is taken for granted) might "feel" that it is in a foreign language.

TRANSLATIONS ARE LIKE buildings. If they're any good, the patina of time makes them look better: Florio's Montaigne, North's Plutarch, Motteux's Rabelais . . . (Who was it who said, "The greatest Russian writer of the nineteenth century, Constance Garnett"?) The most admired, and long-lived, are not the most accurate.

And, like building (the verb), translating produces something increasingly ephemeral now. Few people believe in a definitive translation—that is, one that would not need to be redone. And then there is the force of novelty: a "new" translation, like a new car. Submitted to the laws of industrial society, translations seem to wear out, become obsolete more rapidly. With respect to a few (admittedly a very few) books there is actually a glut of translations. Between 1947 and 1972 there were eleven German translations of *The Picture of Dorian Gray*, and since the 1950s at least ten new English translations of *Madame Bovary*. Translation is one of the few cultural practices that still seems ruled by an idea of progress (in contrast to, say, acoustics). The latest is, in principle, the best.

The new cultural populism, which insists that everything should be available to everyone, carries with it the implication that everything should be translated—or, at least, be translatable. Recall, as a counter-example, that the old *New Yorker*—call the magazine snobbish or anti-populist, as you will—didn't, as a matter of policy, print fiction in translation.

Consider the force of the locution "language barrier"—the barrier which language interposes between one person (or community) and another, the barrier which translation "breaks down." For language is the enforcer of separateness from other communities ("You don't speak my language") as well as the creator of community ("Anyone speak my language around here?").

But we live in a society pledged to the ceaseless invention of traditions—which is to say, the destruction of fealty to and knowledge of the specific, local past. Everything is to be recombined, remade—ideally, in the most portable, effortlessly transmissible form.

A leading feature of our ideology of a unitary, transnational capitalist world culture is the practice of translation. I quote: "Translation today is one of the communicational lifelines of our global village." In this perspective, translation becomes not merely a useful, desirable practice but an imperative one: linguistic barriers are obstacles to the freest circulation of commodities ("communication" is a euphemism for trade) and therefore must be overcome. Underpinning the ideology of universalism is the ideology of unlimited business. One always wants to reach more people with one's product. Besides the universalist claims implicit in this goal of unlimited translation, there is another implicit claim: namely, that anything can be translated, if one knew how. *Ulysses*, Gerard Manley Hopkins, whatever. And there is a good argument for saying this is true. (Perhaps the only important book that can't be translated is *Finnegans Wake*, for the reason that it is not written in only one language.)

The inevitable instrumentation of this idea of the necessity of translation, the "translation machine," shows us how the ancient dream of a universal language is alive and well. Saint Jerome took it for granted, as did most Christians of the early centuries, that all languages descend from one Ur-language (Hebrew, the original speech of mankind, until the presumptuous building of the Tower of Babel). The modern idea is that, via the computer, all languages can be turned into one language. We do not need an actually existing universal language as long as we have, or can imagine as feasible, a machine which can "automatically" give us the translation into any foreign language. Of course, the poets and fancy prose writers will instantly weigh in with their old lament about what is, inevitably, "lost in translation" (rhyme, flavor, wordplay, the grit of dialect) even by experienced, individual, "real" translators. Imagine the dimensions of the loss if the translator is not a person but a program! The directions on a Tylenol bottle can be translated without loss into any language. This is hardly the case with a poem by Marina Tsvetaeva or a novel by Carlo Emilio Gadda. But the project of a translation machine proposes quite another idea of language, one which identifies language with the communication of information: statements. In the new Platonic praxis, the poets will not need to be banished from the Republic. It will suffice that they will have been rendered unintelligible, because the artifacts they make with words cannot be processed by a machine.

This universalist model exists side by side with the persistence of language separatism, which asserts the incommensurability of cultures, of identities (political, racial, anatomical). So, in the former Yugoslavia, one language is being turned into many, and there is the farce of a patriotic *call* for translations. Both models exist simultaneously, perhaps interdependently. Language patriotism may continue to grow as a country pursues economic politics that sap national sovereignty, just as the most lethal myths of national distinctiveness can maintain their hold on a population even as it becomes ever more attached to the cultural paraphernalia of consumer capitalism, which is blandly supranational (made in Japan, made in the U.S.A.), or to computer technologies, which promote inevitably the growth of a world language, English.

I BEGAN WITH an anecdote that illustrated some of the ideological paradoxes embedded in the practice of translation. I'll end by evoking another fragment of personal experience: my participation in the transmitting of my own books into other languages. This has been a particularly wrenching task in the case of *The Volcano Lover*, with its multiplicity of narrative voices and levels of language. Published in 1992, the novel already exists or is about to exist in twenty foreign languages; and I have checked, sentence by sentence, the translations in the four principal Romance languages and made myself available to respond to countless questions from several of the translators in languages I don't know. You might say I'm obsessed with translations. I think I'm just obsessed with language.

I don't have time to tell you any stories about my dialogue with the translators. I'll end by saying that I wish I could stop wanting to be available to them. I wish I could give up trying to see the words, my own sentences, English, shine through. It's melancholy as well as enthralling work. I do not translate. I am translated—in the modern sense and in the obsolete sense deployed by Wycliffe. In supervising my translations, I am supervising the death as well as the transposition of my words.

[1995]

ACKNOWLEDGMENTS

"A Poet's Prose" was written as an introduction to Marina Tsvetaeva, *Captive Spirit: Selected Prose* (Virago Press, 1983).

"Where the Stress Falls" appeared in *The New Yorker*, June 18, 2001.

"Afterlives: The Case of Machado de Assis" is the foreword to a reprinting of *Epitaph of a Small Winner* (Noonday Press, 1990).

"A Mind in Mourning" appeared in the *Times Literary Supplement*, February 25, 2000.

"The Wisdom Project" appeared in *The New Republic*, March 16, 2001.

"Writing Itself: On Roland Barthes" is the introduction to *A Barthes Reader*, ed. Susan Sontag (Hill and Wang, 1982).

"Walser's Voice" is the preface to Robert Walser, *Selected Stories*, ed. Susan Sontag (Farrar, Straus and Giroux, 1982).

"Danilo Kiš" is the introduction to Danilo Kiš, *Homo Poeticus: Essays and Interviews*, ed. Susan Sontag (Farrar, Straus and Giroux, 1995).

"Gombrowicz's *Ferdydurke*" is the foreword to a new translation of Witold Gombrowicz, *Ferdydurke* (Yale University Press, 2000).

"*Pedro Páramo*" is the foreword to a new translation of Juan Rulfo, *Pedro Páramo* (Grove Press, 1994).

"DQ" was published in Spanish translation in a National Tourist Board of Spain catalogue, "España: Todo bajo el sol," in 1985; it has never before appeared in English.

"A Letter to Borges," written on the tenth anniversary of Borges's death and published in Spanish translation in the Buenos Aires daily *Clarin*, June 13, 1996, has never before appeared in English.

"A Century of Cinema" was written for and first published in German translation in *Frankfurter Rundschau*, December 30, 1995.

"Novel into Film: Fassbinder's *Berlin Alexanderplatz*" appeared in *Vanity Fair*, September 1983.

"A Note on Bunraku" was a program note for performances of the Bunraku Puppet Theatre at the Japan Society in New York City on March 12–19, 1983.

"A Place for Fantasy" appeared in *House and Garden*, February 1983.

"The Pleasure of the Image" appeared in *Art in America*, November 1987.

"About Hodgkin" was written for *Howard Hodgkin Paintings*, the catalogue of an exhibition organized by the Modern Art Museum of Fort Worth, Texas, in 1995, and subsequently seen at the Metropolitan Museum in New York. It was first published in Britain by Thames & Hudson in 1995.

"A Lexicon for *Available Light*" appeared in *Art in America*, December 1983.

"In Memory of Their Feelings" was written for the catalogue *Dancers on a Plane: Cage, Cunningham, Johns*, which accompanied an exhibit at the Anthony d'Offay Gallery in London from October 31 to December 2, 1989.

"Dancer and the Dance" first appeared in French *Vogue*, December 1986, in French translation and in English.

"On Lincoln Kirstein" is a revision, done in 1997 for a publication by the New York City Ballet, of a tribute to Lincoln Kirstein written ten years earlier, on his eightieth birthday, which appeared in *Vanity Fair*, May 1987.

"Wagner's Fluids" was the program essay for a production of *Tristan und Isolde* staged by Jonathan Miller at the Los Angeles Opera in December 1987.

"An Ecstasy of Lament" was the program essay for a production of *Pelléas et Mélisande* staged by Robert Wilson at the Salzburg Festival in July 1997.

"One Hundred Years of Italian Photography" is the foreword to *Italy: One Hundred Years of Photography* (Alinari, 1988).

"On Bellocq" is the introduction to a new edition of E. J. Bellocq, *Storyville Portraits* (Jonathan Cape and Random House, 1996).

"Borland's Babies" is the preface to Polly Borland's *The Babies* (powerHouse Books, 2001).

"Certain Mapplethorpes" is the preface to Robert Mapplethorpe's *Certain People: A Book of Portraits* (Twelvetrees Press, 1985).

"A Photograph Is Not an Opinion. Or Is It?" was written as an accompanying text to Annie Leibovitz's *Women* (Random House, 1999).

"Homage to Halliburton" was published in *Oxford American*, March/April 2001.

"Singleness," one of a group of essays inspired by Borges's "Borges y yo," was collected in *Who's Writing This?*, ed. Daniel Halpern (Ecco Press, 1995).

"Writing As Reading," a contribution to a series called "Writers on Writing" in *The New York Times*, appeared on December 18, 2000.

"Thirty Years Later . . ." is the preface to a new edition of the Spanish translation of *Against Interpretation* (Alfaguara, 1996). It was first published in English in *Threepenny Review* (Summer 1996).

"Questions of Travel" appeared in the *Times Literary Supplement*, June 22, 1984.

"The Idea of Europe (One More Elegy)" started as a talk delivered at a conference on Europe held in Berlin in late May 1988. It has never before appeared in English.

"The Very Comical Lament of Pyramus and Thisbe (An Interlude)" was written for the catalogue of an art exhibition in Berlin and first published there, in German translation, in *Die Endlichkeit der Freiheit Berlin 1990*, ed. Wulf Herzogenrath, Joachim Sartorius, and Christoph Tannert (Edition Hentrich, 1990). It appeared in English in *The New Yorker*, March 4, 1991.

"Answers to a Questionnaire" was written in July 1997, in response to a questionnaire sent by a French literary quarterly. It was published, in French, in "Enquête: Que peuvent les intellectuels? 36 écrivains répondent," *La Règle du Jeu*, n.s. 21 (1998), and has never before appeared in English.

"Waiting for Godot in Sarajevo" was first published in *The New York Review of Books*, October 21, 1993.

" 'There' and 'Here' " appeared in *The Nation*, December 25, 1995.

"Joseph Brodsky" was written in 1997 as the afterword to Mikhail Lemkhin, *Joseph Brodsky/Leningrad Fragments* (Farrar, Straus and Giroux, 1998).

"On Being Translated," a speech given in November 1995 at a conference on translation held at Columbia University and organized by Francesco Pellizzi, the editor of *Res*, was printed in *Res* 32 (Autumn 1997).